The Increasingly United States

D1563337

Chicago Studies in American Politics

A SERIES EDITED BY BENJAMIN I. PAGE, SUSAN HERBST,
LAWRENCE R. JACOBS, AND ADAM J. BERINSKY

Also in the series:

Additional series titles follow index

The Increasingly United States

*How and Why American Political
Behavior Nationalized*

DANIEL J. HOPKINS

THE UNIVERSITY OF CHICAGO PRESS   CHICAGO AND LONDON

The University of Chicago Press, Chicago 60637
The University of Chicago Press, Ltd., London
© 2018 by The University of Chicago
All rights reserved. No part of this book may be used or reproduced in any manner
whatsoever without written permission, except in the case of brief quotations in critical
articles and reviews. For more information, contact the University of Chicago Press, 1427
East 60th Street, Chicago, IL 60637.
Published 2018
Printed in the United States of America

27 26 25 24 23 22 21 20 19 18   1 2 3 4 5

ISBN-13: 978-0-226-53023-9 (cloth)
ISBN-13: 978-0-226-53037-6 (paper)
ISBN-13: 978-0-226-53040-6 (e-book)
DOI: 10.7208/CHICAGO/9780226530406.001.0001

Library of Congress Cataloging-in-Publication Data

Names: Hopkins, Daniel J., author.
Title: The increasingly United States : how and why American political behavior
    nationalized / Daniel J. Hopkins.
Other titles: Chicago studies in American politics.
Description: Chicago : The University of Chicago Press, 2018. | Series: Chicago studies
    in American politics
Identifiers: LCCN 2017049888 | ISBN 9780226530239 (cloth : alk. paper) |
    ISBN 9780226530376 (pbk. : alk. paper) | ISBN 9780226530406 (e-book)
Subjects: LCSH: Central-local government relations—United States—History—20th cen-
    tury. | Nationalism—Political aspects—United States. | Political psychology—United
    States—History—20th century. | United States—Politics and government—20th century. |
    Political participation—United States—History—20th century.
Classification: LCC JK325 .H66 2018 | DDC 324.973—dc23
LC record available at https://lccn.loc.gov/2017049888

♾ This paper meets the requirements of ANSI/NISO Z39.48-1992 (Permanence of Paper).

Contents

*Online appendixes are available at http://www.press.uchicago.edu/sites
/hopkins/.*

Acknowledgments

One of the great pleasures of finalizing this manuscript has been the realization of just how many insights from colleagues, friends, and family members are scattered throughout these pages. In parts of the book where other readers are likely to see discussions of political behavior, I see instead places and conversations in which colleagues helped sharpen these arguments. To me, these pages bring to mind conversations on city streets and college greens, as well as the occasional late-night email. While I cannot adequately highlight everyone's contributions here—and while I have almost certainly neglected someone's contribution—I do wish to express my most sincere thanks to friends and colleagues, including John Aldrich, Asad Asad, Joe Bafumi, Chris Bail, Jay Barth, Nicholas Beauchamp, Chris Berry, Sarah Binder, Nate Birkhead, Rachel Blum, Leticia Bode, Richard Boyd, Jordan Boyd-Graber, Richard Brisbin Jr., David Broockman, John Bullock, Andrea L. Campbell, Dave Campbell, Tom Carsey, Erin Cassese, Devin Caughey, Joshua Cherniss, Peter Thisted Dinesen, Kyle Dropp, Jamie Druckman, Ryan Enos, Pablo Fernandez-Vazquez, David Fontana, Rob Ford, Linda Fowler, John Freemuth, Paula Ganga, Claudine Gay, Elisabeth Gerber, James Gimpel, Kimberly Gross, Eitan Hersh, Leslie Hinkson, Frederik Hjorth, David Hopkins, William Howell, Kosuke Imai, Charles King, Karin Kitchens, Justin Koch, Vladimir Kogan, Ken Kollman, Dean Lacy, Eric Lawrence, Frances Lee, Jan Leighley, Gabe Lenz, Jacob Levy, Neil Malhotra, T. J. Mayotte, Nolan McCarty, Tali Mendelberg, Marc Meredith, Peter Miller, Colin Moore, Ryan Moore, Jonathan Mummolo, Clayton Nall, Brendan Nyhan, Eric Oliver, Danilo Petranovic, Lindsay Pettingill, Alison Post, Eleanor Powell, Karthick Ramakrishnan, Philip Resnik, Steven Rogers, Tom Sander, Jack Santucci, Eric Schickler, Deborah Schildkraut, Danny Schlozman, Chris Schorr, Jas Sekhon, Boris Shor,

B. K. Song, Gaurav Sood, Chris Tausanovitch, Alex Theodoridis, Emily Thorson, Jessica Trounstine, Eric Uslaner, Milan Vaishnav, James Vreeland, Chris Warshaw, Margaret Weir, Antoine Yoshinaka, and Hye-Young You. I especially appreciate the assistance, advice, and thoughts of those outside the academy, including journalists, analysts, and political professionals: Kevin Collins, Jay Cost, Kevin Drum, Tom Glaisyer, Drew Linzer, Alex Lundry, Reihan Salam, and Aaron Strauss. Even friends and family were pressed into service on occasion, with particular thanks due to Rona Gregory, Alex Horowitz, Luke McLoughlin, and Elizabeth Saunders.

This book draws on many data sets, some of which were compiled and kindly shared by colleagues, including Stephen Ansolabehere, Vin Arceneaux, Danny Hayes, Shigeo Hirano, Jennifer Lawless, James Snyder, Jessica Trounstine, and Ryan Vander Wielen. Dan Coffey, Dan Galvin, Gerald Gamm, John Henderson, Joel Paddock, Justin Phillips, and Eric Schickler teamed up to collect some of the state party platforms analyzed in chapter 7. This research also draws on a grant of survey time provided by Time-Sharing Experiments in the Social Sciences (TESS) to me, Jens Hainmueller, and Teppei Yamamoto. TESS is funded by the National Science Foundation (SES-1628057), and its principal investigators are James N. Druckman and Jeremy Freese.

Several individuals and institutions deserve special note. Much of the work on this book was conceived and undertaken while I was at Georgetown University, and it bears the indelible imprint of Georgetown colleagues and fellow Americanists Mike Bailey, Bill Gormley, Jonathan Ladd, Hans Noel, and Clyde Wilcox. Their insights fill these pages. More generally, Washington, DC, is home to an incredibly vibrant, thoughtful, and generous group of American politics scholars, and this book is much stronger for their feedback and advice. In particular, I gratefully acknowledge Lee Drutman, Danny Hayes, Matt Hindman, David Karol, Eric Lawrence, John Sides, and Matthew Wright, who joined with my Georgetown colleagues and other DC-based political scientists to provide incisive feedback at a May 2014 book conference and throughout the book-drafting process.

A BIGDOG grant from the Georgetown Department of Government made a second book conference possible in August 2014. For their time, participation, tireless efforts, and spirited advice, I thank Vin Arceneaux, Justin Grimmer, Richard Johnston, Diana Mutz, and Andrew Reeves.

Colleagues at the University of Pennsylvania picked up where those at Georgetown University left off, answering endless queries and providing still more invaluable advice. In particular, I gratefully acknowledge the thoughts, insights, experience, camaraderie, and fist bumps of Dan Gillion, Guy Grossman, Brielle Harbin, Michael Jones-Correa, John Lapinski, Yph Lelkes, Matt Levendusky, Michele Margolis, Marc Meredith, Diana Mutz, Anne Norton, Brendan O'Leary, and Rogers Smith. I am grateful to the Penn Program on Opinion Research and Election Studies as well.

The Arlington Public Library, the Enoch Pratt Free Library in Baltimore, and the DC Public Library all provided excellent places in which to move this manuscript forward, day by day and data set by data set.

Colleagues at varied institutions were kind enough to invite me to present this work and to provide feedback when I did. In particular, I am grateful for thoughtful feedback from seminars at the University of Michigan's Institute for Social Research and its Center for Political Studies; the University of Maryland's computer science department; Georgetown University's Political Economy Lunch; Harvard University's Malcolm Wiener Seminar on Inequality and Social Policy; Dartmouth College's American Politics Workshop; the University of North Carolina; the annual meetings of the Midwest Political Science Association; Duke University's American Politics Seminar; Princeton University's Center for the Study of Democratic Politics; Yale University's Center for the Study of American Politics; Vanderbilt University's Department of Political Science; the University of Chicago Department of Political Science; the Computational Linguistics Lunch and the Annenberg School for Communication's Elihu Katz Colloquium at the University of Pennsylvania; the University of Southern California; McGill University's Centre for the Study of Democratic Citizenship; and the University of Copenhagen.

As an editor of the Chicago Studies in American Politics series, Adam Berinsky played a crucial role in sharpening and improving this manuscript; I am in equal measure grateful for and embarrassed by the length of time that he has been striving to improve this manuscript. Likewise, John Tryneski and Chuck Myers provided crucial advice and assistance as the senior editors at the University of Chicago Press. I am grateful to Holly Smith, Christine Schwab, and Melinda Kennedy at the press, along with editorial project manager Carol McGillivray, for extensive work on this manuscript as well.

As my advisers in graduate school, Robert Putnam and Gary King shaped my questions, thinking, and tool kit in countless ways. (OK, Gary, maybe "countless" is the wrong word. But a lot.) I find the products of their long hours of advice and conversation spread across this book's pages and hope that they can do likewise. They are model social scientists, and this book takes their work, thinking, and teaching as its primary models. I should note as well that I would not have pursued a PhD in political science without the inspired teaching of Steve Levitsky.

Although this manuscript has one author, it is the product of many people's work. Specifically, I wish to acknowledge the research assistants at Georgetown University and the University of Pennsylvania whose tireless work tracking down obscure facts and performing so many other unsung tasks made these pages possible. They include Tiger Brown, Julia Christensen, Zoe Dobkin, Henry Feinstein, Katherine Foley, Patrick Gavin, August Gebhard-Koenigstein, Gregg Gelzinis, Jackson Gu, Victoria Hay, Saleel Huprikar, Max Kaufman, Roger Li, Louis Lin, Colin Mack, Daniel Maldonado, Katherine McKay, Eric Mooring, Thomas Munson, Owen O'Hare, Ashwin Ramesh, Gabrielle Rothschild, Andrew Schilling, Anton Strezhnev, Graham Welch, Amelia Whitehead, and Elena Zhou.

To my mom, you have always been my model of an engaged scientist. To my late father, although our world is a profoundly different place than it was in 2001, I like to think that you would have enjoyed seeing some of your insights develop from our late-night dog walks into the pages of this book. To my kids, I apologize that this book has neither the pacing of Harry Potter nor the characterizations or illustrations of a Beatrix Potter story. But your boundless energy and curiosity have inspired me on countless occasions. There is nothing that I enjoy more than exploring these fifty united states (and our capital) with you. And to Emily, whose dedication to truth and service continually inspires me, I dedicate this book. A more perfect union, indeed.

CHAPTER ONE

Introduction

The Increasingly United States

S igned into law in 2010, the sweeping health care reform known as the Patient Protection and Affordable Care Act, or Obamacare, remained a major issue for candidates years later. And not simply for candidates running for the US House or Senate, where the legislation was drafted and where the law's repeal was undertaken in 2017. The health care law played a role even in races as removed from national politics as a 2014 retention election for the Tennessee State Supreme Court. There, three incumbent justices found themselves targeted by TV advertisements denouncing them because "they advanced Obamacare in Tennessee." The justices had not actually heard any cases related to the federal law. But they had appointed the state's attorney general, and he later chose not to join an anti-Obamacare lawsuit, providing ammunition to their opponents (Fuller 2014; Fox17 2014).

On their own, low-profile contests like a state supreme court retention election rarely attract much voter interest, so tying opponents to divisive national issues is a common campaign tactic. It is also one employed by both sides of contemporary US politics. In a 2013 special election to the Washington, DC, Council, one candidate found himself fending off attacks over his support of GOP presidential candidate Mitt Romney (Craig 2013). One of his opponents even bothered to post a negative website headlined with a simple message: "Patrick Mara is a Republican." Mara responded by arguing that national allegiances are not relevant in a local race, and his campaign mailers urged voters to "vote your conscience, not your party." Despite high-profile endorsements, including the *Washington Post*'s and the Sierra Club's, he failed to win the at-large seat in an overwhelmingly Democratic city.

From the candidates' vantage point, the rationale behind such attacks seems obvious. National politics is rife with people and issues that are evocative to voters. To say "Obamacare," "Mitt Romney," or "Donald Trump" is to cue a set of meaningful associations with the national parties, the social groups that support them, and the positions that they take. Contemporary state and local politics are presumed to be devoid of such symbols, meaning that national politics can serve as a ready benchmark against which to evaluate otherwise unknown state and local candidates.

It is not only candidates and campaign staffers who assume that today's electorate is nationalized. The discipline of political science has tracked American citizens' growing fixation with Washington, DC. In recent decades, scholarship on American political behavior has focused overwhelmingly on national politics, with much more limited research at the state and local levels. Berry and Howell (2007) report that fully 94 percent of articles on US elections in five leading political science journals between 1980 and 2000 focused on elections for federal offices (845). To ignore state and local politics is a costly omission, as it means ignoring the politics that elect the vast majority of officials in the United States as well as the policy areas where states and localities hold sway. States and localities account for forty-eight cents of every dollar of total government spending in the United States (Congressional Budget Office 2014; US Census Bureau 2016). They also incarcerate 87 percent of all prisoners nationwide (Carson 2015). But they are far from receiving corresponding levels of attention from political scientists.

Even those studies that do analyze states and localities frequently conceive of them as independent polities, more like ancient Athens than Athens, Georgia. It is also a mistake to treat state and local politics as independent and autonomous when many of the same voters, candidates, parties, and interest groups are politically active across multiple levels of the federal system simultaneously. Surely the fact that state and local electorates are drawn from the same population as the national electorate is politically consequential, as is the fact that they are frequently choosing between the same two political parties at different levels of government. The goal of this book is to stop taking today's highly nationalized political behavior for granted and instead make it a puzzle to be documented and explained.

In other realms of American life, nationalization is so apparent as to be indisputable. Consider retail. The United States has over thirty-five thousand cities and towns, and they vary tremendously in their size, geography, and demographics. Yet, over the twentieth century, their storefronts came to look increasingly similar, as large chains like Walmart, Subway, and CVS replaced smaller, locally owned stores throughout the country (Rae 2003). In earlier generations, many purchases required local knowledge, since stores and their products varied from place to place. Today's chains offer the same products nationwide, often in the same parts of similarly designed stores. In important respects, the nationalization of American political behavior parallels the nationalization of retail. Just as an Egg McMuffin is the same in every McDonald's, America's two major political parties are increasingly perceived to offer the same choices throughout the country.

To understand today's nationalization, we need new concepts as well as new evidence, and this book aims to provide both. Conceptually, it distinguishes between two different ways in which political behavior can be nationalized. In the first, vote choices are nationalized when voters use the same criteria to choose candidates across the federal system. If voters' choices in state and local races echo those in national races, their voting is nationalized in this respect. On the second dimension, political behavior is nationalized when voters are engaged with and knowledgeable about national politics to the exclusion of state or local politics. This distinction proves important, as the two elements need not move in tandem. A Tennessee Supreme Court retention election, for instance, could in theory see high levels of engagement as the vote breaks down along national party lines, making it nationalized along one dimension but not the other.

To measure the ebbs and flows of nationalization's two dimensions, this book presents a wide variety of quantitative and qualitative evidence drawn from all fifty states and the District of Columbia. It employs many surveys, some conducted decades ago for other purposes and others conducted in recent years exclusively for this book. To demonstrate how key factors interrelate, this book presents a series of survey experiments as well. It also considers varied election returns from gubernatorial and mayoral races, some dating back nearly a century.

Along the way, this book discusses examples as varied as concern about climate change among those living near the coasts, statements of American identity in nineteenth-century books, the shifting emphases of state party platforms, the expansion of local television news in the 1960s, and the 2016 election of Donald Trump. This book draws more heavily on state-level evidence than on local evidence, both because it is more readily available and because of localities' subordinate legal status in American federalism. Still, as the example of DC Council candidate Patrick Mara makes clear, nationalization has implications at the local level, several of which are detailed in the paragraphs and chapters that follow.

Although the streams of evidence are many, the results are consistent. American political behavior has become substantially more nationalized along both its dimensions. Since the 1970s, gubernatorial voting and presidential voting have become increasingly indistinguishable. What is more, Americans' engagement with state and local politics has declined sharply, a trend that has unfolded more consistently over decades.

Why Nationalization Matters

Both of these nationalizing trends have profound implications for how voters are represented in contemporary American politics. In part, that is because today's nationalization stands in sharp contrast to some of the core assumptions made by the framers of the US Constitution. In their view, citizens' state-level loyalties were expected to be far stronger than those to the newborn nation (Levy 2006, 2007). In "Federalist 46," Madison gives voice to this belief, explaining that "many considerations . . . seem to place it beyond doubt that the first and most natural attachment of the people will be to the governments of their respective States" (Hamilton, Madison, and Jay 1788, 294). Hamilton provides a similar view in "Federalist 25," noting that "in any contest between the federal head and one of its members the people will be most apt to unite with their local government" (Hamilton, Madison, and Jay 1788, 163–64). The states had key advantages over the federal government in winning citizens' loyalties, as their purview included most of the issues that were familiar, local, and important to citizens' daily lives (Levy 2007). In fact, so strong were state-level loyalties that Hendrickson (2003) explains the US Constitution as a peace pact that averted conflict between separate countries.

At the time the US Constitution was written, the assumption that citizens' primary loyalties would lie with the more proximate state governments was uncontroversial. Although today's America spans a far greater area than did the America of 1787, the distances covered by the original thirteen states represented a more formidable barrier to imagining a singular, unified nation. In the late eighteenth century, the country's primary transportation system was horse, oxen, and wagon, and a traveler could expect to go no more than ten miles per day most of the year (Nettles 1962, 307). In fact, transportation in the new nation was sufficiently poor that the Constitutional Convention was delayed for two weeks past its May 14 start to allow delegates time to brave mud-choked roads (Padula 2002, 44). Without broadcast media sources like radio or television, information traveled no faster than the horses and boats that carried it. Living before the Erie Canal, before transcontinental railroads or interstate highways, the framers held the reasonable expectation that political loyalties would wane over great distances.

The framers' assumptions about citizens' state-level loyalties are not merely of historical interest. Americans today have inherited the political institutions the framers crafted, institutions whose operation hinges partly on whether those foundational assumptions hold true today. Consider one of the innovations of the US Constitution, a federal system that divides sovereignty between the central and state governments (LaCroix 2010). Stable federal systems are necessarily the product of a careful balancing act in which neither the centrifugal forces of state-level disagreement nor the centralizing forces of pressing national problems dominate for long (Riker 1964; Derthick 2004; Greve 2012; Kollman 2013). In one analysis of federalism, Levy (2007) considers the problem of protecting subnational authority from centralization and ultimately concludes that federalism relies on strong emotional attachments between citizens and the subnational governments. In his words, the argument in the *Federalist Papers* "depends on the citizenry's natural loyalty and attachment to their states as against the federal center. That is, a prediction about the affective relationship citizens will have to states is built into the account of what will make the constitutional structure work" (464). For the framers, citizens' state-level loyalties were a critical counterweight to the centralizing tendencies inherent in a federal system. Understanding contemporary Americans' engagement with state-level politics will thus help us understand whether that counterweight continues to work as the framers envisioned (see also Pettys 2003; Young 2015).

The extent to which political behavior is local or national in orientation also has the potential to influence political accountability by shaping the incentives that state and local officials face. Think about politics from a governor's vantage point. If voters are well informed about state politics and liable to vote differently in state and national elections, the threat of a general-election challenge is a real one. In that scenario, the governor has a significant incentive to deliver what voters—or at least a pivotal segment of them—want. But if voters are likely to back the same party as in presidential elections irrespective of the governor's platform or performance, the governor's incentives change. When political behavior is nationalized, governors may well come to see their ambitions as tethered more closely to their status in the national party than their ability to cater to the state's median voter. If so, their actions in office might well reflect the wishes of the people most likely to advance their careers, whether they are activists, donors, or fellow partisans from other states.

In a similar vein, as political behavior becomes more nationalized, national issues may come to dominate state and even local political debates. For voters, that is not necessarily a bad thing—if they previously knew little about state and local politicians, knowing their stance on national issues provides a meaningful heuristic. Presumably, voters in Tennessee's 2014 Supreme Court elections had more actionable information after seeing ads linking some incumbents to health care reform. Nonetheless, those national issues have the potential to crowd out more local concerns. A national emphasis may also influence the political agenda, shifting voters' attention from tangible local issues to more symbolic national ones.

Even at the federal level, nationalization has consequences for political representation. Both houses of the US Congress elect their members through geographically defined districts. Since the earliest days of the United States, voters' places of residence have determined the constituencies in which they can vote. There are several reasons that a political system might opt for geographically based districts, and the notion that neighbors are likely to share political interests is just one of them (Rehfeld 2005). Still, in a political system that represents people based on where they live, nationalization can undercut each district's claim to have its own unique communities of interest.

That, in turn, has implications for governance and polarization. In recent years, scholars and pundits alike have become alarmed by the rise of political polarization among federal politicians and its impacts in a system that divides powers between the branches of the federal government (Fiorina, Abrams, and Pope 2005; McCarty, Poole, and Rosenthal 2006). The divergence in policy preferences between congressional Democrats and Republicans has grown dramatically since the 1970s. Between 2011 and 2017, the collision between a White House controlled by Democrats and a House of Representatives controlled by Republicans led to a period of legislative gridlock punctuated by occasional high-stakes negotiations (Lee 2016; Mann and Ornstein 2016). And while this polarization and legislative gridlock have many causes (Barber and McCarty 2013), nationalized political behavior is an underappreciated one. When voters are national

in orientation, legislators have little incentive to bargain for benefits targeted to their constituents. Rather than asking, "How will this particular
bill affect my district?" legislators in a nationalized polity come to ask,
"Is my party for or against this bill?" That makes coalition building more
difficult, as legislators all evaluate proposed legislation through the same
partisan lens.

In short, nationalized political behavior has widespread implications
for political representation. Nationalization is likely to influence everything from how campaigns are run to who wins elections and how politicians are held accountable for their actions in office. Its impacts stretch
beyond the ballot box to the halls of our governments as well. Nationalized political behavior has the potential to foster elite-level political polarization and to create a disconnect between the issues voters face in
their daily lives and those that dominate political debates. Our federalist
division of authority and heavy use of geographic districting allow for the
expression of varied local interests and issues. But if state and local politics focus on the same issues as national politics, contemporary America
may not be taking full advantage of its political institutions.

How Can Politics Be Nationalized If Communities Differ?

A quick glance at recent maps of election outcomes seems to argue
against nationalization, with states and towns differing dramatically in
their support for the two major parties. Those differences appear to have
hardened in recent years as more and more states and localities grow reliably Republican or Democratic (Hopkins 2017). In 2016, for instance,
Hillary Clinton won 87 percent of the votes for president in New York's
Manhattan, while Donald Trump won 80 percent of the vote in Randall
County in the Texas Panhandle. The very fact that calling Patrick Mara
a Republican constituted an attack in Washington, DC, is evidence that
political preferences vary greatly in different parts of the country. So we
need to ask: Do such pervasive geographic differences refute the claim
that contemporary US politics is nationally oriented?

No, in a word, although such objections do illustrate the value of defining nationalization precisely. One feature of nationalized political behavior is that it is oriented toward the national government and its divisions,
to the near exclusion of the state or local levels. Still, how people engage in national politics is known to be related to various individual-level

factors, from their social class (Berelson, Lazarsfeld, and McPhee 1954; Gelman et al. 2008) and racial and ethnic backgrounds (Dawson 1994; Abrajano and Alvarez 2010) to their religious backgrounds and engagement (Kellstedt et al. 1996), age cohorts (Campbell et al. 1960; Miller and Shanks 1996), and other characteristics. People with different individual-level characteristics tend to live in different places, so a nationally oriented politics is fully compatible with significant differences in partisanship or political behavior across space. Even in a nationalized political system, places can and do differ markedly. But those differences are primarily due to *compositional differences* in who lives where rather than the *contextual effects* of living in specific places. When political attitudes and behavior are nationalized, similar people subject to similar information and mobilization efforts should respond in similar ways. The core issues that animate politics will be similar, too.

To contend that American political behavior is nationalizing is not to argue for the death of distance or the irrelevance of geography. To the contrary, this book is motivated precisely by the fact that geography remains a powerful determinant of so many aspects of Americans' social and economic lives. The quality of schools, the danger of crime, the availability of jobs, the presence of pollution—all of these concerns affect some neighborhoods, municipalities, and regions far more than others (e.g., Sampson 2012; Chetty and Hendren 2015; Chetty, Hendren, and Katz 2015). Americans living on one block can be served by dramatically different schools—or subject to dramatically different tax rates or crime threats—than their neighbors on adjoining blocks. So if today's political behavior is nationalized, it is also likely to be divorced from many of the local issues that Americans confront in our daily lives. Political nationalization is important not because it heralds the end of geography but because it complicates political representation on the many issues where geography continues to matter greatly in Americans' day-to-day lives.

Engines of Nationalization

What is behind today's nationalization of both vote choice and political engagement? Contemporary social science excels at examining the effects of a single, well-defined cause, such as the introduction of television. But our tools for identifying the varied causes of a single trend are more limited, however important that trend might be. This constraint is especially pronounced when our interest is historical and our capacity to conduct experiments or ask new survey questions is limited. Still, while this book cannot quantify the relative importance of all the would-be explanations precisely, its second half does devote sustained attention to the potential causes of contemporary nationalization. It identifies separate pathways that explain the two facets of nationalization. One pathway highlights the role of the political parties, while the second emphasizes the interplay of Americans' identities and our changing media markets. At the same time, this book downplays other would-be causes, such as changes in residential mobility.

I turn first to nationalization's first dimension and to the question of why elections for state offices increasingly feel like reruns of the presidential election. As this book contends, the increasing alignment of national and state-level voting is to an important extent the product of a party and interest-group constellation that is funded nationally and that increasingly offers voters similar choices in all parts of the country. Political scientists have long argued that party cues allow voters to connect their own policy preferences with the choices on the ballot in a straightforward way (Campbell et al. 1960; Fiorina 1981; Popkin 1994). Here, I add the important caveat that those party cues are national ones. Contemporary state parties do not vary markedly in the platforms they offer voters, and even those differences that do exist do not appear to influence voters' perceptions or their votes. Today, party labels convey very similar meanings in jurisdictions across the country. In short, one proximate cause of nationalized vote choices is the increasingly similar options the parties offer across the nation (see also Hopkins and Schickler 2016).

What, then, explains why parties nationalize? Although that question is more peripheral to this project, prior research provides some potential answers. That research has highlighted three factors: the centralization of governmental authority (Chhibber and Kollman 2004), the decline of Democratic dominance in the South (Mickey 2015), and the increasing homogeneity of the American economy. In analyzing the United States, I do not find evidence of a straightforward link between any of these factors and nationalized vote choices—the trend lines simply don't align. For example, state and national vote choices became decoupled in the 1960s, at the very time that the flood of Great Society legislation was increasing the federal role in many policy areas traditionally handled by states and localities. Still, the evidence presented here is quite compatible with claims of indirect connections, as each of these factors is likely to have influenced voters over time by shaping the parties' policy goals and platforms. This connection from the centralization of state authority, the decline of the one-party South, and economic convergence to nationalizing party brands and then ultimately to vote choices constitutes the first explanatory pathway emphasized here.

When explaining nationalization's second facet—the decline in state and local political engagement—our explanation shifts to the transformation of the US media market. Older media outlets tend to have audiences that are bounded geographically. Given the limits inherent in distributing a print newspaper, someone waking up in Oklahoma City in 1930 could not expect to read that day's *Los Angeles Times*. Those geographic limitations provided economic incentives for some media outlets to foreground state and local politics. In recent decades, as audiences shift away from print newspapers and local television news, they are also shifting away from the outlets most likely to provide extensive state and local coverage. These changes are especially likely to affect Americans' knowledge about and engagement with state and local politics, which is the second element of nationalization.

Yet today's strongly national orientation among voters is not simply a product of our changing media markets. Canada and the United Kingdom have seen similar shifts in their media markets without a concurrent nationalization of their political behavior, as the September 2014 referendum on Scottish independence and the continued success of the Parti Quebecois in Quebec, Canada, vividly illustrate. In both places, there are powerful political movements seeking to break up the country. One critical difference between the United States and those countries relates to the structure of national and subnational identity.

In political science as well as psychology, a growing body of scholarship pays attention to the role of identities in shaping individuals' interactions with their social worlds. People think about themselves as members of varying social groups, and those attachments prove critical in explaining how they handle new information, the attitudes they adopt, and the actions they take (Zaller 1992; Taber and Lodge 2006; Achen and Bartels 2016). Two people might be categorized as identical based on demographic categories, for instance, and yet may differ dramatically in what they understand those categories to mean for their lives (Theiss-Morse 2009; Wong 2010; Schildkraut 2011, 2014). National and ethnic identities are among the more enduring (Gellner 1983; Anderson 1991), even as their political import can shift quite suddenly. Yet while Americans' regions, states, and communities of residence remain a component of their self-image, they are not very strong sources of identity, especially when compared with identities based on family roles, religion, or occupation. And more importantly, place-based identities are not very politicized in today's United States. One doesn't have to espouse particular political views to be a proud Rhode Islander or South Dakotan.

The strength of contemporary American identity, especially as compared to state- or local-level attachments, anchors the second explanation outlined in this book. Absent strong or politically charged attachments to their states and localities, Americans are not chronically engaged by subnational politics. If information about state and local politics is readily available, they will pick it up (see also Prior 2007). If state or local politics generate some unusual threat, residents may well mobilize in response (Dahl 1961; Oliver, Ha, and Callen 2012). But in a transforming media market characterized by growing consumer choice, the structure of Americans' identities means that they are unlikely to go out of their way to seek out information about state or local politics. The interplay of Americans' identities and changes in media markets explains the declining engagement with state and local politics.

Certainly, this account of the causes of contemporary nationalization is not exhaustive. For one thing, the pathways identified here are conceived of as two separate tracks, but it is possible for them to intersect. As the media environment shifts, for example, so too does the capacity of the subnational parties to distinguish themselves. And while this book emphasizes how identities interact with the changing media environment to shape political information, it is also possible that in the long run, the media environment shapes identities.[1] To claim that three factors—the political parties, Americans' identities, and the changing media market— played critical, proximate roles in nationalizing our politics is not to say that they were the only factors at work.

Chapter Outline

This book is divided into two sections. The first seeks to define and describe trends in nationalization while the second identifies two causal pathways that partly explain it.

Trends in Nationalization

Above, we saw that nationalized political behavior is likely to have varied impacts on American politics. Chapter 2 ("Meanings of Nationalization, Past and Present") expands that discussion by examining what nationalized voting behavior means for political representation. This project is not the first to take up questions of nationalization, so chapter 2 then details what we already know before fixing the term's meaning for the remainder of the book. Occasional studies have considered political nationalization within the United States, but their focus has been principally on shifts in government, parties, or political institutions (Lunch 1987; Gimpel 1996; Paddock 2005; Klinghard 2010) and not on voter behavior. That said, a separate body of scholarship has uncovered a variety of trends that are clues of nationalization in American voters' political behavior, from the declining incumbency advantage to the changing base of party activists. To date, though, we have not understood those observations within a single framework. We have seen them as isolated symptoms, not as evidence of a common diagnosis. After reviewing existing evidence on nationalization, we are then in a position to define its two elements.

Chapter 3 ("The Nationalization of American Elections, 1928–2016") presents empirical evidence on the first aspect of nationalization, the alignment of national and subnational divisions. Specifically, it measures the level of nationalization in American voting behavior and partisanship over time, and it does so using a combination of county-level election returns and individual-level survey data. Writing in 1967, political scientist Donald Stokes saw the nationalization of American voting behavior as a steady trend, one he linked to ongoing changes in communications technology. Yet the chapter's varied analyses provide a more nuanced and up-to-date picture. The analyses focus chiefly on gubernatorial elections, as governors are at once sufficiently visible and influential that it is plausible their elections could generate distinctive geographic patterns of political support.

The evidence shows that nationalization had been rising in the 1930s and 1940s, but it peaked and then declined in the 1960s and 1970s, precisely at the time Stokes was writing. Since around 1980, the nationalizing trend in gubernatorial elections has resumed and accelerated, a conclusion reinforced by analyses of individual-level survey data from exit polls and the American National Election Studies. In fact, by 2014, the relationship between presidential and gubernatorial county-level voting was almost perfect, meaning that returns in governors' races could be predicted quite accurately without knowing any state-specific information. As compared to the past, the present era is undeniably a nationalized one. But the nationalization of political divisions is not a secular trend, increasing inexorably as revolutions in communication and transportation reduce the connection between distance and information. Instead, it waxes and wanes in ways indicative of a more complex causal story. These patterns are further reinforced through analyses of partisan identification, presidential home-state advantages, and 2016 presidential election returns. In its conclusion, this chapter also outlines why nationalized vote choices have tended to advantage Republicans over Democrats in recent years.

In chapter 4 ("Staying Home When It's Close to Home"), I consider the second element of nationalized political behavior, citizen engagement across the levels of the federal system. The chapter also charts how that engagement has varied over time. There are reasons to think—as the framers of the Constitution did—that local and state governments would win the loyalties of the citizens over the more remote federal government. Local politics frequently means face-to-face politics, and it addresses tangible issues that are likely to have a direct bearing on voters' lives (Fischel 2001; Oliver, Ha, and Callen 2012). But, as this chapter shows, Americans today are primarily engaged with national and above all presidential politics. The evidence is extensive: contemporary Americans' disproportionate engagement with federal politics is evident in their knowledge, descriptions of politicians, web searches, campaign contributions, and turnout decisions.

There are ongoing debates about whether Americans know enough to fulfill their democratic responsibilities in national elections. But however one assesses knowledge about national politics, knowledge about state and local politics is markedly lower. Chapter 4 also brings to light what I term the "presidential paradox." At the same time that voters express their disproportionate interest in the federal government, they acknowledge that mayors and governors can have more influence on their day-to-day lives. This effect is especially pronounced when asking about the president as a person, suggesting that the overwhelming media attention on the US presidency might be one factor behind the disproportionate interest in national politics. The fact that the president is a single individual may also help personalize politics and so attract citizens' interest.

The conception of nationalization advanced in this book focuses partly on the alignment between national and subnational divisions in voting behavior. To conclude that today's electorate is nationalized, we thus need to consider the dogs that didn't bark—the many state and local issues that could have given rise to indigenous political conflict in a less nationalized system. Precisely because such issues are typically of interest in only some parts of the country, they are not frequently included in nationally representative surveys. Indeed, prior studies of the effects of local context have focused overwhelmingly on just a handful of factors, such as the ethnic and racial diversity of the community or the state of the local economy.

Chapter 5 ("Local Contexts in a Nationalized Age") takes up the task of studying a variety of political issues with disparate spatial impacts, issues that have the potential to give rise to distinctive, localized political divisions. The issues it considers vary markedly, from nuclear power and economic inequality to immigration, defense spending, and federal lands. Yet the analyses uncover a fact common to many of them: once we account for political partisanship, Americans' political attitudes are not strongly correlated with attributes of their communities. Americans living near federal lands are no more opposed to the federal government than people living elsewhere, just as Americans who live on an ocean coast are only imperceptibly more concerned about climate change. In the contemporary United States, once we know basic demographic facts about an individual, knowing her place of residence adds little to our understanding of a variety of political attitudes. The consistency of that pattern reflects the imprint of a nationalized political system, one in which citizens react not to local interests but to national symbols.

To be sure, there are some local conditions that show meaningful and consistent associations with political attitudes, just as the extensive research on local contextual effects would lead us to expect. But ironically, the issues that do show disparate spatial patterns prove to be those salient in national politics, such as immigration, crime, or the economy. Far from being an alternative grounds of political division, local issues appear to become politically meaningful precisely when citizens can use national debates to understand and politicize them. All politics is decidedly not local.

Explanations of Nationalization

The book's sixth chapter ("Explaining Nationalization") inaugurates its second section focusing on the potential causes of nationalization. This chapter briefly summarizes a range of potential explanations of nationalization, from economic transformations and geographic mobility to changes in US media markets or political parties. The chapter then outlines the two causal pathways that are our focus here. The first emphasizes how shifting party platforms and brands lead to highly nationalized voting patterns, possibly as a long-term consequence of changes in state authority. The second details how Americans' identities and the changing media environment produce low knowledge of and engagement with state and local politics.

In chapter 7 (*"E Pluribus Duo"*), I take up the political parties, the first proximate cause emphasized here. Are they heterogeneous national coalitions, with state parties enjoying considerable leeway to tune their platforms and strategies to the state context? Or are they unified and nationalized parties in which the parties differ little from state to state? Both depictions are ideal types, but this chapter uses various data sources to demonstrate that the state parties themselves, and especially as voters perceive them, have increasingly come to mirror their national counterparts. In particular, it employs automated analyses of state party platforms to extend our view back to World War I. As the evidence makes clear, state party platforms have less state-specific content over time.

Parties' positions and voters' perceptions of those positions need not be the same (Lenz 2013), so chapter 7 then shifts from actual records of party positions to voters' perceptions of the parties. Analyzing a 2014 GfK survey conducted on a population-based sample, I show that the contemporary state parties are perceived with a bit less clarity than their national counterparts—but in almost identical terms. The chapter demonstrates that very few voters have different partisan identifications at different levels of government, further undermining the capacity of state or local politics to sustain divisions that are not animated nationally. It also shows that even those differences in actual state party positioning that scholars do detect are not reflected in gubernatorial voting: by 2006, there was essentially no advantage to gubernatorial candidates when their state party had taken more moderate positions in the outgoing legislative session.

Yet shifts within the parties are not as well matched to explain the second face of nationalization, Americans' declining engagement in state and local politics relative to national politics. For that, I turn to two factors operating in tandem: the structure of Americans' loyalties and the changing ways in which they get political information.

How federalism operates hinges on citizens' relative connections to the different levels of government and thus on their identities (Riker 1964; Levy 2006, 2007; Kollman 2013; Young 2015). Yet assessments of contemporary Americans' geographic identities and their connections to the different levels of government have been few and far between (but see Wong 2010; Young 2015). In chapter 8 ("Sweet Home America"), I consider the role of

place-based identities in American politics. Using a database of books, I
show that statements of state-level identity have declined relative to statements of American identity since the 1960s. Even today, many Americans
feel attached to their place of residence. Yet they report far stronger connections to their family and to America as a whole, making those identities
more fertile ground for political mobilization. What's more, among their
various spatially defined communities, Americans' strongest connections
are to their neighborhoods and not to more explicitly political units, such
as their towns, cities, or states. The content of these place-based identities
is not usually political, a fact that further undermines state and local identities as a potential bedrock for durable political engagement.

Contemporary Americans' identities are unlikely to motivate them to
seek out information about state and local politics when that information
isn't readily available. That observation makes the structure of the information environment critical. Accordingly, I then turn to the changing media
market in chapter 9 ("The Declining Audience for State and Local News
and Its Impacts"). Over American history, the primary sources of political
information have shifted repeatedly, as pamphlets, newspapers, and radio
have been joined and in some instances replaced by broadcast television,
cable television, and the Internet. Researchers have devoted considerable
attention to how such changes in the media market might influence the partisan and ideological slant of the news available to Americans. But these
changes are also likely to have profound influences on the available information about state and local government, as the shift in media technologies
since 1900 has generally been away from media outlets with audiences that
are bounded in space. Given limits in their distribution and dissemination,
print newspapers have significant incentives to specialize in the news of
a given spatially defined community. Local television stations do as well,
although the strength of the incentive depends on the fit between their
broadcast area and local political jurisdictions. For Internet and cable news
outlets, that is far less true. Yet despite the likely impact of the shifting media environment on the balance of information about different levels of the
federal system, the topic has received little scholarly attention.

Existing technologies surely influence the information available to citizens, but the relationship between a medium of mass communication and
its content is by no means deterministic. Media outlets' relative attention
to the different levels of government needs to be analyzed, not assumed.
Accordingly, chapter 8's empirical analysis begins by using automated
content analyses to identify the levels of attention to state and local politics since 1920. For two big-city newspaper outlets—the *Chicago Tribune*

and the *Los Angeles Times*—it shows that state politics has long been an overlooked topic, even in the more spatially oriented media environment of years past. For the period since the 1980s, digital archives provide access to far more media content, enabling the analysis of fifty-one of the largest American newspapers. Those analyses reinforce the core conclusion that state-level politics receives markedly less attention than local politics, which itself is neglected relative to national politics. There is some noteworthy spatial variation, with newspapers in state capitals providing more state-level coverage than their counterparts elsewhere. Somewhat unexpectedly, analyses of select local television transcripts in the post-2006 period indicate that even in recent years, local television news has given significant attention to state politics and government.

Chapter 9 also considers what these trends have meant for audiences. While there has not been a notable decline in the relative coverage of state and local politics *within* a given medium of communication, there have been critical shifts in the relative sizes of audiences *across* the different types of media since around 1990, with newspaper readership and local television viewership declining as the audiences for Internet-based news and cable television have grown. Put differently, spatially bounded media sources are losing their audiences, and so citizens are likely to be losing information about state and local politics.

After documenting these facts, chapter 9 examines their political implications. Using survey data, it shows that people's knowledge about state politics is strongly associated with their sources of news. People whose primary news sources have significant state and local content are more likely to know their governor or to name in-state representatives and US senators than other citizens. The chapter then substantiates the claim that these changes in the media environment are a *cause* of declining state and local political engagement. To do so, it uses the leverage afforded by the varied relationships between state capitals and TV's designated market areas (DMAs). In the 1960s and 1970s, living in a state capital DMA increased gubernatorial turnout, while living in a DMA dominated by another state had the opposite effect. Such patterns are expected: local television news became a major source of political information in the 1960s (Prior 2006, 2007). Yet these effects are much more muted after around 1990, as local TV news lost viewers to cable news and then the Internet. Where people live—and the amount of information local television provides about state politics as a result—is no longer as influential on their participation in gubernatorial elections as it was thirty years ago. These case studies make the underlying causal claim credible: as news audiences move to cable television and the Internet, the effects of their access to television coverage about state politics have declined. In theory, the Internet has the potential to vastly increase the local news available to Americans—local news from any part of the country is but a few computer keystrokes away. In actuality, that potential goes largely unused, as new media outlets serve to concentrate attention on a small number of national news sources (Hindman 2009).

The Consequences of Nationalization

The nationalization of American retail is inscribed on our landscape, visible to any passerby. The nationalization of our politics is at once less easily observed and yet potentially more consequential. In fact, the breadth of nationalization's impacts is part of what makes the topic so important, as it touches on many of the core questions of contemporary politics and political science. If voters' political information and behaviors are primarily oriented toward national politics, and if political agendas are set nationally, those facts have implications for elections and accountability in state and local politics. Similarly, enquiring about citizens' relationship to particular subnational spaces and polities clearly speaks to questions about representation and the role of spatially defined legislative districts. Studying the changing role of space in American political behavior might also illuminate aspects of voter decision making, party strategy, party organization, and campaign finance. These research questions are related to still more general questions posed by social theorists, such as the impact of the size of the political community (e.g., Dahl and Tufte 1973), changing communications technology, the transforming economy, or geographic mobility on political behaviors and identities.

On a more prosaic note, nationalization has implications for key features of contemporary US politics. It might explain why in 2014, during a period of relatively even and fiercely contested partisan competition nationally, thirty-six of the fifty states had unified party control of their statehouses, a fraction higher than it had been in six decades (Nagourney 2014). Certainly, nationalization is a critical part of the explanation for contemporary Republican dominance in many statehouses and the US House of Representatives: even among parties with roughly equal levels of strength nationally, it advantages parties with majority support in many jurisdictions over those whose support is more spatially concentrated (Chen and Rodden 2013; Jacobson 2015; Abramowitz and Webster 2016). Similar factors help explain how Donald Trump won the presidency in November 2016 while losing the popular vote by more than 2 percentage points.

In nationalized eras, it is also plausible that the political agenda will be set nationally and will be outside the control of state or local actors. The risk, then, is of a mismatch between the political system's relentless focus on national issues and the important decisions made at the state and local levels. It was that mismatch that Republican Patrick Mara pointed to when arguing for his election to the DC Council.

Among the many potential consequences of nationalized political behavior, this book's conclusion highlights two. First, nationalized political behavior has important implications for representation and accountability in state and local politics. States and localities make critical decisions across a broad array of policy areas, ranging from what is taught in their schools and how land can be developed to who can marry and what constitutes a crime. Yet in a nationalized polity, many votes cast for governors, state legislators, and even sometimes mayors are cast with an eye toward the candidates' alignment in national politics (see also Rogers 2016, 2017). Such voting patterns have the potential to dampen the electoral connection between voters and officials, as state and local officials may come to believe they are insulated from the threat of losing at the ballot box.

Second, the conclusion details how nationalized political behavior can foster polarization and gridlock in federal policy making. Even at the federal level, nationalized political behavior is likely to change politicians' incentives in ways that make it harder to build legislative coalitions. In a less nationalized political system, any given bill will raise idiosyncratic trade-offs for individual legislators. A conservative legislator's large uninsured population might push her to back an expansion of health insurance while a liberal legislator from an area with low-performing schools might back vouchers. Yet as politics becomes more nationalized, legislation's local impacts have come to matter less than its partisan hue. It's why even congressional Democrats with many elderly constituents opposed prescription drug coverage in 2003 and why Republican governors with high numbers of uninsured residents turned down the Medicaid expansion that was part of the Affordable Care Act. In a nationalized era, the costs of defying one's constituents pale in comparison to the costs of defying one's national party. Put differently, nationalized political behavior is a critical but overlooked ingredient in today's political polarization.

CHAPTER TWO

Meanings of Nationalization, Past and Present

A political machine relentlessly giving state-funded jobs and contracts to its supporters and being vindictive in pushing opponents out of politics. Armed men appearing in the night to seize voting records and guarantee the election of a friendly candidate. Taxes designed to drive unfriendly newspapers out of business. A popularly elected executive who has to move out of his office whenever one of his predecessors—the man actually calling the shots—returns to town.

These descriptions could come from any number of modern-day autocracies, with the distribution of jobs and the threat of violence used to cement the autocrat's power and subvert democratic institutions. But in truth, those events all took place in Huey Long's Louisiana, a state that he formally oversaw as governor from 1928 to 1932 and ran with essentially unchecked power until his assassination in 1935 (White 2006).

While Huey Long cuts something of a unique figure in American history, his reign is emblematic of an earlier, less nationalized political era. In Long's day, control over state patronage was a major prize in itself, one that could anchor state-level political divisions very different from those at the national level. Indeed, Louisiana's Democratic Party was divided into the Long and anti-Long factions not just in the early 1930s but for decades after the "Kingfish's" death (Key 1949). Although one needs to view vote totals from Long's Louisiana with skepticism, in 1928, 34 percent more Louisiana voters were reported to have voted in the January Democratic primary that put Huey Long in power than in the subsequent presidential election. State-level politics was fought over different issues, and yet it engendered as much or more interest than federal politics.

The goal of this chapter is to lay the conceptual groundwork to make sense of figures like Huey Long—and of the possibility that state-level politics might cut along lines quite different from national politics. Specifically, this chapter answers three related questions: First, why study nationalization? Second, what is already known about nationalization in the United States, both from studies that consider the question explicitly and from those that address it only incidentally? And finally, how is nationalization defined in this book?

As the introduction outlined, whether a political system is nationalized or not can have effects on outcomes as varied as citizens' trust of government and the issues likely to top the political agenda. This chapter's next section focuses on nationalization's potential impacts on political representation as one especially important reason to study it in depth. In a nationalized polity, there is a potential mismatch between the focus of voters' attention and the issues that state and local officials are able to influence.

Next, this chapter outlines a small but insightful group of studies that discuss the nationalization of American politics explicitly. That research focuses almost exclusively on the federal level, using the local–national dichotomy as a way to understand voting for president or Congress. Considered jointly, these studies illustrate that political nationalization has not consistently risen but has instead proceeded in fits and starts over US history. In subsequent chapters, that over-time variation will prove critical in helping us rule out or qualify certain explanations of nationalization. Still, there is an irony in prior work: by studying voting for federal offices while ignoring voting in state and local races, these studies have concentrated on the elections in which nationalization is the least remarkable.

The chapter then juxtaposes a series of seemingly unrelated findings about American politics that, although not typically discussed in terms of nationalization, provide hints of its contours. Changes in the makeup of party activists, the role of membership organizations, the structure of political campaigns, the declining incumbency advantage: all of these disparate observations are clues that broader nationalizing processes are at work. In the postwar period, American politics has transitioned from elections centered on local party organizations to elections focused on candidates and now to elections dominated by national partisan identities. That transformation has important implications for the choices the parties present to voters.

In past work, the meaning of nationalization has varied from study to study. Still, having identified the varied conceptions of nationalization animating prior research, we are then able to define nationalization. For our purposes, nationalized political behavior has two facets. The first is when the political conflict and issues dominant at the national level are reflected in subnational political competition and voter behavior. The second is when political engagement is primarily oriented nationally, to the exclusion of subnational governments or political affairs. Distinguishing these two elements of nationalization is critical, as it is quite plausible that they have different explanations. This conception of nationalization applies primarily to multilevel systems, meaning not only the federal systems in the United States, Canada, and Germany but also to transnational institutions such as the European Union. By this definition, Huey Long's Louisiana was decidedly not nationalized. The Longs and the anti-Longs were both overwhelmingly Democrats in national politics. What's more, for many of those involved, the stakes of Louisiana politics in the Long era dwarfed those of federal politics.

Why Study Nationalization?

The study of nationalization has largely been the province of scholars interested in countries other than the United States, as detailed in chapter 6. But historians and social scientists have occasionally considered processes of nationalization within the United States. In fact, past scholarship points to several potentially nationalizing moments. To Clinton Rossiter (1956), the "first American Revolution" took place well before 1776, with colonists coming to think of themselves as a single distinctive people. McCormick (1973) detected the germs of nationalization in the political parties of the 1830s, as the two parties' desire to win the presidency induced them to compete throughout the country. The Reconstruction following the American Civil War was undeniably another period of national reintegration, however contentious (Foner 1988). So, too, were the final decades of the nineteenth century: then, the major political parties became national organizations in their leadership and organizational capacity (Klinghard 2010).[1] These examples leave unmentioned the New Deal, the world wars, and still other potentially nationalizing moments. They also omit a variety of economic and technological changes that have been thought to knit the United States together, from the construction of the Erie Canal and the transcontinental railroads to the interstate highway system.

Despite the variety of definitions of nationalization, the underlying motivation for studying political nationalization is often similar: whether

votes are cast with an eye toward national or local factors has critical implications for how voters are represented within government. In democratic
systems, a lynchpin of representation is that voters use elections to communicate their preferences (e.g., Downs 1957). In turn, how politicians act
in office hinges on their perceptions of voters' priorities (Mayhew 1974).
Think about a member of Congress. If she sees voters as prioritizing local
issues, she may respond in kind, perhaps by working for tangible benefits
for her constituents (e.g., Grimmer, Messing, and Westwood 2012). If she
instead thinks voters are nationally oriented, she may prioritize national-
level policy advocacy or leadership within her party.

Still, there are over five hundred thousand elected officials in the United
States, only 537 of whom serve at the federal level (US Census Bureau
1992). The remainder are state and local officials, from governors and state
treasurers to mayors, city council members, and school board representatives. If voters care principally about national issues, members of Congress
can plausibly redirect their efforts to focus on national priorities. But faced
with a nationally oriented electorate, it is unclear how a small-town mayor,
a state legislator, or even a state governor should respond. One risk is that
they might conclude that their reelection hinges on national-level factors
beyond their control, threatening the electoral connection and the premise
of democratic representation.

So long as state and local officials believe that their actions will have
a meaningful impact on their reelection prospects, they are incentivized
to work in ways that will win them votes (Ferejohn 1986). They will fill
potholes, help their constituents navigate bureaucratic processes, push
legislation that will improve local schools—whatever they see their constituents as passionate about. But should their belief in electoral accountability wane, they may prioritize other incentives, whether those of their
career, their party, allied interest groups, or their family and friends. In a
nationalized polity, for example, a governor may have stronger incentives
to pursue the policies favored by members of her party nationally than
those backed by her constituents. Likewise, a mayor may worry less about
allegations of corruption if voters' gaze is fixed on Washington, DC.

Evidence from Rogers (2016, 2017) indicates that such concerns are
not far-fetched. After analyzing state legislative outcomes, he concludes
that "presidential evaluations and the national economy matter more for
state legislators' elections than state-level economic conditions, state policy
outcomes, or voters' assessments of the legislature" (1; see also Schleicher
2008). State legislative races appear to depend far more on outcomes

outside of state legislators' control—say, the national economy or presidential approval—than outcomes they might plausibly influence. Or consider the example of 2006, when the Democratic Party won around three hundred new seats in America's statehouses (Johnson 2006). Those victories were fueled partly by voters' opposition to the Iraq War, a war that state legislatures had no say in or control over. In a federalist system, nationalization risks disconnecting the policy areas that state and local officials are responsible for from those that voters prioritize (but see Arceneaux 2005, 2006).

Nationalization has implications for political systems as well as individual officials. For one thing, the extent to which a nation's politics are nationalized or localized has profound implications for the issues it is likely to address—and for who is likely to win a given conflict. For Schattschneider (1960), to nationalize a political conflict is to involve a broader range of actors and to change the balance of power. In his words, "One way to restrict the scope of conflict is to localize it, while one way to expand it is to nationalize it" (10). The nationalizing example par excellence was the civil rights movement, a movement that was unfolding as Schattschneider wrote. Civil rights leaders worked consciously to draw northern whites into what had previously been considered a regional issue (e.g., McAdam 1982). Nationalization influences both the political agenda and the likely outcome on a given issue, as national issues eclipse local issues.

National issues are not simply broader in scope than local issues; they may be qualitatively different as well. Whether the question is a zoning ordinance or a property tax hike, many local issues are grounded firmly in property values and other questions of self-interest (e.g., Einhorn 2001; Fischel 2001; Self 2003). What is more, with many local issues, deducing self-interest is relatively straightforward. National issues, by contrast, are frequently symbolic (Sears 1993): they pit groups against each other based more on their values and identities than on their concrete interests. A more nationalized politics is potentially a more symbol-driven politics, a possibility examined in chapter 5.

Nationalization can also be reflected in the party system. In the words of Chhibber and Kollman (2004), "Having national parties, as opposed to fragmented, localized parties, tends to channel the choices of voters and politicians into a small number of coalitions and to force governments to confront national-level problems" (10). In the Canadian federal elections between 1993 and 2008, for example, the Bloc Quebecois won a majority or near majority of Quebec's seats while only running candidates within

Quebec. As a result, political competition in Quebec took place on different grounds than it did elsewhere in Canada, complicating the mapping from public preferences to legislative policy making (see also Johnston and Blais 2012).

To be sure, as the examples of the civil rights movement and the Bloc Quebecois make clear, nationalization is not inherently good or bad. It can be either, depending on the normative hue of the issues that are brought to the foreground or submerged as a result. The same could be said of nationalization's impacts on vote choice. If voters are more familiar with the national parties and their reputations, they might cast more informed votes when those same parties compete in subnational elections. Think back to the example of the Tennessee Supreme Court retention election highlighted in this book's introduction: if voters would otherwise know only the candidates' names, knowing their connection to the state's attorney general and the Affordable Care Act might lead to more informed votes. But nationalization might also crowd out legitimate local issues, inducing a mismatch between the issues on which voters evaluate candidates and the issues politicians can address in office. Whether nationalization helps voters cast ballots that reflect their preferences hinges on the baseline—on the information that voters would otherwise have used in figuring out whom to support. However we evaluate it normatively, nationalization surely merits study, as it influences who wins office as well as the priorities that officials and parties pursue while in office.

The Nationalization of American Elections: What We Already Know

Intermittently, scholars of American politics have studied the nationalization of voting behavior explicitly. One group of studies conceives of nationalization as a long-running trend. Focusing on political behavior, for example, Stokes (1967) finds a substantial decline in constituency-specific turnout patterns dating to the 1930s and then a subsequent decline in local influences on partisan voting. But while Stokes sees an unbroken trend of increased nationalization, his analyses stop in 1960—and according to Bartels's 1998 extension of Stokes's research, the nationalization of voting since then has proceeded more fitfully. Decomposing presidential voting from 1868 to 1996, Bartels charts the relative influence of partisanship, national, and state-level factors in explaining presidential election outcomes in the states over time. He finds that state-level factors were more influential in explaining patterns of support for the two parties from the 1870s to the 1920s and that they declined in influence between the 1920s and the 1940s. That is consistent with claims of rising nationalization around the time of the New Deal in the 1930s.

Still, Bartels also shows that state-specific factors regained influence in the 1950s and 1960s. Nationalization is not a one-way street. Nor is Bartels (1998) the only source of evidence that nationalization was incomplete well into the twentieth century. Using data up to 1990, Gimpel (1996) considers the related question of electoral incongruence between state and nation, "meaning that local electoral coalitions are constituted differently from national coalitions" (4). For Gimpel, the relationship between national and state politics varies in important ways across regions. While northeastern and midwestern states have significant demographic heterogeneity, strong political parties, and state-level divisions that are closely aligned with national divisions, those characterizations do not hold in the West.

Yet the post-1980 evidence in Bartels (1998) suggests that the nationalizing trend did resume, as state-level political forces proved less influential after Ronald Reagan's election. In summary, he writes that "on a broad historical scale, [these results] might be read as a reflection of long-term nationalization of the mass media and of American political culture more generally" (286). That certainly might be true. Yet, by separately accounting for each state's partisan leanings, Bartels (1998) employs a measure in which nationalization is distinct from partisanship. In that approach, nationalized elections are those in which states swing from their partisan baselines in tandem. Later, we instead consider partisanship as a potential vehicle of nationalization.

Another group of studies considers nationalization as a characteristic of particular congressional elections. For example, Brady, D'Onofrio, and Fiorina (2000) illustrate patterns of nationalization in congressional voting that are similar but not identical to those in presidential voting. They report that the national component of House voting dropped in the late 1950s and 1960s before recovering in the 1970s and early 1980s. Still, they chart another drop in the mid-1980s before a spike in the 1994 midterm elections, as voters nationwide turned against Democratic congressional candidates. And 1994 is not unique. In recent decades, some of the most nationalized congressional elections have come in midterm "waves," such as 1994, 2006, 2010, and 2014. The fact that these waves always target the members of the president's party suggests that negative reactions to a sitting president are one engine of nationalized voting (Abramowitz and Webster 2016). Still, as Burden and Wichowsky (2010) write, "Precisely why some election years appear to be little more than a collection of local elections while other years look like national referendums remains unclear" (454).

The Rise and Fall of Candidate-Centered Elections

The research that explicitly considers political nationalization in the United States is limited, with virtually no work on nationalization's impacts in state and local elections. But a largely separate body of research has detected various elements of nationalization, even if its authors rarely understand their findings in those terms. Nationalization proves to be an unseen unifying thread helping to stitch together disparate patterns in American voting behavior.

In a country with thoroughly nationalized politics, voters support or oppose candidates based on their affiliation with national political parties, parties that have fixed platforms and consistent symbolic associations across all parts of the country. To be sure, nationalized political behavior does not imply that the parties will perform equally well across space. If one party has disproportionate support among voters of a certain income or ethnicity, and if those groups are distributed unevenly across space, party support will differ across space even in a highly nationalized polity. But as a system grows more nationalized, the capacity of individual candidates to build a "personal vote" that is loyal only to them should decline absent some offsetting factor. The magnitude and causes of the personal vote in the postwar United States have been central questions in political science in recent years (e.g., Jacobson 2015), so it is valuable to consider that research and its implications for the nationalization of American political behavior.

Political scientists have long argued that the 1960s marked the beginning of a fundamental shift in the relationship between voters and elected officials, as television and a host of other legal, organizational, institutional, and technological changes led to increased candidate-centered voting. In the elections just after World War II, voting had been very party oriented, with strong party organizations (Aldrich 1995; Skocpol 1999), low levels of split-ticket voting (Hirano and Snyder 2013), and a modest electoral advantage for incumbent office holders (Ansolabehere and Snyder 2002;

Jacobson 2015). In the 1960s and 1970s, however, individual candidates were increasingly empowered relative to party organizations. Aided by television (Prior 2006) and professional offices, they were able to communicate directly with voters—and to build their own bases of support, which included voters whose loyalties were to them as individuals, not to their party. The rising incumbency advantage in the 1960s was evident for a variety of federal and state offices (Ansolabehere and Snyder 2002), some highly visible and some not, suggesting that it is "part of a nation-wide political transformation" (321) not limited to federal or legislative offices.

During that same period, the resources political parties could offer their candidates were changing as well. Prior to the 1960s and 1970s, the political parties in many places were deep, federated organizations with extensive local roots and armies of community-based activists (Aldrich 1995; Campbell 2007). In the period before widespread political appeals through television advertising or direct mail, those activists provided a means by which the parties could use social relationships and face-to-face contact to mobilize voters (Gerber and Green 2000). For example, as late as 1970, approximately 7 percent of Americans reported having worked for a political party (Putnam 2000, 41). To win the nomination of a local, state, or national political party in that context was to enlist these organizations in support of one's candidacy.[2] The varying strength of organizations in different jurisdictions provides one limit on the extent of nationalization (Trounstine 2008). In some places, party strength might be partly a legacy of the past, as party organizations successfully sustain themselves through the decades (Mayhew 1986). This social model of party organization also allowed for substantial heterogeneity in party platforms, organization, and strength across states. In many instances, party activists were motivated by tangible rewards like jobs, as we saw in the Huey Long example that opened this chapter. As a result, they were loyal principally to the group, not the particular policies it espoused (e.g., Key 1949; Phillips 1969).

By around 1970, however, that model was endangered. Like other political groups, the two major political parties were transitioning from organizations with large memberships and physical presences in many communities to professionalized organizations located primarily in Washington, DC (e.g., Aldrich 1995; Skocpol 1999, 2003; Putnam 2000). Whereas parties once offered candidates extensive community-level political networks, they increasingly offered services including polling and fund-raising instead (Aldrich 1995; Paddock 2005). By 1980, winning a party's nomination was far less likely to bring with it a corps of experienced party activists with close connections to local voters. As a result, candidates had increasing incentives to build their own organizations. From the viewpoint of voters, direct contact with a political party increasingly meant fund-raising letters from strangers, not house calls from neighbors. By 1996, the share of Americans who had worked for a political party had fallen to under 3 percent (Putnam 2000, 41) at the same time that American political campaigns had become vastly more expensive.

Beyond Candidate-Centered Elections

Although less remarked upon, the decades since approximately 1980 have brought another transition in the relationship between voters, candidates, and parties. While the 1960s and 1970s saw increasingly candidate-centered elections and a sizable personal vote, candidates' capacity to build personal bases of support appears to have waned more recently. Consider trends in the incumbency advantage, which is the additional vote share that accrues to candidates of either party when they are seeking reelection. The incumbency advantage rests on candidates' ability to build support not based on partisanship—and offers us one metric of the strength of the personal vote. Although it might be higher than its pre-1960 levels, the incumbency advantage has undeniably receded in recent years (Gelman and Huang 2008; Fowler 2015; Jacobson 2015), a trend that began in the 1990s for federal offices (Ansolabehere and Snyder 2002). Erikson (2017), for example, shows that the improved performance of sophomores in the House of Representatives—one measure of the incumbency advantage—peaked in 1980 and that it has been generally declining since. In 2010, the so-called sophomore surge was a 2–3 percentage point vote share bonus, a low incumbency advantage similar to those observed during the 1950s (see also Jacobson 2015; Abramowitz and Webster 2016).

It is not just incumbency advantage that has been waning. Studies of various aspects of voting behavior all point to the declining relationship between individual candidates and specific blocs of voters, often defined geographically. For instance, there is less geographic carryover from primaries to general elections than there was in 1980 (Hirano and Snyder 2013), meaning that candidates' patterns of support in primary elections are less evident come the general election. That fact is consistent with

the decline of local party organizations. Examining gubernatorial elections between 1965 and 2011, Meredith (2013) reports that the advantage
a candidate receives in her home county reached a peak of around 8.5 percentage points between 1977 and 1988 and then declined to 6.5 percentage
points between 1989 and 2000 and 5.6 percentage points between 2001
and 2011. Put differently, the friends-and-neighbors effect declined by
around 34 percent between the 1980s and the first decade of the 2000s.

As in the period just after World War II, federal elections in the years
since 2000 have seen a detectable but small personal vote. As was true
then, party-line voting in the last decade has proven to be an important
limit on the size of the personal vote. To build a personal vote is to win
support among voters who would otherwise have backed a candidate
from another party (Jacobson 2011). Thus, where party-line voting is
strong, the personal vote is likely to be limited. The 1990s and 2000s saw
a pronounced uptick in party-line voting, with 1994 representing a turning point (Jacobson 2016). The correlation between presidential voting
and voting for the House of Representatives reached a nadir at 0.51 in
1972 and then climbed to 0.95 by 2012 (Jacobson 2015, 2016), meaning
that presidential performance had become a near-perfect predictor of the
relative strength of the two parties in House races.[3]

Contemporary candidates are also having substantial difficulty winning voter support through their policy positions. In a study of seventy-
five thousand voters and eleven hundred congressional elections between
2006 and 2012, Tausanovitch and Warshaw (2015) find a "negligible" connection between incumbents' voting while in office and citizens' subsequent support for them. Today's voters appear to give far more weight
to *parties'* policy positions than to individual *candidates'* policy positions
(see also Schleicher 2008; Nyhan et al. 2012; Sniderman and Stiglitz 2012;
Hall 2015).

As explained in more depth in chapter 7, polarization and ideological
sorting are likely to have changed the electoral calculus decisively, making
it increasingly difficult for candidates and state parties to maintain platforms that are distinct from their national copartisans. Unsurprisingly, in
analyses of voting behavior, Ansolabehere and Snyder (2002) find that
"the differences in party divisions across the states have shrunk enor-
mously since the 1940s. . . . In most states, local party monopolies over
government have broken down" (328). It is thus incomplete to simply say
that the pendulum has swung back in favor of party-centered elections
in the period after about 1980. To be more accurate, we might say that

we have transitioned from elections centered on local party organizations to elections centered on candidates in the 1960s and 1970s and to elections centered on national partisan identities more recently. V. O. Key famously distinguished between parties as organizations and parties in the electorate. That distinction proves crucial in understanding why today's party-centered voting differs from the party-centered voting of the 1950s. And that, in turn, has crucial but little-noticed consequences for the nationalization of American political behavior.

In short, while recent research on American politics has not focused on nationalization or its causes, that research has nonetheless generated a wealth of findings relevant to it. The capacity of individual candidates to cultivate a personal vote—whether through their social networks, status as incumbents, or voting in office—has declined in recent decades. Today's vote choices are simply too nationalized for politicians to build much of a reputation separate from their party's. Still, to fully understand what these varied trends tell us about nationalization, we need to define the term precisely, our next task.

Defining Nationalization

Comparative research has conceived of nationalization primarily as an attribute of party systems, with nationalized polities being those in which the same slate of parties competes across the regions of a given country (e.g., Caramani 2004). But as applied to mass-level political behavior, nationalization might mean multiple things. For example, we might define nationalization in terms of the sources of behavior at different levels of the political system. To the extent that people are divided over the same issues locally and nationally, we might term such a politics "nationalized" (see also Gimpel 1996). Yet we might also use the term "nationalized" to refer to a political system in which voters are principally engaged with national-level politics and devote less time and attention to the politics of the various states, localities, or other subnational units.

For conceptual clarity, it is helpful to turn to spatial representations of political conflict (Downs 1957; Fiorina, Abrams, and Pope 2005; Jessee 2012) and to conceive of voters as having fixed but differing preferences across two policy dimensions. By "dimension," we mean a single continuum on which public policy might be set, such as the level of taxes or extent of government intervention in a given arena. Figure 2.1 illustrates

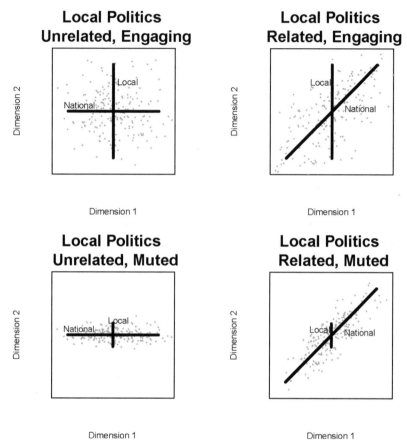

FIGURE 2.1. Possible configurations of national and local politics
This figure illustrates four possible configurations of the relationship between the animating dimensions of local and national politics. The solid black lines indicate the active dimensions at each level of politics, while the gray dots indicate the positions of would-be voters on two different issue dimensions. The bottom-right panel depicts nationalization along both dimensions.

four possible configurations of cleavages at the national and subnational levels. The space is Euclidean, so voters who are further apart in a given dimension hold more dissimilar views. We further simplify things by asserting that distance captures preference intensity as well: when preferences are further apart, mobilization and contestation are fiercer. The question then becomes about the choices that candidates and parties offer to voters and the dimensions on which those choices do or do not differ. The black lines indicate the dimensions active in local and national politics—and we'll set aside a mesolevel such as states for the moment, although one could extend this framework to include them as well, or else think of states as "local." Each gray dot represents a voter's position in this two-dimensional space.

In the top-left panel, national politics is defined by the horizontal issue cleavage and so is entirely on the first dimension, which we might imagine to be about the role of the government and the level of taxation. But with respect to local politics, the disagreement is exclusively on the second dimension. This second dimension could be about preferences for growth versus community preservation, or it could be about social issues like abortion and same-sex marriage. This dimension is at a right angle to the first, making it "orthogonal" or unrelated. One's views on the first dimension tell us nothing about one's views on the second dimension. Importantly, in this configuration, the issues dividing people in local politics are wholly divorced from the issues dividing people in national politics. And each level of politics is equally divisive (and perhaps equally engaging), as the equal lengths of the two lines make clear. That is, the stakes are equal. In this scenario, one could imagine separate party systems emerging at the two levels of government. For instance, after Huey Long's assassination in 1935, Louisiana politics was defined for decades by a split between the "Longs" and the "anti-Longs" that existed only in that state and that was contested primarily within the state's Democratic Party (Key 1949).

Another possibility is shown in the bottom-left panel. Here, too, local politics is fought over a different dimension than national politics. And here, too, knowing where someone stands in local politics tells you nothing about her views in national politics. But in this case, there is less disagreement about local politics and, quite possibly, less engagement with it. To the extent that there is political mobilization, it is likely to be primarily on national issues, as the disagreement on such issues is far more substantial. This configuration of muted local political conflict is quite compatible with theories that the scope of local politics is limited by local political institutions and competition between jurisdictions (e.g., Peterson 1981; Burns 1994; Rae 2003; Hajnal and Trounstine 2010; Gerber and Hopkins 2011).

Turning to the top-right panel, we see a different configuration. Here, local politics continues to be fought over the second dimension—and there are real differences of opinion on that dimension. But now, national political divisions encompass the second dimension as well as the first.

In this case, we might expect similarities in behavior targeting national and local politics, since the content of national politics now overlaps with local politics. Holding an attitude on the second dimension determines one's stance in local politics, but it also helps determine where one stands in national politics. National political competition includes elements of two separate issues. Local politics only divides voters on the second dimension. So while local politics is not merely an extension of national cleavages, nor is it entirely divorced from them. But local politics remains consequential in its own right. In this scenario, candidates and political parties face incentives to coordinate their efforts across the levels of government but also to offer meaningful views about local issues.

The bottom-right panel provides yet another scenario. As with the scenario just above, local political differences are exclusively on the second dimension, while national political differences are on both dimensions. But notice that the differences of opinion in both dimensions track the national political cleavage closely. Relatedly, the difference of positions represented in local politics is not wide, implying little room for conflict or mobilization. This fourth scenario depicts nationalization as it is defined in this book: national and local politics are fought over related dimensions, and the scope for disagreement in national politics is much wider. As a consequence, national political divisions infuse subnational politics, and political engagement is primarily national in orientation.

This conception of nationalization is distinctive in a few important respects: it focuses on political behavior rather than organizations or institutions, and it considers not just behavior directed at the national government but behavior targeting governments at all levels of the federal system. As a result, it is likely to vary in a continuous fashion over time. Some political moments are more or less nationalized, but nationalization is unlikely to ever be absolute. What is more, different aspects of political attitudes and behavior—from engagement and information to vote choice—can be nationalized to different extents.

This conceptual exercise says nothing about the crucial question of how national and local political cleavages come to be defined—or about where political attitudes or engagement come from. To the extent that we observe a relationship between national and local cleavages, it could be induced by voters' attitudes, by the choices elites offer, or both. Still, the exercise is helpful in defining nationalization, which we take here to have two separate but related elements. The first is about overlapping bases of political mobilization and division, with politics considered more nationalized when voters face and make similar choices across the levels of government. In the figure above, we might measure this aspect of nationalization by considering the angle between the national and local cleavages. More generally, to analyze nationalization defined in this manner, we need to focus on the choices offered by candidates and made by voters. The second aspect of nationalization is about engagement, with mass politics considered more nationalized when citizens allocate disproportionate time and attention to the national level.

To the extent that larger divisions on issues are more mobilizing, these two definitions will overlap. But they are analytically distinctive. One can imagine a nationalized politics where the presence of national issues in local politics serves to mobilize and foster engagement. Local candidates like DC's Patrick Mara are frequently unknown, but casting them in national terms also infuses the race with some of the energy of national politics. Local elections become a continuation of national politics by other means, and they become more engaging as a consequence. In that view, nationalization might serve to mobilize otherwise uninterested citizens, giving them a ready-made reason to care about state or local politics and so heightening participation. Still, one can also imagine a polity where interest in national politics crowds out interest in local politics and where local engagement is low. Sorting between these possibilities empirically is one task of this book, a task we begin in the next chapter. So, too, is the relative placement of state and local politics within this conceptual framework. Are they equally nationalized? In theory, either state or local politics could be nationalized while the other is not, making the extent of nationalization in those two arenas separate but related questions. It is to those empirical questions that we now turn.

CHAPTER THREE

The Nationalization of American Elections, 1928–2016

D an Bongino was born in New York City in 1974, and that is where he went to college. After a stint with the New York Police Department, he joined the Secret Service and moved to Maryland in 2002. Ten years later, he was the Maryland Republican Party's candidate for the US Senate—and in 2014, he contested the state's Sixth Congressional District, which stretches from Washington, DC's, Montgomery County suburbs north and west into the state's rural panhandle. Bongino's residence at the time was not in the Sixth District, and it was not especially close. In fact, residents of Cumberland in western Maryland could get to Pittsburgh, Pennsylvania, more quickly than to Bongino's home near Annapolis. But he contended that his place of residence should not be decisive: "Do you want a guy who geographically is your next-door neighbor but philosophically is a million miles away, or do you want the opposite?" Bongino asked (Schleifer 2014).

For Dan Bongino, it is self-evident that contemporary politics is nationalized. To represent someone politically *is* to represent them ideologically. But the idea that Americans might want to be represented by a neighbor— or more generally, by someone who lives in and is oriented toward the same geographic community—has a rich history in US politics (e.g., Fenno 1978; Grimmer, Westwood, and Messing 2014). Indeed, politicians' connections to a given district are frequently a prominent part of their advertising (Vavreck 2014). It is hard to watch television during election season without hearing about a candidate fighting for "Arkansas values" or "standing up for New Hampshire." In this chapter, we test whether contemporary voters' decisions and partisan identities are as nationalized as Bongino's question presupposes. Specifically, we examine empirical evidence on the alignment of political divisions across the offices and levels of government, the first face of nationalization as defined in the preceding chapter. The subsequent chapter turns to empirical tests of Americans' relative levels of political engagement across the federal system, which is the other face of nationalized political behavior.

Already, there is some evidence on the nationalization of America's federal elections (e.g., Burden and Wichowsky 2010; Jacobson 2015; Abramowitz and Webster 2016). Writing based on election returns up through 1960, political scientist Donald Stokes (1967) reports increasing homogeneity in turnout and partisan support across America's regions. From his vantage point, nationalization appeared to be consistently rising, making factors that have unfolded over many decades—like improved communications technologies—likely causes. But if Bartels (1998) is right that the nationalization of presidential ballots waned in the years after 1960, we need an explanation that can account for its falls as well as its jumps.

Still, the existing evidence has important limitations, as we saw in the last chapter. Most prior studies on the United States have not considered nationalization directly, and those that have focus on presidential and congressional elections without examining the impact of nationalization at other levels of the federal system. Moreover, even the most recent evidence is more than a decade old, leaving open the possibility of accelerating nationalization since the 1990s.

This chapter seeks to fill those voids by providing evidence from American voting patterns on the first component of nationalized political behavior, the alignment of political divisions across levels of government. It brings a wealth of data on Americans' partisanship and vote choices to bear. When studying the past few decades, analyses of nationalized voting can draw upon survey data, including the large-scale exit polls conducted by a consortium of media outlets. Yet our goal is not simply to quantify today's nationalized voting patterns. We also seek to document their variation over many decades so as to assess potential causes in subsequent chapters. To do so, we turn to county-level election returns dating back to 1928.

These analyses focus primarily on gubernatorial elections. That emphasis is a corrective to the singular focus on federal elections in prior work. But a more important motivation is the central role of governors in American federalism: governors are at once sufficiently visible and powerful that their elections should be a hard case for claims of nationalized political divisions (Ansolabehere and Snyder 2002; Kousser and Phillips

2012). If elections to any office are capable of generating state-specific divisions and dynamics, they should be races for governor.

We begin with analyses of voters' identification with the two major parties. Americans' identities as Republicans, Democrats, or neither have long been singled out as a uniquely powerful influence on vote choice (Campbell et al. 1960; Bartels 2002; Green, Palmquist, and Schickler 2002; Carsey and Layman 2006; Lavine, Johnston, and Steenbergen 2012). In typical situations, most partisans can be counted on to back their party's nominees, lending stability to federal elections in the United States (Zaller 2004). Put differently, since most voters are committed partisans, and since most partisans vote for their party's candidates, election results tend not to fluctuate wildly from year to year. Still, in prior decades, partisanship was thought to have a regional or state-specific element to it: people whose demographic and social characteristics might make them likely to be Democrats in some parts of the country could well be Republicans elsewhere (Dahl 1961; Phillips 1969). Consider a leading local businessman in the 1950s. In many parts of the North, he was likely to be a Republican, but in much of the South, the GOP was an anathema. Accordingly, this chapter opens by analyzing individual-level survey data on partisan identities. Americans' partisan identities have become less state specific since around 1980. For recent elections, once we know an individual's basic demographic characteristics, we learn essentially nothing about her partisanship by also learning her state of residence.

Much of the research on nationalization to date has made use of aggregated election returns, so our next analyses do the same. Using county-level data from 1928 to 2014 and exit poll data for more recent years, we find that presidential and gubernatorial vote choices have become increasingly integrated. Voting patterns in contemporary gubernatorial races are almost indistinguishable from those in presidential races, in spite of the sometimes pronounced differences in the candidates and their platforms. Still, this rise in nationalization has not been monotonic. Nationalization declined in the 1960s and 1970s, suggesting that factors internal to the political system might be behind its rises and falls. Moreover, county-level election returns and individual-level exit polls tell the same story, increasing our confidence in the patterns uncovered.

In reviewing past research, chapter 2 identified a variety of concomitant trends that bolster the claim that voting patterns are becoming increasingly nationalized. The decline in the congressional incumbency advantage and drops in "friends-and-neighbors" voting both are consistent with increasingly nationalized vote choices. In this chapter's final empirical analysis, we add one more such piece of evidence by charting the decline in presidential candidates' home-state advantage over time. Presidential candidates used to enjoy sizable advantages in their home state but do not today. Voters no longer buck their party to support a favorite son or daughter. And although nationalization can advantage either political party in specific moments, it has advantaged the Republican Party in recent decades.

The last chapter introduced us to Huey Long and the idiosyncratic but sustained political divisions that his reign brought to Louisiana state politics. Huey's grip over Louisiana politics has passed, and so too has the era when gubernatorial candidates were likely to induce novel geographies of electoral support. Considered jointly, this chapter's over-time findings point to nationalizing factors operating in the decades between 1930 and 1950 and again since 1980. The candidates that the major parties nominate for governor surely differ across the fifty states, but the geographic distribution of support they receive is increasingly indistinguishable from what their party's presidential nominees earn.

Partisan Identification and the Declining Political Distinctiveness of States

The book *In the Shadow of FDR* includes a description from a 1956 novel worth quoting at length. In that novel, the author "told his readers of 'Joe Wilson of Burlingame, San Francisco Peninsula, who was once Jere Wilzweski of Pittsburgh.' As he moved from the blast furnaces to a white-collar job and then to an executive position, he detected 'that everyone in the block, all of the barbecue-pit owners, the mechanical lawn-mower owners, the Chrysler and Mercury owners, the commuters, the Peninsulates, the Fortune-reading people, were Republican.' So he and his wife unobtrusively changed their registration to the Grand Old Party, 'and, finally, even began to reconstruct their memory of Roosevelt and remembered him as a socialist, father of much-marrying children, fomenter of discontent, upsetter of the peace, and heard and believed that Eleanor had never loved him'" (Leuchtenburg 1989, 57). Though fictional, the story of how Democrat Jere Wilzweski of Pittsburgh became Republican Joe Wilson of Burlingame is instructive. It certainly captures the role of partisan identities as a perceptual filter that shapes how people view political events past and present (Zaller 1992; Lodge and Taber 2013). But it also depicts that in earlier eras, Americans' partisan identities were related to both their social class and their social milieu (Berelson, Lazarsfeld, and McPhee 1954; Campbell et al. 1960).

As late as 1969, Phillips (1969) described an American party system in which many of the states had distinctive patterns of party allegiance. Like Joe Wilson, people who might be Democrats in one context could be Republicans in another. To test that possibility more generally, this section considers individual-level survey data. Its goal: to assess whether otherwise similar Americans have different partisan identities depending on their state of residence. As the central units in American federalism, and as the focal points for subnational party organization, states are a logical starting point in examining subnational clustering in Americans' partisanship. For these analyses, we focus on partisanship because it behaves like a persistent social identity (Green, Palmquist, and Schickler 2002; Huddy, Mason, and Aarøe 2015), making it less subject than actual vote choice to election-specific changes such as campaign targeting. It is important to add that as compared to the vote choices analyzed later in this chapter, partisanship is likely to be a lagging indicator of political change. Specifically, we analyze the American National Election Study's (ANES) cumulative file, which provides data on partisanship in most even years since 1948. The ANES is the flagship survey within the study of American politics, as it involves lengthy, face-to-face interviews with randomly sampled Americans. We specify the outcome as the classic seven-point scale of partisan identification, with strong Democrats coded as a 1 and strong Republicans coded as a 7.[1] Given the realignment of many southern voters over this period (Carmines and Stimson 1989; Green, Palmquist, and Schickler 2002), these analyses focus on 36,363 nonsouthern respondents to the surveys conducted in presidential and most midterm years between 1956 and 2012.

The primary quantity of interest is the intraclass correlation (ICC) from multilevel models (Gelman and Hill 2006), where states are the grouping of interest.[2] The ICC is a straightforward estimate of the share of state-level clustering: it represents the fraction of the total variation in partisanship that can be explained by knowing which state the respondent lives in. An ICC of 0 indicates that knowing which state a respondent calls home tells us nothing about her partisanship, while an ICC of 1 indicates that everyone in a given state shares the same partisanship and that states are thus perfect predictors of party identification. A score of 0 indicates no clustering, while 1 indicates complete clustering.

Of course, differences across states might simply reflect composition effects, or differences in who lives in a given state. For instance, African Americans are geographically segregated from non-Hispanic whites, so if Americans' racial backgrounds increasingly correlate with their partisan-

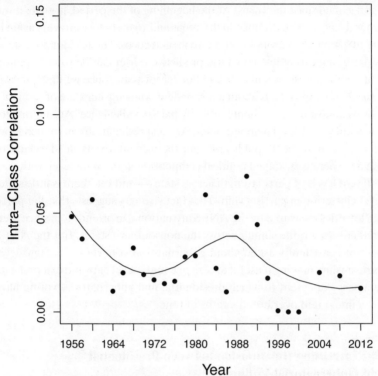

FIGURE 3.1. State-level variation in partisanship
This figure uses the American National Election Studies between 1956 and 2012 to predict partisan identification measured on a seven-point scale. The x-axis denotes the year of the survey; the y-axis depicts the intraclass correlation indicating the shared variance among respondents within a given state.

ship, we should expect to see rising ICCs irrespective of the impact of living in a specific state. To differentiate such compositional effects from the contextual effects of interest, we estimate the models of partisanship by year conditional on several individual-level demographic factors, including the survey respondents' education, income, race, gender, and religious identification.[3]

Figure 3.1 illustrates the results. The first thing to note is that the ICCs are never very large, meaning that the vast majority of the variation in how Americans outside the South identify politically is within-state variation. That said, the share of the variation explained by one's state of residence has declined since the 1980s. At the beginning of the period, in 1956, it was around 0.05. It then dropped in the 1960s and 1970s before growing again in the 1980s and then dropping in the 1990s and 2000s. The ICC for 2012 stood at 0.012, indicating just how little predictive power can be found in information about respondents' states.[4] For recent years, once we know several basic demographic facts about a respondent, knowing her state of residence tells us almost nothing about her likely partisan allegiance. Accounting for a few individual-level demographics, Arizona residents are not much more or less likely to be Republicans than their counterparts in Maryland or Maine. There is sustained political competition at the state level, with very different levels of party strength across states—and yet, there is little state-level clustering in partisanship. That fact strongly suggests that the partisan loyalties measured by the ANES are national in orientation, since their predictors are quite similar across the nonsouthern states. But the ANES has not consistently asked about gubernatorial vote choice or state-level partisanship, making it useful to turn to county-level data and exit poll data to assess the extent to which presidential and gubernatorial voting have been integrated over broad swaths of time.

The Increasing Relationship between Presidential and Gubernatorial Voting

Already, there is extensive evidence that Americans' voting patterns in federal elections have become increasingly anchored by partisanship in the past few decades (Bartels 2002; McCarty, Poole, and Rosenthal 2006; Levendusky 2009). Whereas in earlier decades, American voters were open to presidential and congressional candidates from the other political party, fewer and fewer voters are now willing to back out-party candidates (Jacobson 2015; Abramowitz and Webster 2016). Different parts of the country differ quite markedly in their baseline partisan leanings (e.g., Gimpel and Schuknecht 2003; Rodden 2013), so one likely consequence of rising party-line voting is increasingly stable geographic patterns (Hopkins 2017). States and counties that are reliably Republican or Democratic in one election should not appear in the other party's column two or four years later. And, in fact, analyzing presidential election returns through 2004, Glaeser and Ward (2005) find precisely that. To date, though, there is little evidence on the extent to which parallel trends are unfolding in state-level politics.

Here, we use county-level election returns to test the claim that state-level political divisions have become more nationalized. Specifically, this section examines the relationship between presidential and gubernatorial voting for the major parties between 1928 and 2014. The underlying data set was compiled by combining a variety of sources, including the county-level data set developed by Hirano and Snyder (2007), Congressional Quarterly, David Leip's Atlas of U.S. Presidential Elections, and various secretaries of state and state boards of elections. Our presidential-year data include the Democratic Party's share of the two-party vote for between 3,090 and 3,153 US counties, depending on the year in question.

To be sure, there are limits on what we can learn from aggregated election returns. Very different political processes can be obscured by aggregation, and it is unclear whether a given change is the product of a change among voters, candidates, or both.[5] Still, county-level election returns are available dating back many decades, allowing us to establish a time series—a data set with observations from different points in time—that begins before the New Deal. They are also a key source for earlier work, including Stokes (1967), and so facilitate comparisons with prior results.

If the same political divisions now animate national and state politics, we should expect to see certain features even in county-level election returns. One such expectation relates to electoral persistence, meaning the extent to which counties back the same parties in subsequent elections. If gubernatorial vote choices are driven by election-specific factors, we should expect over-time stability to be low, even if it is high in presidential races. In that scenario, each election would divide the state's electorate anew, and knowing how a county voted in a given election would not be of much use in predicting its support in the next election. However, if gubernatorial vote choices are driven instead by stable political identities, we should expect considerable persistence in county-level results from election to election. In figures 2 and 3 in this chapter's online appendix, we show strong evidence of the latter by tracing persistence in presidential and gubernatorial elections since the New Deal. Even in midterm gubernatorial elections, county-level patterns of support for the two parties have grown increasingly stable over the past few decades, with a particular spike after 1994. In their persistence at least, gubernatorial elections have come to look more and more like presidential elections. These trends are suggestive of a common set of factors that has been stabilizing both gubernatorial and presidential voting across space.

Still, evidence of county-level persistence in gubernatorial elections is not in itself evidence of nationalized political divisions. If elections are dominated by state-specific factors, organizations, or subnational identities that are stable over time, we should observe high levels of persistence across elections despite low levels of nationalization. Certain parts of Louisiana were consistently anti-Long, for instance (Key 1949). For that reason, we now examine a second, more central expectation from the nationalization hypothesis. If voters see choosing between a Democrat and a Republican for president in the same light as they see making that choice for governor, counties that lean one way in presidential races should have similar leanings for governor.

To test that possibility, we focus initially on thirty-two states outside the South that have held their gubernatorial elections during midterm years during at least some of the period from 1930 to 2014. Given Chhibber and Kollman's argument about the centrality of the New Deal in tipping the balance of power and interest toward the federal government—which we return to in chapter 6—observing elections as early as 1930 is important in evaluating different hypotheses about the nationalization of voting behavior in gubernatorial elections. And again, the absence of two-party competition in the pre-civil-rights-era South makes it critical to consider southern states separately (e.g., Key 1949; Carmines and Stimson 1989; Mickey 2015). Even after the Republican Party became competitive at the presidential level, it took at least a generation for the GOP to build strong organizations and field competitive candidates at the state and local levels.

For each midterm election and the elections immediately before and after, we use linear regression to estimate the relationship between the share of the two-party vote accruing to the Democratic candidate in a given gubernatorial election and the share earned by the Democratic presidential candidate two years prior. We do so while weighting by each county's total number of presidential votes. This metric tells us how close the relationship is between the geographic distribution of support for major-party presidential and gubernatorial candidates. A relationship of 0 would indicate that knowing which counties backed the Democratic presidential candidate tells one nothing about which candidates will back the Democratic gubernatorial candidate, while a relationship of 1 indicates a perfect linear correspondence. It is thus one measure of the nationalization of gubernatorial elections. In 1930, for example, 1,311 US counties met our criteria, and the estimated relationship when pooled with 1934 was 0.50 with a standard error of 0.02. For every additional percentage point that the Democratic candidate won in the prior presidential election, the Democratic gubernatorial candidate could expect an increase of half of a percentage point in support.

In the left panel of figure 3.2, we illustrate the same relationship for each midterm year. Depending on data availability and electoral calendars, the number of counties varies between 1,332 and 1,502. From 1930 to the early 1950s, the connection between presidential and gubernatorial voting rose, peaking in 1946—the first midterm election of the Truman presidency—at 0.76. It then slid sharply to 0.16 in 1962, when John F. Kennedy was president, and to 0.11 during the first election after Richard Nixon's 1968 victory. It rebounded to 0.44 in 1974, months after Nixon's resignation. Subsequently, it grew slowly, reaching 0.67 in 1986 and 0.84 in 2006. The 2014 midterms saw an increase to 0.93, the highest estimate observed in this time span. Counties' relative support for President Barack Obama in 2012 proved to be a very strong predictor of the relative support for Democratic gubernatorial candidates two years later. By this metric at least, 2014 represented the apogee of nationalized voting in gubernatorial elections. In that year, for the twenty-eight nonsouthern states that had gubernatorial elections, the distribution of partisan support was almost identical to that for the presidential election two years prior. The 2012 and 2014 elections had very different outcomes in terms of partisan support, with the Democrats winning in 2012 and the Republicans dominating in 2014, but the geographic distribution of relative support was essentially identical across those two years. The 2014 elections saw different candidates on the ballot in each state, and yet we can forecast the two-party vote share almost perfectly without accounting for any state-level factors.

By holding gubernatorial elections during the midterm year or especially during an odd-numbered year, earlier generations of politicians hoped to influence who votes for governor as well as the relationship between voting across different levels of government (Rosenstone and Hansen 1993; Anzia 2013). Without a presidential election on the ballot, fewer people vote, and those who do might have more state-specific factors in mind. Accordingly, in the right panel of figure 3.2, we consider the relationship between presidential and gubernatorial voting for states with on-cycle elections. Note that over the period in question, some states shifted from two-year gubernatorial terms to four-year gubernatorial terms, a fact that explains why twenty-nine states are included in this analysis.

As is clear, the on-cycle gubernatorial elections have seen a similar pattern, with rising nationalization in the 1930s and 1940s, a steep decline in the 1960s, and a rebound more recently. Intriguingly, though, in the most recent years, the level of nationalization has actually been higher in states that hold gubernatorial elections in midterm years (see also Javian 2012). This pattern was certainly evident again in 2016, with the GOP winning governors' seats in Democratic strongholds like Vermont while the Democrats prevailed in GOP-leaning Montana, North Carolina, and West Virginia. These less nationalized results are possibly a product of the particular states that currently hold on-cycle elections, a group of

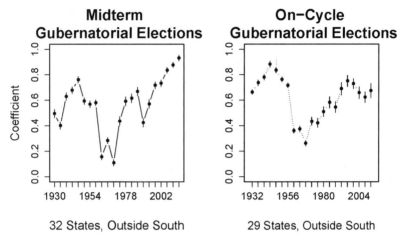

FIGURE 3.2. Relationship between presidential and gubernatorial voting
For counties in nonsouthern states, these graphs plot the coefficients when estimating the two-party share of the gubernatorial vote going to the Democratic candidate using the two-party vote share that went to the Democratic presidential candidate in the most recent prior election. On the left are the results for gubernatorial elections held during the midterm year; on the right are the results for those held during the presidential year. Each election year is smoothed with that before and after.

predominantly smaller states that also includes Delaware, Indiana, Missouri, New Hampshire, North Dakota, Utah, and Washington. The more personalized politics of smaller states (Lee and Oppenheimer 1999), perhaps coupled with incumbency advantage, could explain the relative disconnect between presidential and gubernatorial voting.

It is also plausible—though certainly not proven here—that the lower turnout in midterm elections has led to increasingly partisan electorates.[6] According to this interpretation, in recent decades, midterm electorates have diverged from presidential electorates as weak partisans sit out midterm elections. If so, that is another potential explanation for the lower correlation between presidential voting and gubernatorial voting when they appear on the ballot simultaneously. Still another possibility is that voters might feel more free to back an out-party gubernatorial candidate if they have just registered their partisan allegiance through their presidential vote. These issues undeniably merit more research. Either way, the results for presidential years serve as a useful benchmark for just how nationalized gubernatorial elections in midterm years have become.

To be sure, we expect to find evidence of nationalization in the South, given the increasing two-party competition there during the second half of the twentieth century (Black and Black 2009). We focus here on the eight southern states that hold gubernatorial elections in at least some midterm years, including Alabama, Arkansas, Florida, Georgia, South Carolina, Tennessee, Texas, and Virginia.[7] The number of observed counties varies between 422 and 866 depending chiefly on state election calendars. As figure 3.3 illustrates, the story for the South does appear to be one of increasing nationalization, with a pause in the late 1960s and 1970s when Republican presidential candidates were competitive while Republican gubernatorial candidates were less so. The relationship between

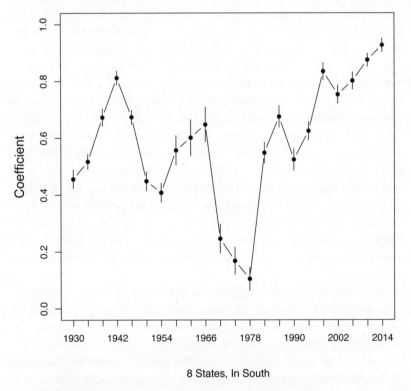

8 States, In South

FIGURE 3.3. Relationship between presidential and gubernatorial voting in the South, midterm gubernatorial elections

For counties in eight southern states, this figure plots the coefficients when estimating the two-party share of the gubernatorial vote going to the Democratic candidate using the two-party vote share that went to the Democratic presidential candidate in the election two years prior. Each election year is smoothed with that before and after.

presidential and gubernatorial voting is relatively low in the 1930s but then grows into the early 1960s before waning in the subsequent elections. In general, the elections after 1982 and especially after 1994 show consistently high levels of nationalization. In fact, the pooled coefficient for 2006, 2010, and 2014 is 0.87, making it indistinguishable from the 0.88 figure recorded for the nonsouthern states.

Evidence from Exit Polls

To this point, evidence of nationalization has come primarily from analyses of aggregate election returns. Yet to state the obvious, counties are not people. When analyzing aggregate data, there are persistent concerns about the problem of ecological inference, a statistical problem that appears when drawing individual-level conclusions from aggregate-level data (Achen and Shively 1995; King 1997). Another way to gauge the connection between presidential and gubernatorial voting over time is to look at the exit polls done for a consortium of news outlets during midterm elections.[8] Beginning in 1990, the exit polls consistently asked respondents about their choice in their governor's race as well as their vote (if they cast one) in the most recent presidential race. As their name implies, these exit polls are typically administered right as voters are leaving the polls. Exit poll respondents are by definition voters, meaning that exit polls provide an image of the electorate largely free from concerns about who actually turned out to vote. What's more, the sample sizes are quite large—in the six midterm elections between 1990 and 2010, we observe gubernatorial vote choices for a total of 68,059 respondents, including at least 6,299 in each year.

In figure 3.4, we use the exit poll data to chart the relationship between presidential and gubernatorial voting over time for all respondents in states with governors' races. On the vertical axis, we illustrate the correlation between reporting voting for the Democratic presidential candidate two years earlier and voting for the Democratic gubernatorial candidate in the midterm election in question.[9] These correlations range from −1 to 1, where a −1 means a perfect linear negative relationship, a 0 means that there is no linear relationship, and a 1 indicates a perfectly linear positive relationship.

In 1990, the correlation for all voters nationwide was 0.61, indicating a sizable but not perfect relationship between gubernatorial voting and

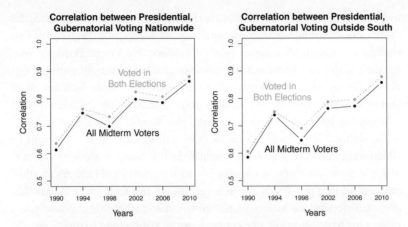

FIGURE 3.4. Growing relationship between presidential and gubernatorial voting
This figure illustrates the polychoric correlations between self-reported vote preferences in presidential elections and subsequent midterm gubernatorial elections. The gray line indicates voters who participated in the midterm gubernatorial election as well as the presidential race, while the black line indicates voters in the midterm election even if they did not cast a ballot in the presidential race.

presidential voting. Four years later, the correlation grows markedly to 0.75. The 1994 Republican wave not only ushered in GOP majorities in the House of Representatives and the Senate but also saw increasingly nationalized governors' races, as prominent Democratic incumbents including New York's Mario Cuomo and Texas's Ann Richards lost. But as the figure makes clear, 1994 was not the high-water mark for nationalized voting. The relationship between presidential and gubernatorial voting dropped somewhat in 1998, in part because Bill Clinton's resounding reelection in 1996 included a significant share of GOP-leaning voters. It then grew to a peak in the post-9/11 election of 2002. Strikingly, it remained high in 2006, at a time when the electorate swung from its 2004 support of George W. Bush to a widespread repudiation of GOP candidates. And while 2008 and 2010 represented another substantial swing in public preferences, from the first Obama victory in 2008 to the Republican resurgence in 2010, the correlation there was the highest during this span: 0.88. As the gray line makes clear, the basic trend is highly similar when we look only at people who voted in both elections.

The realignment of political loyalties and organizations in the South took decades, meaning that even in an analysis of the 1990s and 2000s, we need to check whether the results are driven by the South. In this case, the design of our sample makes that unlikely, as several southern states (including Louisiana, Mississippi, North Carolina, and Virginia) do not vote for their governors in midterm years. Nonetheless, the right panel of figure 3.4 illustrates that the removal of other southern states does not affect the substantive conclusion: between 1990 and 2010, the individual-level relationship between gubernatorial and presidential voting grew tighter.

As defined in chapter 2, one facet of nationalization is the extent to which national-level politics is fought over the same issues—and generates the same divisions or cleavages—as state-level politics. As another measure of that possibility, we now turn to a more technical analysis that does not depend on voters to remember whom they backed two years prior. Our basic question: does gubernatorial voting tend to divide people in the same ways as the previous presidential election? To answer it, we first develop a statistical model of presidential voting in a given election including a series of thirteen basic demographic predictors.[10] We then use that model to predict gubernatorial voting in the subsequent midterm election. If state-level idiosyncrasies lead to different political configurations, a single nationwide model of presidential voting will not do an especially good job of predicting how people will vote in their state's gubernatorial elections.

As figure 3.5 shows, we see an increasingly strong relationship between presidential voting and gubernatorial voting. The figure shows two lines. The top one indicates the model's average predicted probability that someone would vote Democratic for those who actually did vote for the Democratic candidate for governor. In other words, this number indicates how good the model is. A perfect model would score a 1, meaning that everyone who actually voted for the Democratic candidate was predicted to do so. In 1990, of actual Democratic gubernatorial voters, the model gives them a 59.8 percent chance of voting Democratic on average. The bottom line illustrates the average predicted backing for the Democratic gubernatorial candidate among those who did not actually vote for that candidate, which was 30.3 percent in 1990. The gap between these two figures gives an estimate of the model's predictive power and its capacity to predict gubernatorial voting using a presidential model. In 1990, the gap is 0.29, which is neither bad performance nor perfect. By 2002, however, the gap in predicted voting between actual Democratic voters and non-Democratic voters grows to 0.46, meaning that gubernatorial voting is increasingly predicted by the same factors that predict presidential voting.

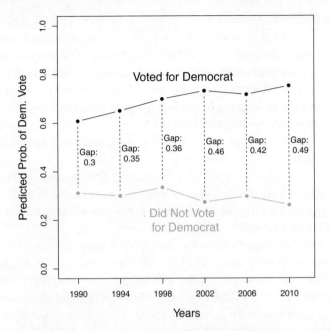

FIGURE 3.5. Predicting gubernatorial voting using presidential races
Using exit poll data, this figure shows the results when using models fit to presidential voting to predict gubernatorial voting in the subsequent midterm election. The black line indicates the average predicted probability of a Democratic vote for those who actually supported the Democratic candidate, while the gray line indicates the same quantity for those who did not support the Democrat. A growing gap between these two measures is indicative of the increasing capacity of presidential voting to predict gubernatorial voting.

The elections of 2004 and 2006 were very different ones. But despite the significant swing toward the Democrats between those two years, the gap in 2006 remains 0.43, well above its level in the 1990s. The gap then grew sharply in 2010, to 49 percentage points. To an increasing extent, gubernatorial voting looks like presidential voting.

Presidential Home-State Advantage

This chapter has focused on voting in gubernatorial elections—and for good reason. Governors are high-profile executives with a range of critical responsibilities (Kousser and Phillips 2012). As compared to other state and federal offices, governors enjoy the largest incumbency advantages

(Ansolabehere and Snyder 2002). If governors aren't able to distinguish themselves from their national party brand, down-ballot candidates for statewide office are unlikely to be able to do so, either. Still, if voting behavior is increasingly nationalized, that nationalization is likely to influence a variety of elections up and down the ballot. If candidates for governor can no longer count on local ties to win support from voters outside their party, then we shouldn't expect candidates for down-ballot state offices to do so, either. Already, we know that the once-pronounced incumbency advantage in congressional elections has declined markedly in recent decades, to levels not seen since the 1950s (Jacobson 2015; Abramowitz and Webster 2016; Erikson 2017). In fact, the incumbency advantage has declined in recent years for a range of offices, from down-ballot statewide offices to mayors (Fowler 2015).

But what about candidates for president? Scholars and pundits alike have long speculated about the vote premium presidential candidates earn from their home states (e.g., Lewis-Beck and Rice 1983). Indeed, party elites clearly consider candidates' home states and their electoral implications when deciding whom to back. But anecdotal evidence suggests that a pronounced home-state advantage may be declining along with the incumbency advantage. In the 2000 presidential election, Democrat Al Gore lost his home state of Tennessee by 3.9 percentage points, a state that had backed the Democrat in the prior two presidential elections and that could have made Gore president. In 2012, Republican presidential nominee Mitt Romney won just 37.5 percent of the vote in Massachusetts despite having served as the state's governor, barely outpacing the 36.0 percent won by Republican John McCain in a 2008 election that was less friendly to Republicans overall. The year 2016 was unusual, with both major-party candidates hailing from New York State. But even so, Donald Trump lost ground among the voters closest to his Manhattan residence: while 14.9 percent of Manhattanites had backed Mitt Romney in 2012, only 9.7 percent of Manhattanites backed Trump in 2016.

Here, we estimate the home-state advantage using regression models fit to every group of five consecutive elections between 1928 and 2012.[11] As figure 3.6 makes clear, in the 1930s and 1940s, there is considerable uncertainty about the estimated home-state presidential advantage. But the pattern since then is quite clear, with the home-state advantage growing to as large as 9 percentage points for the five-election window from 1972 to 1988 before declining in more recent years. For the period between 1996 and 2012, it stood at just 2.4 percentage points. There does

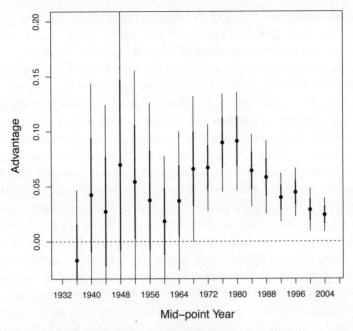

FIGURE 3.6. Declining presidential home-state advantage
This figure presents estimates of the home-state advantage for presidential candidates, estimated from samples of five consecutive presidential elections between 1928 and 2012. The dots
depict coefficients indicating the magnitude of the home-state advantage, with thick lines denoting standard errors and thin lines denoting 95 percent confidence intervals.

continue to be a home-state premium—but one that is a shadow of its
former self.

Nationalized Voting in 2016

The 2016 election saw the Republican Party's leadership lose control over
its nomination process (Cohen et al. 2016) and then the unexpected general-
election victory of Donald Trump. In theory, a populist outsider like Trump
has the capacity to scramble existing voting alignments and so might challenge the trend of increasingly nationalized voting documented throughout
this chapter. Although this book's analyses were largely complete prior to
the 2016 election, we now turn briefly to county-level election returns from
forty-one states to provide one final test of the claim that voting divisions

are increasingly nationalized.[12] Building on the analyses of partisan identification above—and anticipating the analyses in chapter 5—we employ
a different metric of nationalization by considering the consistency of the
mapping between demographics and presidential voting across regions.

Political scientists have long noted the different voting patterns of
non-Hispanic whites in the South and elsewhere (Key 1949; Bartels 2006;
Acharya, Blackwell, and Sen 2016). Earlier in this chapter, we saw evidence that the correlation between presidential and gubernatorial voting was increasingly similar in the South and the non-South. Even so, one
overlooked element of Barack Obama's victories in his 2008 and 2012
races was a vestige of regional distinctiveness: while Obama performed
quite poorly among southern whites, he won support from larger numbers
of white, noncollege voters outside the South. While Obama didn't win
white voters in either of his bids, one analyst concludes that 34 percent
of Obama's 2012 supporters were white voters without a college degree
(Cohn 2016). Such regional differences were crucial to Obama's wins in
heavily white, midwestern states like Wisconsin and Iowa. Given that, one
threat to the Democrats' post-Obama presidential fortunes was the prospect
that white voters without a college degree outside the South might come
to vote more like their southern compatriots.

The county-level evidence suggests that that's precisely what happened
in 2016. For both 2012 and 2016, we fit regression models predicting the
Democratic Party's share of the two-party vote using a variety of demographics. Those demographics include each county's percentage with a
college degree, its population density, its logged median household income, its share of Hispanic residents, and its share of residents who were
non-Hispanic white, black, Asian American, or American Indian. These
basic demographics prove more predictive in 2016 than they were in 2012,
as the R-squared statistic grows from 0.47 to 0.66. Moreover, in 2012,
voting in the South was distinctive. There was a more negative relationship between a county's percentage of white residents and its support of
Obama in the South than elsewhere—the coefficient associated with the
interaction between the percentage of white residents and being a southern county was −0.093 (SE = 0.030). Yet that same interaction dropped
to −0.041 (SE = 0.026) in 2016, as the relationship between counties' percentage of white residents and their support for the Democratic candidate in the South became less of an outlier. A postelection analysis by
Sean Trende and David Byler (2017) reaches a similar conclusion, noting that "even when you remove counties that have populations that are
more than 10 percent black, the rural South and Pennsylvania are roughly

equally Republican." This evidence is consistent with the claim that Donald Trump was elected president in part because a key group—white voters without college degrees—voted somewhat more consistently across the country. Far from undermining the hypothesis of rising nationalization, Trump's election appears to reinforce it.

Summary and Conclusion

In November of 2014, Republican Dan Bongino stood before the voters of Maryland's Sixth Congressional District. Bongino's disadvantages were considerable. The district had been gerrymandered to favor a Democrat, combining the Democratic-leaning DC suburbs with the far western reaches of the state. Bongino lived well outside the district he sought to represent; he grew up in another state. What's more, the particular Democrat Bongino faced was an incumbent who had won his prior election handily. But 2014 was a strongly Republican year, and Bongino came within 2 percentage points of victory. In an era of nationalized vote choices, neither Bongino's outsider status nor his opponent's incumbency did much to redirect the national tides.

The evidence presented in this chapter indicates that Dan Bongino's experience is increasingly the norm—and that it applies to elections for governor as well as elections for Congress. Overall, Americans' gubernatorial vote choices were nationalizing in the decades between 1930 and 1950 and again since 1980. While we will consider explanations of nationalization in depth beginning in chapter 6, it is worth briefly commenting on how these trends match up with a few common explanations for nationalization. While vote choices certainly became more nationalized in the American South, they also did so throughout the country, meaning that this isn't simply a story about the end of the one-party South. On their own, hypotheses based on political competition are not well suited to explain these findings, either: states in the Northeast, Midwest, and West have nationalized despite the consistent presence of two-party competition throughout this period. Nor do patterns in the centralization of political authority explain these trends straightforwardly, seeing as nationalization declined at the same time that the Great Society expanded the federal government's purview. Yet these results also undercut Stokes's conjecture that the cause is the expansion of communications technologies in some straightforward way—why should the expansion of television in the 1960s have reduced nationalization, while the expansion of radio and cable television had the opposite effect?

However, trends in political polarization match those in nationalized voting closely, providing a clue about one cause of nationalization.

What are the implications of the nationalizing trend in Americans' vote choices for the two parties' electoral fortunes? In specific districts and elections, nationalized political differences can help either of the two political parties win elections. In 2006, for example, Democratic candidates were the ones tying their down-ballot opponents to an unpopular president, while in 2014, the tables were turned. But on balance, the nationalization of vote choice since roughly 1980 has favored the Republican Party (Edsall 2015; Jacobson 2015; Abramowitz and Webster 2016). The advantage is most pronounced for legislative races, whether for Congress or for statehouses. Democratic voters tend to be very highly concentrated in larger urban areas, whereas Republican voters are more evenly spread out across suburbs, smaller cities, and rural areas (Rodden 2010, 2013). As a consequence, even legislative districts that are drawn with seemingly apolitical criteria such as spatial compactness will typically produce more GOP seats, as their voters are distributed more efficiently across space (Chen and Rodden 2013). In New York State, for example, there was no pro-Republican gerrymander as of 2014. But even so, the highest GOP margin of victory in congressional races was just 72 percent, while nine Democrats—mostly from in and around New York City—won their races by larger margins. From the point of view of maximizing seats, Democratic voters are inefficiently concentrated, even when Democrats have a hand in drawing the districts.

For the Democratic Party to win a congressional majority given the spatial concentration of its voters, its candidates need the votes of a sizable number of citizens who lean right in presidential politics (Rodden 2010). When the only political divisions are national ones, and when appeals to local loyalties and service fall flat, that task becomes exceedingly difficult. Consider 2012, a year in which the Democratic Party's US House candidates received 1.4 percentage points more votes than their GOP opponents and yet fell thirty-three seats short of capturing the House. The nationalization of voting divisions is thus part of the story of why a forty-year Democratic majority in the US House of Representatives gave way to a period of sustained GOP control with only brief interruptions (Jacobson 2015).

The same geographic skew also advantages the GOP overall in statewide elections for Senate or governor, although to a lesser degree. In 2012, Barack Obama won 51.1 percent of the vote, to Mitt Romney's 47.2 percent. Yet in a national victory of nearly 4 percentage points, Obama took only twenty-six of our fifty states, and he took two of those states (Florida and Ohio) by less than his nationwide margin. In 2016, the skew was more striking still: Hillary Clinton won the popular vote by 2.1 percentage points while winning only nineteen states. In either election, if we assume a uniform partisan swing, a fifty-fifty election nationally would have produced a decisive GOP majority when counting each state equally.

These facts about political geography may also help to explain why we saw nationalized voting ratcheting up most sharply during Democratic presidents' midterm elections, whether in 1994 or 2010. Such elections are ripe for nationalization: they combine vulnerable Democratic office holders whose partisanship is out of step with their constituents and an electorate mobilized by its opposition to a Democratic president (Erikson 1988; Patty 2006; Abramowitz and Webster 2016). Even in the wake of the 1980 election, when Ronald Reagan swept to victory, the Democrats held twenty-seven governorships, including in pro-Reagan states like North Carolina, Utah, and Montana. By early 2017, as Donald Trump took office, Democrats held only sixteen of the nation's governorships, including only four in states won by Trump.

Our focus in this chapter has been on the state level, partly because of the centrality of governors in state-level politics (Kousser and Phillips 2012), partly to counterbalance the federal focus of prior work, and partly because of data availability. Simply put, there are very few surveys about local policy preferences, especially covering multiple cities (but see Oliver, Ha, and Callen 2012). Yet even at the local level, there is evidence that attitudes on local public policy questions are closely integrated with national policy attitudes. In an investigation of residents' ideology across sixteen hundred US cities and towns, Tausanovitch and Warshaw (2014) report "no evidence that separate forces are at work in determining citizens' positions on municipal policy questions and federal policy questions" (10). They find that liberal-conservative ideology, defined with respect to national issues, tracks municipalities' overall spending levels closely. That reinforces the evidence we have seen throughout this chapter, evidence indicating an ever-closer alignment between national and subnational political divisions.

From the point of view of state and local political participation, it is not immediately clear whether nationalized vote choices are likely to be mobilizing or demobilizing. If voters are primarily interested in national politics, it is possible that infusing state or local politics with a national dimension might increase interest and engagement, as state and local elections become proxy wars. But it is also possible that the absence of durable divisions in state and local politics will lead voters to wait for the federal or even presidential elections that move them before casting their ballots. Americans' levels of engagement across the federal system—and any changes over time—are the topic of the next chapter.

CHAPTER FOUR

Staying Home When It's Close to Home

In Chicago politics, 1983 was a landmark year. In that year, incumbent mayor Jane Byrne was challenged in the Democratic primary by both Harold Washington and Richard M. Daley. Washington, a US congressman, sought to make history as the city's first black mayor. For his part, Daley was the son of Richard J. Daley, the Democratic Party chieftain who had served as the city's mayor for more than twenty years. The Democratic primary alone drew 1.17 million voters to the polls—and turnout was higher still in the general election, when 1.29 million voters narrowly chose Washington over his Republican opponent, Bernard Epton (Hajnal 2007). The following fall, when it came time to choose between incumbent president Ronald Reagan and his Democratic challenger, Walter Mondale, turnout in Chicago dropped by nearly three hundred thousand voters. More Chicagoans wanted a say in their mayor than in their president.

Chicago's 1983 mayoral election was undeniably unusual, with racial divisions between black people and white people providing a powerful motivation for political engagement (Hajnal 2007). Epton's campaign even briefly employed the slogan "Before it's too late," an obvious reference to whites' fears of black takeover. But while that election engendered atypical interest, it was not unique when compared to local or state elections of earlier eras. In some moments of American political history—and in some other countries in recent years (Horiuchi 2005)—subnational elections have seen voter interest that equals or even outpaces that of national elections. As this book's introduction made clear, that pattern of subnational primacy is in line with what the framers of the US Constitution anticipated: as compared with the national government in Washington, the state governments were more proximate and were expected to enjoy deeper voter loyalty (Levy 2007). This chapter thus presents over-time evidence on the second face of nationalization identified in chapter 2: Americans' political engagement and participation across the levels of the federal system.

People are unlikely to participate if they lack the motivation to do so. And although existing research on political engagement focuses over-whelmingly on *federal* politics, engagement is likely to underpin partici-pation in state and local politics as well. Accordingly, in its opening sec-tion, this chapter considers what two well-developed perspectives on why people vote lead us to expect about participation in subnational politics. From the first—the instrumental perspective—we might expect citizens to be highly engaged in state and local politics. States and localities are charged with a range of responsibilities that have a direct bearing on Americans' lives. If self-interest is a primary motivation for participation, the state and local levels are central venues in which to defend that inter-est (Fischel 2001; Schleicher 2008). Also, the smaller sizes of states and especially localities make a given voter much more likely to be pivotal. An expressive or symbolic perspective, by contrast, leads us to expect people to participate in politics in large part because it engages with social groups and identities to which they feel attached. In this view, we should see dis-proportionate engagement at whatever level identities and emotional at-tachments are strongest.

Empirically, the chapter then uses data from various surveys to docu-ment that Americans today are markedly more engaged with national pol-itics than state or local politics. Among the evidence presented, we see that the ability to name one's governor has declined in recent decades, even as the ability to name the vice president has remained roughly constant. Today, Americans' favorite and least favorite politicians are overwhelm-ingly at the federal level. Americans care more about the party who con-trols the federal government, and they can describe their president in more detail than their governors. In fact, the lure of the presidency is so strong that in virtually every US state, web search traffic is higher for the presi-dent of the United States than for the state's governor—and that is usu-ally true even during the months when those governors are standing for election while the president is not.

Survey data also illustrate that Americans are not paying disproportion-ate attention to the federal government because they believe its actions have the greatest impact on their daily lives. Even as voters acknowledge the substantial impact of state and local government, they remain fixated on national politics, a finding that this chapter terms the "presidential paradox." This result undercuts the claim that nationalized engagement is driven straightforwardly by the migration of authority to the federal government, as Americans continue to recognize the authority of states and localities. The expressive approach, with its emphasis on identity, attachments, emotions, and narratives, gives us a straightforward way to make sense of the disproportionate attention to the nation and the presidency. Politics in the United States has become a contest of evocative symbols, and state and local politics are largely devoid of such symbols.

To illustrate that these patterns are no mere artifact of survey responses, we turn to analyses of campaign contributions, a real-world political behavior. In 1990, approximately two-thirds of all itemized, individual-level political contributions went to candidates in the same state as the respondent. By 2012, just one-third of contributions went to in-state candidates, as donors increasingly prioritized candidates who did not formally represent them. We also see that while individual-level contributions to gubernatorial candidates have grown slowly, contributions to Senate candidates have spiked in recent years. These patterns provide compelling evidence of the increasingly national focus of political behavior, since donors are now giving more and more across state lines and to candidates who influence partisan control of national institutions. In light of extensive research on campaigns' and parties' central role in mobilizing voters (Wolfinger and Rosenstone 1980; Rosenstone and Hansen 1993; Verba, Schlozman, and Brady 1995; Green and Gerber 2008; Hersh 2015), these findings also suggest that nationally visible campaigns are more likely to have the resources needed to mobilize voters than state- or local-level campaigns. To some extent, the national interests of political donors could be contagious, as they influence campaigns' capacity to mobilize voters. Nationalized giving begets nationalized voting.

In representative democracies, voting is arguably the central mechanism through which citizens at large influence policy making, so it is critical to measure whether Americans' differential engagement in national politics translates into nationally oriented patterns of voter turnout as well. Accordingly, the chapter closes by considering voter turnout data from big-city mayoral and gubernatorial elections. Using presidential election turnout as a baseline, it documents the relative declines in turnout at the state and local levels. There have been ongoing debates about how to assess the levels of voter turnout in national politics and the decline in voter turnout after 1968 (Rosenstone and Hansen 1993; Putnam 2000; McDonald and Popkin 2001; Franklin 2004; Leighley and Nagler 2014). But however one assesses turnout nationally, turnout is frequently much lower in state and local politics. When the election is closer to home, voters are more likely to stay home. These differences in engagement and turnout across the federal system also give us new insights about the expressive motivations underpinning Americans' turnout decisions, a point developed in this chapter's concluding paragraphs.

Adapting Theories of Participation for a Federal System

Political engagement—that is, interest in politics, a sense of political efficacy, and basic political knowledge—is an important attitudinal prerequisite to political participation (Verba, Schlozman, and Brady 1995; see also Delli Carpini and Keeter 1996). Put simply, people who know more about politics and are more interested in politics are more likely to get involved. Understanding political engagement is especially important in the United States, both because political participation is strictly voluntary and because the litany of federal, state, and local elections provides so many opportunities to vote (Rosenstone and Hansen 1993; Anzia 2013). In recent years, research on Americans' political engagement has been almost entirely research on their engagement with *federal* politics. How does their engagement with state- and local-level politics compare?

Even casual observers of American politics know that voter turnout is highest in presidential elections—and that holding off-cycle elections is an effective strategy for changing the composition of the electorate and keeping turnout down (Oliver, Ha, and Callen 2012; Anzia 2013). But assume the vantage point of someone unfamiliar with our modern-day political system, and Americans' differential turnout in federal elections becomes less a self-evident fact and more a puzzle to be explained. Here, we consider two broad classes of theoretical explanations for political participation and draw out their implications for voters' relative engagement across the levels of the federal system.

Instrumental Explanations

From Madison to the present, one line of thinking about voter participation in America has emphasized instrumental motivations: people participate in politics to influence how they are governed. Under the classic "calculus of voting" approach, voters are more likely to vote as the benefits of doing so and the probability of casting the decisive vote rise (Riker and Ordeshook 1968; Aldrich 1993). The benefits of voting, in turn, are the difference in policies to be enacted by the different candidates. The more candidates' views on policy diverge, the more it matters who wins.

One element in the calculation of instrumental impact is the size of the group in question. As Schuessler (2000) explains, "Economically, small groups provide greater returns to individual action, in that both the individual's share of the public good as well as the individual's instrumental responsibility of bringing about the public good, are increased" (34; see also Olson 1965). Voters are far more likely to be pivotal in local or state elections than in national elections, since the number of voters for president is frequently thousands of times larger than the number for mayor or state legislator. Elections that are exactly tied, almost unheard of in national politics, do occur in state and local politics (Enos and Fowler 2014). Even in Florida in 2000, 537 votes separated George W. Bush and Al Gore. By contrast, in November 2015, a race for the Mississippi statehouse ended in a tie, with both the Democrat and Republican winning exactly 4,589 votes.

What's more, the policy questions that animate local or even perhaps state elections might have a direct impact on voters in ways that national politics might not. In the United States, the homeownership rate at present is around 64 percent, and in 2010, the median home sold for $222,000 (Callis and Kresin 2015). For many voters, their single most valuable asset is their home. The value of those homes can be powerfully affected by local decisions about school district boundaries, zoning, development, or transportation (Burns 1994; Fischel 2001). If political participation is to an important extent instrumental, it is not obvious that voters' engagement and participation should be primarily national.

Outside the instrumental approach, there are still other reasons to suspect that local politics should have the advantage in the race for public attention. One of the key insights of recent scholarship on voter participation is the capacity of social networks to catalyze political participation (Putnam 2000; Gerber, Green, and Larimer 2008; Bond et al. 2012; Sinclair 2012). People are more likely to take part in politics when asked to do so—and especially when asked by someone they know. In local politics, it is not uncommon for would-be voters to know the candidates personally and for outreach to take place largely through networks of friends and neighbors (Oliver, Ha, and Callen 2012). The evidence bears this out, at least as of 1990. In that year, Verba, Schlozman, and Brady (1995) found that when it came to volunteering on political campaigns, 50 percent of those who volunteered had worked on a local campaign as compared to just 22 percent at both the state and federal levels (55). Under some conditions, and for some people, local politics can be the main political event.

Taking an international perspective reinforces that claim. Horiuchi (2005) documents a variety of cases in which lower-level elections saw higher turnout than did national elections, from rural Japan to pre-1924 Australia and specific elections in Canada, Finland, India, Northern Ireland, Spain, and Switzerland (3–4; see also Sellers et al. 2013). At times, more voters have turned out in provincial elections than in federal elections in the Canadian provinces of Newfoundland, Prince Edward Island, and Quebec. In fact, in Canada's 2015 federal election, Quebec's turnout was 67.3 percent, putting it nearly 4 percentage points lower than the turnout recorded during the 2014 provincial election. That set of international examples also furnishes a clue about the conditions under which subnational politics is likely to become the marquee event. Many of those examples are societies with some level of subnational autonomy and significant ethnic divisions. Whether in Chicago, Quebec, or Northern Ireland, elections that are infused with questions of ethnic identity can drive up subnational engagement (Levy 2007).

Expressive Explanations

These cross-national observations track more closely with the second class of theoretical explanations, ones that explain political participation as the product of expressive or symbolic rather than instrumental considerations (e.g., Sears 1993; Schuessler 2000). The expressive view of participation typically builds from observations about people's attachments to social groups (e.g., Huddy, Mason, and Aarøe 2015). Across a variety of situations, people's sense of themselves depends to an important extent on the status of the social groups with which they identify (Tajfel 1981). In some cases, these social groups can be very narrowly defined, whether as a single high school class or the residents of a city block. But meaningful groups are often much larger and more abstract. As any sports fan can attest, you don't need to know every group member personally—or even know how many group members there are—to feel a strong allegiance to the group. Indeed, one of the mysteries of contemporary nationalism is how people can feel so passionately about an "imagined community" when they will never meet more than a tiny fraction of its members (Anderson 1991).

In different situations, there are a wide variety of social identities that might be operative (Roccas and Brewer 2002; Klar 2013). National identities (e.g., Theiss-Morse 2009; Schildkraut 2011, 2014) and other place-based identities (e.g., Wong 2010) are one common and influential class of social identities, but they are far from alone. Americans' identities as Republicans, Democrats, or Independents can powerfully influence how they think, feel, and act as well (Green, Palmquist, and Schickler 2002; Hajnal and Lee 2011; Iyengar, Sood, and Lelkes 2012; Klar 2014; Theodoridis 2015). Under the right conditions, there are many social groups that can generate intense attachments and in turn influence people's emotions, attitudes, and behaviors. Connections to their companies were critical in keeping Union soldiers on the front lines during the Civil War despite the incredible risks involved (Costa and Kahn 2010). Or as another example of the power of group connections, consider that college students who identified with a political party felt positive emotions when exposed to undeniably bad news about economic performance or US troop deaths that nonetheless boosted their party's prospects (Combs et al. 2009). The positive implications for their political party outweighed the negative implications for other social groups.

Whether the social group is defined by service, geography, partisanship, or something else, these strong emotional attachments to groups can in turn motivate behavior in defense of the group and its status (Sears 1993; Ethier and Deaux 1994; Marcus 2006). As a consequence, people's political attitudes and behavior are likely to depend on how closely connected they feel to the relevant social groups (Ethier and Deaux 1994; Deaux 2000; Combs et al. 2009; Lavine, Johnston, and Steenbergen 2012; Huddy, Mason, and Aarøe 2015). They are also likely to depend on the norms that are central to the social identity in question (Theiss-Morse 2009; Schildkraut 2014). If being a good American, a Democrat, or a Republican entails voting, those attachments might prove especially potent engines of political engagement. In a 2002 survey, Theiss-Morse (2009) finds that at least 89 percent of American respondents cite "respecting US institutions" as important in truly being American.

The situation can shape how social identities translate into attitudes and behavior as well. For one thing, threats to the group and its status have a particular power to mobilize people (Sherif et al. 1961; Miller and Krosnick 2000; Huddy 2013). More generally, different situations are likely to invoke different identities and the different social norms that come along with them (e.g., Klar 2013). For example, as a general rule, people do not identify strongly with the particular hotel room to which they are assigned. Nonetheless, Goldstein, Cialdini, and Griskevicius (2008) find that if you want to encourage hotel guests to reuse towels, telling them that "75 percent of guests who stayed in this room participated in our new resource savings program" is more effective than appealing to them as citizens or as men and women. This finding illustrates how different situations can evoke different identities: when in a hotel room, the relevant norm is how other guests in that room acted. The influence of a given social identity comes not just from its overall strength or salience but also from its relevance to a particular decision.

With this background in social identities, we can turn back to the question at hand: in a federalist system, are people more likely to participate in national, state, or local elections? Instrumental vantage points emphasize the role of interests in participation: people will vote more frequently at the level where doing so is most likely to advance their interests. But from the expressive vantage point, people vote because of their connections to relevant social groups. In the words of Schuessler (2000), "Individuals often are motivated by a desire to express their tastes, or preferences, because such expression has a direct influence on who they are—on their identity" (3). In some cases, to be a group member is to perform certain acts: part of one's identity as a Republican or a Democrat is voting for those parties. In others, people participate to connect themselves to different outcomes or states of the world. For instance, Schuessler (2000) explains that under the expressive view, "my motivation to participate is grounded not in the calculative realm of strategically producing states of the world, but in the interpretative realm of attaching myself to those states" (15). Here, people join protests, vote, or otherwise engage in politics because of what it says about themselves (see also DellaVigna et al. 2014).

One challenge with theories emphasizing expressive motivations is their flexibility. Clear predictions emerge from expressive accounts only when they provide an explanation of why people want to attach themselves to certain outcomes or to identify with certain groups. That said, to the extent that political participation has expressive motivations, political engagement should be connected to the strength and content of different identities. Higher engagement in national elections should reflect stronger attachments to relevant national-level groups, whether those groups are defined by partisanship, nationality, or in other ways. The content of group identity is also likely to matter: if one key element of American national identity is a commitment to democratic politics, adhering to that identity is especially likely to encourage participation. In chapter 8, we take up questions of Americans' attachments to their nation, states, and localities in more depth, considering the strength and content of those various attachments. Here, our goal has been to outline an expressive account of political participation that indicates when we should expect national engagement to outstrip state or local engagement. We turn now to empirical assessments of Americans' engagement and participation across the levels of the federal system.

Our Declining Knowledge of Governors

Some knowledge about politics has long been seen as a prerequisite to effective participation (Mill 1869). In the decades after World War II, American society saw a vast expansion of education, as Americans were increasingly going beyond high school to seek college and even professional degrees. Education is a well-known correlate of political knowledge. People who have spent more time in school are more likely to know specific facts about politics and government (Delli Carpini and Keeter 1996). Those observations set up a puzzle for political scientists: if education levels rose markedly, why were Americans no more knowledgeable about politics in 1995 than they were in 1965 (Delli Carpini and Keeter 1996; Prior 2007)? Still, our measures of political knowledge have been almost entirely measures of federal politics, and it remains unclear whether state- and local-level knowledge has remained roughly constant as well.

Given that people who are more knowledgeable about politics are more likely to participate—and more able to participate meaningfully—assessing knowledge in subnational politics is critical. To do so, we turned to the Roper Center's iPoll archive and identified various questions that were asked about voters' knowledge of their governors over the years. Figure 4.1 illustrates the results—and shows that the share of Americans who are able to name their governor has dropped substantially in recent decades, from the 85 percent recorded in 1949 to the 66 percent recorded in 2007. There is less evidence that knowledge of national politics has declined in a similar way (e.g., Delli Carpini and Keeter 1996). For instance, a June 1996 Gallup/CNN/*USA Today* survey found that 69 percent of Americans could correctly name the vice president, a figure that differs little from the 64 percent who could name the vice president in a February 1945 Gallup poll.[1] In the

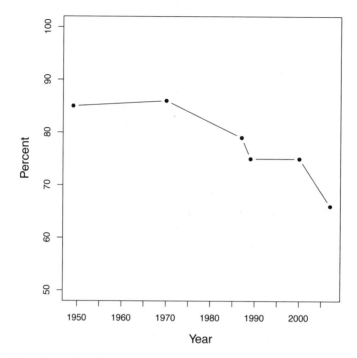

FIGURE 4.1. Knowledge of state's governor over time
Drawing on surveys from various sources, this figure presents the share of US adult survey respondents who can correctly name their state's governor. Note that there was no check for accuracy in the 2000 survey.

postwar period, Americans' educational attainment improved markedly, their knowledge of national political figures remained flat, and their knowledge of state-level figures declined. This evidence is one indication of nationalized political engagement, as the trends in Americans' knowledge of state-level politics and of national politics have diverged in recent decades.

Describing Executives

Another approach to measuring voters' relative interest in different levels of the federal system is less direct but perhaps more satisfying. Both our 2013 and 2015 Survey Sampling International (SSI) online surveys included open-ended questions asking respondents to describe their president, their governor, or both to "someone from elsewhere." Our respondents could type as much or as little as they liked—and the length of those descriptions provides us with another measure of respondents' relative interest and engagement across the federal system. For instance, one 2013 respondent described his governor by calling him a "true Texan with conservative and family values, and a defender of the Constitution"; for President Obama, the same respondent explained that "he is an egotistical person who has an agenda and is trying to run the United States without listening to the will of the people." This respondent does identify Texas governor Rick Perry as a "true Texan" but goes on to note Perry's defense of the federal Constitution. In this case, to uphold Texan values is to defend the US Constitution.

As figure 4.2 shows, in both years, respondents had more to say about their president, even (or perhaps especially) when they did not think of him as *their* president. In 2013, the average response was just thirty-six characters for the governors as compared to fifty-two characters for the president ($p < 0.001$). Put differently, responses were 49 percent longer when describing the president, a marked difference depicted on the top of figure 4.2. The difference is still evident but less pronounced in 2015, at fifty characters versus forty-four ($p = 0.05$). Americans' descriptions of their presidents are longer, an indication of their greater knowledge and engagement with presidential politics.

Most contemporary Americans identify with one of the two major parties, and those identifications are themselves a potent motivator of political action (Keith et al. 1992; Green, Palmquist, and Schickler 2002; Lavine, Johnston, and Steenbergen 2012; Klar 2014; Theodoridis 2015). Much as baseball fans' connection with their team encourages them to attend its games, citizens' "rooting interest" in the fight between the two political parties leads them to vote. So, an alternative approach to measuring Americans' relative engagement across the federal system is to ask about whether it is more important to have a governor or a president who shares their political party. Figure 4.3 shows that the preference for a president of the same party is overwhelming, with 71 percent of 2015 SSI respondents preferring that their party win the presidency. And while one might worry that the results are driven by Republicans' reactions to Obama, they are not: the Democrats in the same survey prefer to control the presidency by a 74 percent to 26 percent margin.

As another measure of respondents' relative attention to different levels of government, the 2014 GfK survey asked them to name up to three current representatives in the US Congress, whether in the House or the Senate. We then coded the number of in-state officials (on average, 0.69) and out-of-state officials named (on average, 0.71). Respondents are almost equally likely to name a senator or representative from another state as from their own state. We also asked respondents about their least favorite politician and identified cases where the least favorite politician was in

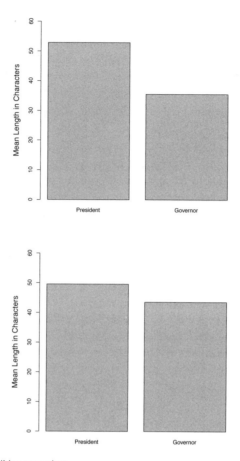

FIGURE 4.2. Describing executives
In the 2013 and 2015 SSI surveys, respondents were asked to describe their governor and/or the president to someone from elsewhere. The descriptions of the president were 49 percent longer in 2013 (*top*) and 14 percent longer in 2015 (*bottom*).

state. Only 15 percent of respondents who named a least favorite politician identified someone in their state of residence. Political action is to an important extent motivated by negative emotions—by threat, dislike, anger, fear, and anxiety (Brader 2006; Brader, Valentino, and Suhay 2008; Gadarian 2010; Iyengar, Sood, and Lelkes 2012; Gadarian and Albertson 2014), and from respondents' least favorite politicians, it is clear that those negative emotions are directed overwhelmingly at politicians on the national stage.

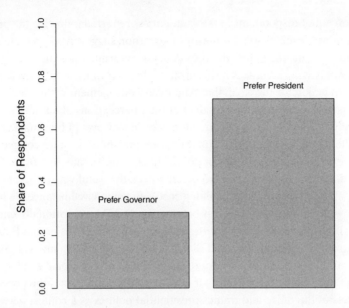

FIGURE 4.3. Prefer same-party governor or president?
This figure shows the distribution of responses to a question in the 2015 SSI survey about whether respondents preferred that their party win their state's governorship or the US presidency.

The Presidential Paradox

Contemporary American voters find their presidents far more engaging and evocative than their governors. From an instrumental perspective, it is possible that Americans' attention is simply tracking the centralization of authority in the federal government (e.g., Walker 1995; Nivola 2002; Derthick 2004; Greve 2012; Kollman 2013). Given the growing federal role in policy areas that used to be the provinces of the states, from education to health care, the migration of Americans' attention to Washington, DC, might reflect self-interest. One might make a similar argument about the presidential focus specifically: in light of presidents' extensive unilateral powers on issues foreign and domestic (Howell 2003), perhaps voters' focus on the presidency is grounded in their perceptions of authority.

To examine this possibility, we asked survey respondents about both their attention to and perceptions of power across the different levels of government. For example, in the GfK survey, only 44 percent of respondents indicated that the president's decisions have the most impact on their day-to-day lives, with the remainder choosing their governor or mayor. But

78 percent of respondents in the same survey reported following the president more closely than their mayor or governor, suggesting a "presidential paradox." Citizens follow the presidency, even while knowing that other, commonly ignored offices have substantial power in their daily lives. This pattern undercuts the claim that Americans' engagement with federal politics is a straightforward by-product of their perceptions of authority.

A full explanation for the lure of the presidency over public imagination is outside the focus of this book. Still, one possibility is quite compatible with expressive explanations of political behavior. In making sense of the world, people find narratives to be an especially useful way of organizing information (Berinsky and Kinder 2006). In some circumstances, a message with individual stories can be more memorable, emotionally engaging, and persuasive than one with statistical evidence (Brosius and Bathelt 1994; Small, Loewenstein, and Slovic 2007; De Wit, Das, and Vet 2008). Similarly, we may well be drawn to the narrative and personal elements of the US presidency, particularly if news coverage emphasizes the personal aspects of the office and frames presidential politics as a contest between individuals (Patterson 1993; Kernell 1997; Druckman 2003). As one example, Goldman (2012) and Goldman and Mutz (2014) illustrate how media coverage of Barack Obama and his family reduced negative stereotypes about African Americans over the 2008 presidential campaign.

Citizens can empathize with and learn from individual presidents in a way that is more challenging when thinking about aggregate, institutional actors such as the US Congress (see also Hibbing and Theiss-Morse 2002). From an institutional viewpoint, the president and vice president are the only US officials elected nationally. In part for these reasons, Lunch (1987) notes that since at least "Franklin D. Roosevelt, the presidency has been the most truly national institution in Washington" (63). It was the particular connection between the president and the national electorate that led then–House Speaker Tip O'Neill to explain Ronald Reagan's success in Congress by noting, "the will of the people is to go along with the President" (Morris 1999, 439). By 2016, the focus on not only Washington but the presidency was so universal that GOP senator and presidential candidate Marco Rubio could invoke it explicitly, declaring that "we're not going to fix America with senators and congressmen" (Goldmacher 2016). Even among members of the House and Senate, there is a clear recognition of the presidency as the focal point of contemporary US politics.

The visibility of the presidency in news coverage might also make it a coordination point for citizens' political attention. Imagine a voter who knows

that some of her coworkers like to talk about politics. Given the disproportionate coverage of the presidency by most media outlets, if she wants to be
ready for the next conversation at the water cooler, following news about
the presidency is a safe bet. The presidency's initial advantages in winning
public attention could thus compound over time as it becomes common
knowledge that talking about politics means talking about the presidency
(see also Chwe 2001). In short, it is quite plausible that the nature of the
presidency and the way contemporary American news media cover the
presidency encourage Americans' disproportionate attention to it.

Evidence from Internet Searches

Attitudes can be divorced from behavior, so it is important to consider
measures of real-world political behavior as well. We begin with one form
of political engagement that is self-driven and low cost, at least for those
with Internet access: web searches. Specifically, we use Google Trends to
compare the number of searches including the string "Barack Obama"
to the number of searches including each governor's first and last name.
We focus on searches conducted from computers in the states in question.
We then plot the relative search volume by week. The scale varies from
0 to 100, with 100 defined as the maximum search volume for either text
string. That maximum is almost always searches for Obama in November
2008 when he was first elected president.

For the period between January 2004 and July 2016, figure 4.4 here and
figures 4–10 in the online appendix present the number of searches for all
fifty states. As the figures make clear, governors receive a tiny fraction of
the attention the president does, even in their own states. In fact, most
governors received fewer searches than did the president during the week
in which they were standing for election. Even seemingly well-known governors typically generate search traffic that is indistinguishable from zero.

In figure 4.4, we present six "least likely" cases, meaning states where
at least some of the governors during this period were high-profile figures.
Some were known for prostitution scandals (New York's Eliot Spitzer),
while others attracted attention for more conventional reasons, such as
their candidacies for national office (Alaska's Sarah Palin, Louisiana's
Bobby Jindal, and New Jersey's Chris Christie), battles over public policy
(Kansas's Sam Brownback), or both (Wisconsin's Scott Walker). In each
panel, the gray lines show search traffic for each governor while the black

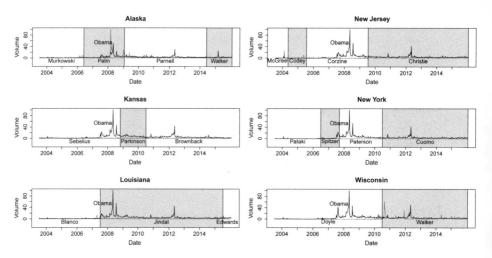

FIGURE 4.4. In-state Google searches
This figure depicts the share of Google searches in the state in question for recent and current governors (*gray lines*) as compared to President Obama (*black line*). The *y*-axis is normed to 100 as the maximum value attained by any politician, and it is typically the attention Obama received upon being elected president in November 2008. Shading distinguishes the period when each governor was in office. Even in each governor's home state, President Obama receives far more interest and attention.

line shows search traffic for Barack Obama. Shading distinguishes the period when each governor was in office. Obama searches commonly dwarf those for the governors, as the gray lines skimming the bottom of each panel illustrate. This pattern holds true even for ostensibly well-known figures such as New Jersey governor Chris Christie, as the top-right panel shows. In the week before Christie's 2009 election over incumbent Jon Corzine, for example, his search traffic was less than half of Obama's within New Jersey—and even in the week of his election, it was only larger by 50 percent, with the pattern reverting to the presidentially oriented norm just one week later. Christie's spike in late 2012 is one exception that proves the rule, since it comes from his keynote address to the Republican National Convention. For governors, getting noticed in their states often means stepping onto the national stage.

In fact, one of the only governors to garner more attention than Obama at his peak was Alaska's Sarah Palin, and that attention among Alaskans came precisely because she joined the 2008 Republican ticket. Another governor who came close was Wisconsin's Scott Walker. Early in 2011, Walker made headlines when he introduced legislation limiting collective bargaining for many public-sector employees. In the ensuing melee, Democratic state legislators went into hiding to prevent the legislature from acting on the bill. Both that legislation and a subsequent recall attempt in June 2012 did lead to spikes in searches for "Scott Walker," as the bottom-right panel of figure 4.4 shows. Yet Walker was widely covered in the national press and so is another rule-proving exception. By contrast, Kansas governor Sam Brownback's 2012 and 2013 tax plans led to widespread dissent among some of his fellow elected Republicans, and yet he virtually never outpaces Obama in searches. And the six states examined here were chosen precisely because of their high-profile governors as compared to the remaining forty-four states illustrated in appendix figures 4–10. Overall, in virtually every week across the governors examined here, President Obama consistently earns more attention from Google searchers who are searching from the governors' states.

Campaign Contributions

In 2012, Shaun McCutcheon was a businessperson, Alabama resident, and Republican activist who sought to donate to twenty-eight different candidates for federal office. Barred from doing so by the aggregate individual federal contribution limit of $46,200, he sued the Federal Election Commission.[2] His 2014 victory in the Supreme Court case that bears his name ended the aggregate contribution limit.

McCutcheon's story illustrates an important way in which campaign contributions are a distinctive form of political participation. In the United States, eligibility to vote is defined by one's place of residence: only residents of spatially delimited jurisdictions are able to participate in a given election. Residents of Alabama cannot vote for governor in neighboring Georgia. But geography does not limit campaign donations in the same way. Regardless of whether he can vote for them or not, a single donor can give to candidates and parties across the federal system. In fact, since there were only seven congressional districts in Alabama at the time of McCutcheon's lawsuit, and since the limit on contributions to any one candidate was $2,700 per cycle or $5,400 per election, McCutcheon's lawsuit implies that he was donating outside his home state. Legally, donations to federal candidates have the same status regardless of whether they are to one's own representative, a point that is so uncontroversial that it played no role in the McCutcheon case or the postdecision

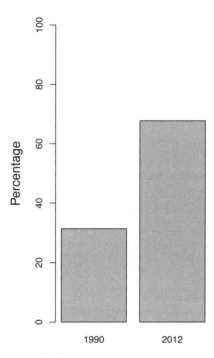

FIGURE 4.5. Out-of-state contributions
This figure depicts the share of US House and Senate candidates' individually reported contributions for the years 1990 and 2012 that came from outside the candidate's state.

Source: Lee Drutman.

commentary. But that observation does make the study of campaign contributions a valuable stopover in assessing whether political behavior is
increasingly nationally oriented. That activists like Shaun McCutcheon
seek to give money in races across state lines is itself a clue about their political engagement.

If Americans are more interested in and engaged with elections that
have national implications than in the past, we should expect to see more
donating to candidates outside their own districts or states. As one measure
of that possibility, we calculated the share of itemized donations—those
over $200—that went to a candidate for House or Senate in the donor's
state using data from the Federal Election Commission.[3] In 1990, the share
of itemized contributions that crossed state lines was just 31.4 percent,
as figure 4.5 illustrates. Most individual donors contributing more than
$200 were giving to in-state candidates (though not necessarily candidates

in their own districts). By 2012, though, the share giving across state lines had more than doubled, to 67.8 percent. Shaun McCutcheon–style out-of-state donations were becoming more common.

This evidence is broadly consistent with research by Gimpel, Lee, and Pearson-Merkowitz (2008) on contributions in elections to the House of Representatives between 1996 and 2004. In an analysis that distinguishes within-district giving from giving to neighboring or distant congressional districts, they find that many donations are coming from considerable distances. To be sure, there are important spatial patterns in donations, with residents of more interconnected regions more likely to give to candidates across the metropolitan area (Bednar and Gerber 2015). In their study, Gimpel and coauthors find that 22 percent of total itemized contributions come from adjacent congressional districts. So, space undeniably shapes giving behavior. Still, one critical trend has been toward nationalization, with 45 percent of itemized contributions coming not just from outside the congressional district but from nonadjacent districts (Gimpel, Lee, and Pearson-Merkowitz 2008). Not only are donors commonly found outside the candidates' districts and even their states, donors are also clustered in a small number of districts that are wealthy and well educated (Drutman 2013). Between 1996 and 2004, one-quarter of US congressional districts accounted for 62 percent of all itemized contributions—the so-called ATM districts (see also Gimpel, Lee, and Kaminski 2006). These giving patterns open up a consequential gap between where candidates raise their money and where they get their votes (see also Fontana, forthcoming).

Another source of leverage in understanding Americans' relative engagement with federal and state politics is to compare contribution patterns across offices rather than across jurisdictions. Candidates for governor and US senator face the same electorates, often at exactly the same time. As a consequence, these two offices provide a clear-cut opportunity to observe increasingly nationalized giving patterns. Accordingly, our analyses draw on extensive federal- and state-level campaign finance data reported in Bonica (2014) to estimate two quantities. The first, illustrated in the top panel of figure 4.6, is the total number of unique, itemized contributors to campaigns for governor and US senator. The second, found in the bottom panel of figure 4.6, is the median total receipts—donations received—in millions of dollars for the campaigns of major-party candidates who ran in general elections for governor or US senator between 1998 and 2012. By using medians, we detect the central tendency in campaign contributions rather than having measures that are driven by outliers. In

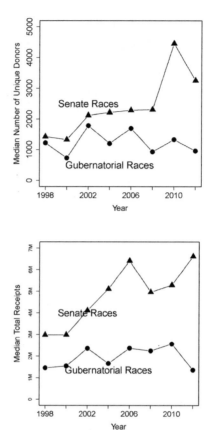

FIGURE 4.6. Campaign finance, campaigns for governor and US Senate
These figures depict the total number of within-jurisdiction donors (*top*) and median total
campaign receipts (*bottom*) for major-party candidates for governor or US senator.

2010, California GOP candidate Meg Whitman alone spent more than
$175 million in her bid to become governor of California and so is one
of the candidacies that risks single-handedly influencing our conclusions.

Both measures indicate growing nationalization in giving. The median
number of itemized, distinct donors to a gubernatorial campaign in 1998
was 1,221, and the comparable figure in 2010 was 1,325, representing 9 percent growth. On the Senate side, the comparable figure is a whopping
314 percent, as the median number of donors rose from 1,422 to 4,459.

Similarly, total campaign receipts also show evidence of disproportionate engagement in races for Senate, with Senate races always drawing at least 75 percent more money than gubernatorial races during the same cycle. Ex ante, we might have expected the opposite pattern, since governors are executives who are likely to draw more media coverage and to be better known than their colleagues in the US Senate (Delli Carpini and Keeter 1996). But it is Senate races that are drawing interest from more contemporary donors, partly because they are elections for federal office with implications for the national balance of power. The organization of the political parties is likely to be part of the explanation as well, with Senate races getting more attention from donors because of the national parties' sophistication in fund-raising.

To this point, this analysis has focused on campaign contributions as an indicator of political behavior—and it has found that contributions are increasingly targeted across state lines and to candidates for federal office. But it is important to consider campaign contributions from the vantage point of the campaigns as well as the donors. In that light, too, the trend has been nationalization in recent years. Changes in campaign finance law and practice—especially in the wake of the Supreme Court's 2010 *Citizens United* decision—are likely to accelerate the concentration of contributions in federal campaigns, as high-end donors can now contribute large amounts to a candidate's efforts via several channels, including Super PACs, 527s, 501(c)(4) organizations, and 501(c)(6) organizations. As vehicles for donors to make contributions much larger than those permitted to the campaigns themselves, the increased use of these tools by a small number of wealthy donors is highly likely to further concentrate resources in elections with national relevance. Put differently, by focusing on itemized contributions made directly to candidates, our analysis has almost certainly understated the extent to which campaign funds now flow from out-of-state sources. And although it is beyond the scope of this book, it is well worth noting that shifting patterns of donations also have the potential to change how elected officials represent their constituents—or even who they consider their constituents to be (Gimpel, Lee, and Pearson-Merkowitz 2008).

Extensive research in political science indicates that political mobilization works. People turn out to vote in part because campaigns ask them to do so, whether through mail, phone calls, or door-to-door canvasing (Wolfinger and Rosenstone 1980; Rosenstone and Hansen 1993; Verba,

Schlozman, and Brady 1995; Gerber and Green 2000; Green and Gerber 2008; Nickerson 2008; Arceneaux and Nickerson 2009; Sinclair 2012; Hersh 2015). If donors are more likely to give to candidates at the federal level, and if campaigns for federal office have more resources to spend on voter mobilization, nationalized giving may produce nationalized voting. But does voter turnout show evidence of nationalization, too? We turn now to that question.

Declining Relative Turnout in Mayoral Races

Today, a big-city mayoral election that drew more voters than a presidential election would be unheard of. The February 2015 Chicago mayoral election pitting incumbent Rahm Emanuel against Chuy Garcia and other contenders drew less than half the turnout of the presidential election two and a half years earlier. That is a far cry from Chicago's engagement in the 1983 mayoral election highlighted in this chapter's opening. Here, we take up the question of big-city voter turnout more systematically. Specifically, we build on and extend the data available in Trounstine (2008) to examine voter turnout in fourteen large US cities, and we integrate presidential election turnout in those same cities.

Presidential turnout is commonly reported by counties, and election returns from historical mayoral elections are not always available. Despite the gaps in the available data, figure 4.7 illustrates a clear pattern across fourteen of America's largest cities: turnout in the most recent presidential elections is markedly higher than turnout in contemporary mayoral elections. In cities like Philadelphia, the ratio of turnout in presidential to mayoral elections for 2011–2012 is nearly four to one; in San Antonio, it gets above six to one. Figure 4.7 does illustrate that the highly racialized mayoral elections of the 1980s and early 1990s drove up turnout in cities beyond Chicago (Carsey 1995; Hajnal 2007). New York City's two elections pitting a white candidate (Republican Rudolphi Giuliani) against a breakthrough black candidate (Democrat David Dinkins) in 1989 and 1993 saw turnout that nearly matched presidential-year turnout. The story was similar in Philadelphia, where Wilson Goode unseated Frank Rizzo in 1983 to become the city's first black mayor. A total of 717,154 voters cast ballots in that 1983 general election, a figure not far from the 772,102 who cast ballots the following November in the Reagan–Mondale presidential election.

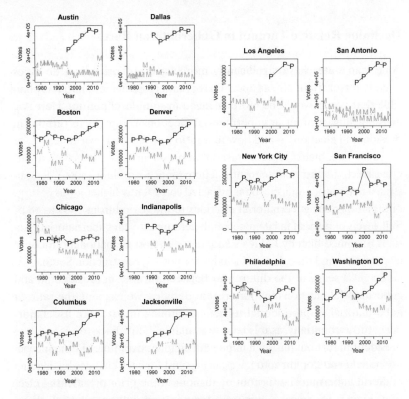

FIGURE 4.7. Big-city turnout in presidential and mayoral elections
This figure illustrates the turnout in presidential elections (P) and mayoral elections (M) for fourteen large US cities. All available data points are illustrated.

But from a contemporary vantage point, those racially charged, high-turnout affairs appear to be behind us, as figure 4.7 makes clear. Today, even the biggest cities typically have low turnout in their general elections (see also Schleicher 2008; Denvir 2015). In 2013, for instance, Democrat Bill DeBlasio took the reins of New York City from the term-limited Michael Bloomberg. Despite the range of policy differences between DeBlasio and his GOP opponent Joe Lhota, only 26 percent of registered voters cast ballots in that election (Denvir 2015). Absent the impetus that comes from strong social identities, many big-city voters can't find the motivation needed to cast ballots in off-cycle elections. The spike in turnout in Austin's 2014 mayoral race comes from a date change that moved the election to November, making it the exception that proves the rule (Anzia 2013).

Declining Relative Turnout in Gubernatorial Races

American states have significantly more legal authority than do cities (e.g., Peterson 1981; Nivola 2002; Gerber and Hopkins 2011), so it is plausible that voters would be more engaged in state-level politics. Here, we consider how turnout in gubernatorial elections compares to turnout in presidential elections—and how that ratio has changed over time.

To be sure, higher levels of turnout in presidential elections than in off-cycle elections are not a recent phenomenon. Kornbluth (2000) demonstrates that presidential elections attracted consistently higher levels of turnout than off-year gubernatorial elections in the period from 1880 to 1898. Still, levels of turnout in late nineteenth-century off-year gubernatorial elections remained high by today's standards, with average national turnout at 66 percent—and that average includes the post-Reconstruction South.

To get a sense of the differences between turnout in presidential and gubernatorial elections in more recent decades, we examine the ratio of gubernatorial to presidential turnout beginning in 1932. We use major-party turnout initially, as it is readily available dating back to 1932. While presidential turnout has seen important changes over time (Putnam 2000; McDonald and Popkin 2001), we can account for such changes by dividing midterm gubernatorial turnout by turnout in the prior presidential election. Figure 4.8 presents this ratio for midterm gubernatorial elections outside the South between 1930 and 2014. Although punctuated by cases where there was a third-party presidential candidate, the general downward trend from the 1950s onward is clear. Both 2006 and 2010 brought significant changes to the partisan makeup of Congress, with the House of Representatives changing hands as a result. And yet, those two years saw the lowest levels of midterm turnout relative to the prior presidential election since the wartime election of 1942.

Beginning in 1970, the data set includes third-party vote totals, allowing us to examine the ratio of total voter turnout in gubernatorial and presidential elections for this more recent period. Figure 4.9 shows the results. The inclusion of third-party data clearly reduces the volatility of the time series. Still, the general trend is one of very gradual decline from 1970's ratio of 0.81 to 1998's ratio of 0.78, and then a sharper decline to 0.64 by 2014. The three lowest levels of relative midterm turnout in gubernatorial races took place in the three most recent elections, suggesting a recent and influential decline in voters' relative interest in state politics.

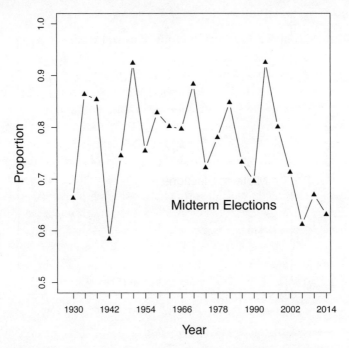

FIGURE 4.8. Ratio of two-party gubernatorial and presidential turnout outside the South
This figure illustrates the ratio of two-party turnout in gubernatorial elections as compared
to presidential elections.

Offices and Turnout Increases over Time

The results in figures 4.8 and 4.9 compare turnout in midterm gubernatorial elections to turnout in presidential years in relevant states. But, of
course, there are other differences between those types of elections, including whether senators are on the ballot and which states are included
in the analysis. While the results above suggest that the turnout premium
in presidential elections has been rising relative to gubernatorial elections, they do not allow us to separate out the effects of Senate versus
gubernatorial elections. We now decompose the presidential-year advantage detailed above. Specifically, this section asks: How much of a turnout
increase is associated with having a gubernatorial, senatorial, or presidential election on the ballot across the fifty states, and how have those
estimates changed over time?

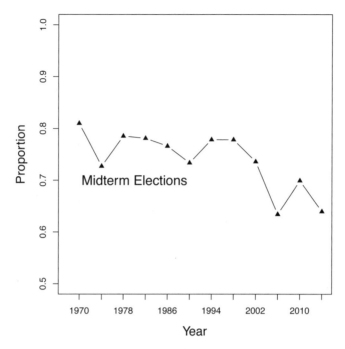

FIGURE 4.9. Ratio of total gubernatorial and presidential turnout outside the South
This figure illustrates the ratio of total turnout in presidential elections as compared to midterm gubernatorial elections.

Today, thirty-six states hold gubernatorial elections during the federal
midterms—that is, during even years that are not presidential elections.
Eleven states hold gubernatorial elections during presidential years,
including the two states on a biannual cycle (New Hampshire and Vermont).[4] As a consequence, candidates for governor frequently appear on
the ballot alongside candidates for Senate and US Congress, and they
sometimes appear alongside candidates for president. This variation, coupled with the variation induced by Senate seats' six-year terms, provides
us with leverage to estimate the impact of different types of elections on
voter turnout.

We begin with data on state-level voter turnout for even years between
1980 and 2014 provided by Michael McDonald's United States Elections
Project.[5] For each even year in that period, we create subsets of the full
data set that include that year, the preceding election year, and the two

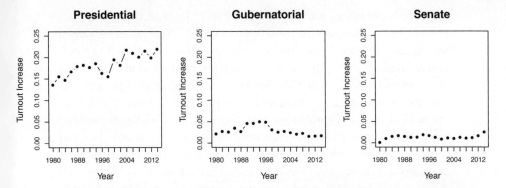

FIGURE 4.10. Turnout premium by office
This figure illustrates the increase in turnout associated with elections to different offices over time as compared to even-year congressional elections. The estimates come from linear regression models of state-level voter turnout fit to eight-year windows of the data for all fifty states.

following election years. These eight-year windows allow us to pool information over time and to separate out the effects of specific offices from those of the particular states holding elections to those offices. For each subset, we then estimate models of total state-level turnout—that is, anyone who turned out to vote for any office in that general election—with indicator variables for whether that state and year had presidential, gubernatorial, or senatorial candidates on the ballot. The models also include state fixed effects to separate out any state-specific differences in turnout rates that persist across elections. The resulting coefficients quantify the voter turnout premium associated with each level of office for each eight-year window in question.

Figure 4.10 illustrates the results and shows a few important trends. First, over this period, presidential elections have always provided a sizable boost of at least 14 percentage points on voter turnout, and by 2014, the premium had grown to 22 percentage points. This evidence reinforces the earlier survey-based claims about the "presidential paradox." Increasingly, presidential elections are the marquee event in American politics. But that premium does not extend to governors, another potentially salient executive office. The turnout premium associated with gubernatorial elections is around 2 percentage points as of 1980, and it grows to 5 percentage points in the mid-1990s before dropping back to just 2 percentage points by 2006.

In analyzing campaign donations above, we saw a spike in the amount of money Senate campaigns are raising in recent years. The voter turnout evidence is consistent with that observation of intensified campaign activity in Senate elections. In 1980, there is almost no premium associated with Senate elections, but the premium creeps upward over time, to 2.5 percentage points by 2014. In short, the gap between turnout in presidential elections and in other statewide elections is growing. And in the most recent elections of 2012 and 2014, the small premium associated with Senate races is ever so slightly larger than that associated with gubernatorial races. This pattern of results is consistent with a small but nonzero bump in turnout resulting from the heightened mobilization efforts of recent Senate campaigns. Some observers have discussed declining voter turnout as if it were a singular phenomenon. But these results illustrate that the trends differ markedly across the levels of government, with a growing gap between presidential elections and others.

Conclusion

This chapter has analyzed varied data sources, from survey responses to campaign contributions and turnout records. The many data sources give rise to a single conclusion: Americans today are markedly more engaged with national and above all presidential politics than with state or local politics. And while there is evidence that Americans were more engaged with national politics than with state politics as far back as the late nineteenth century, it is also clear that the gap between national and subnational engagement has been growing in recent decades. The 1983 Chicago mayoral race, which drew more voters to the polls than the subsequent presidential election, was the product of a bygone era, an era in which racialized elections motivated voters black and white. To the extent that any aspect of American politics is broadly engaging today, it is national politics. National politics—and above all the American presidency—seems to be the sun around which contemporary American political behavior revolves.

These results speak to two of the broad theoretical traditions that seek to explain why people in democratic societies participate in politics. The first centers on the role of self-interest in motivating political participation. According to one long-standing hypothesis in this vein, voters are more likely to turn out when they are more likely to influence the outcome of the election. But the fact that voter turnout is higher in national elections than in state or local elections—that is, in elections with larger numbers of voters—is yet more evidence that the prospect of being the pivotal voter is not a major incentive to vote (Aldrich 1993; Schuessler 2000; Enos and Fowler 2014). The patterns of engagement identified in this chapter also cast doubt on self-interest as a key motive behind participation, as Americans' substantial economic interests in their homes should translate into sustained local engagement but seem not to (Fischel 2001; Self 2003; Oliver, Ha, and Callen 2012). More generally, by relaxing the scholarly fixation on national politics, we can get new perspectives on long-standing hypotheses.

While the results undercut self-interest as a consistent motivation for political participation, explanations emphasizing expressive motivations fare better. To be sure, the expressive approach is not a single predictive model on its own so much as a class of explanations grounded in different social identities. If the framers of the US Constitution were right, and Americans' strongest loyalties were to their states and localities, the expressive approach would yield the same prediction as approaches grounded in self-interest: that political engagement should be high at the state and local levels. The fact that Americans are disproportionately interested in national politics doesn't reinforce expressive explanations generally; it only reinforces particular expressive explanations that emphasize the strength of Americans' national identities and the national focus of their partisan identities. In chapter 8, we take up these questions by examining the strength and content of several geographically defined social identities; in chapter 7, we consider the nature of contemporary partisanship in more detail.

There has been significant concern about the decline in American voter turnout in presidential and congressional elections since the 1960s, coupled with ongoing scholarly debates about the decline's causes, extent, and significance (Rosenstone and Hansen 1993; Putnam 2000; McDonald and Popkin 2001; Franklin 2004; Leighley and Nagler 2014). At the same time, scholars have also questioned whether Americans know enough about politics to cast informed ballots (Delli Carpini and Keeter 1996; Popkin 1994). But however one assesses knowledge, engagement, and turnout in national politics, this chapter shows that those foundational elements of democratic participation are consistently lower at the state and local levels of contemporary American government. Although scholars and other observers have often been concerned about America's levels of voter knowledge and engagement, they have said little about the levels of government at which the deficits are most pronounced.

CHAPTER FIVE

Local Contexts in a Nationalized Age

Two days into 2016, a small armed group seized the headquarters of the Malheur National Wildlife Refuge in eastern Oregon. The protesters sought to create a refuge of a different sort—a safe haven where a local father and son might flee to avoid prison on federal arson charges. The pair's conviction stemmed from a fire that had crossed onto federal lands. The protesters' deeper motivation, however, was hostility to the federal government's control of vast swaths of land in the American West (Johnson, Perez-Pena, and Eckholm 2016). Some of the occupiers had taken part in a similar act of defiance in Nevada in 2014, when rancher Cliven Bundy entered an armed standoff with federal authorities over grazing rights. In fact, two of the occupiers in eastern Oregon were Bundy's sons, Ammon and Ryan (Williams 2016). After the seizure of the federal compound, the *New York Times* and other media outlets quickly set out to explain to readers unfamiliar with the region that the US government actually owns 47 percent of all land in the West (e.g., Bui and Sanger-Katz 2016).

At first glance, the Oregon standoff seems to be evidence against the nationalizing trends documented in previous chapters. After all, the standoff was precipitated by a court decision affecting a pair of Oregon residents, and it was motivated by a political issue wholly unfamiliar to most Americans living outside the West. Indeed, there are a range of political issues that are only meaningful in specific parts of the country, from bike lanes and bus routes to water rights and wolf hunting. But on its own, the existence of issues with disparate regional import does not contradict claims of nationalized political divisions as defined in chapter 2. For an is-. sue to be considered separate from national politics, it needs to generate distinctive political cleavages. What matters is not the content of the issue or its disparate local impact but the way it divides people. If the people who back Cliven Bundy and his sons on the question of federal land ownership are overwhelmingly on the Republican side of national politics, the issue is simply a local instantiation of national political disagreement.

In the contemporary United States, there is little evidence of vibrant, local-level political parties that function independently of the national parties. When local politics involves competition between political parties at all, it is usually between Democrats and Republicans (Schleicher 2008; Oliver, Ha, and Callen 2012).[1] So, in this chapter, we consider a subtler form of local political division. Specifically, we examine the relationship between attributes of Americans' local communities and their attitudes on a wide variety of related political issues. One attitudinal prerequisite of meaningful local political divisions is that ostensibly local issues should have the capacity to divide people in ways that are not derivative of their national political loyalties (see also Hopkins and Mummolo 2017).

Already, there is an extensive literature in political and social science on the ways in which elements of people's local environments shape their attitudes, often referred to as research on "contextual effects" or "neighborhood effects" (e.g., King 1996; Sampson, Morenoff, and Gannon-Rowley 2002). This chapter first briefly summarizes that research, showing how it can shed light on questions about the nationalization of political behavior that have to date been studied separately. Existing research on local contextual effects has focused primarily on racial and ethnic contexts, but as the Oregon example makes clear, there are many local conditions that have the potential to influence attitudes.

Delving into research on contextual effects also helps clarify precisely what nationalized political behavior does and does not imply about political differences across different types of places. Nationalization does not mean national homogenization. A nationalized polity is not one in which place is irrelevant or in which the balance of political forces is similar everywhere. To say that politics is nationalized does not deny that Wyoming is solidly Republican while Massachusetts is heavily Democratic (see especially Gimpel and Schuknecht 2003; Hopkins 2017). Nor is a nationalized polity one in which states and localities confront the same underlying problems. But nationalization does mean that the salient, divisive issues in politics are likely to be the same across otherwise disparate places. From many places, one political division emerges. So, while we should still expect to see different political attitudes in different places, those attitudinal differences should be chiefly a function of individual-level differences, such as income, education, or race. Similar people should have similar attitudes, even when living in different places.

Almost by definition, localized political issues are harder to detect than their national counterparts. What is an issue in one community might not be elsewhere, and so such issues might well fly under the radar of nationally minded analysts or survey writers. What is more, if we were to analyze just one or two local issues, we would risk mischaracterizing the broader set of issues that might be relevant. This chapter thus presents contextual analyses of ten different substantive examples, all drawn from the past twenty years. The issues come from varied political domains, including federal land ownership, defense, the economy, the environment, public safety, and tax policy. The examples differ in several ways, including in the salience of the issue, the issue's valence as clearly negative or more ambiguous, and whether the contextual feature of interest is demographic or geographic. Still, all are issues that have the potential to divide people based on local conditions rather than national party loyalties.

This constitutes a challenging set of tests for claims of nationalization, since people's political attitudes are thought to be more malleable than their political identities and are sometimes divorced from broader political ideologies (Zaller 1992; Bartels 2002; Green, Palmquist, and Schickler 2002; Ahler and Broockman 2017). Finding that attitudes on a specific issue differ systematically across space does not mean that local politics is actually organized along that issue, only that the attitudinal prerequisites for localized divisions are in place. By testing so many distinct issues, we are also allowing for plenty of opportunities to observe contextual effects.

Nonetheless, across the various empirical tests, the core conclusion is of limited contextual correlations. Despite large data sets and varying measures of context and proximity, most local contexts are not strongly correlated with relevant political attitudes. Americans living near military bases are not more supportive of defense spending; those living near federal lands are not less likely to think they receive the most value for their money from the federal government; Idaho and Montana residents living near wolf packs are not more supportive of wolf hunting; Americans living near nuclear power plants are not more or less supportive of nuclear power; Americans living in places with higher levels of air pollution do not perceive more danger from it or support higher environmental spending; Americans living near ocean coastlines are only very slightly more likely to perceive climate change as an important issue; and Americans living in tracts with higher income inequality are no more likely to perceive that inequality is rising or to support the Bush tax cuts.[2] In theory, all of these issues have the potential to generate distinctive, localized political disagreements. But in practice, none seem to generate even distinctive attitudes among those whose places of residence leave them most affected.

That said, we do find contextual effects in select cases. Those who live near the 9/11 targets of New York City and Washington, DC, were more supportive of antiterror spending in 2004 (see also Hersh 2013), while a placebo test indicates that they were not more supportive of defense spending before the attacks. Those who live in high-crime counties are more afraid of crime and in some instances more supportive of anticrime spending as well. Americans living in counties with more unemployment have more negative economic outlooks (see also Books and Prysby 1999; Ansolabehere, Meredith, and Snowberg 2011; Reeves and Gimpel 2012). One common element across these cases of ostensible contextual influence is that all are connected to nationally salient issues, issues that were receiving sustained media coverage and public attention at the time in question. These are issues that are likely to be familiar and cognitively accessible to many prospective voters. We might speculate that this accessibility facilitates connections between place and political attitudes. Put differently, media coverage of an issue might serve to politicize geography or demography and encourage Americans to integrate their political attitudes with aspects of their local contexts. There is an irony here: it is precisely on those attitudes that are salient nationally where Americans' political attitudes appear influenced by their local context. Ostensibly local issues turn out to divide people along familiar national lines. Far from contradicting claims of nationalized political divisions, this chapter's look into political issues with disparate local impacts, like the Oregon standoff, reinforces them.

Contextual Effects and Nationalized Attitudes

The variety of the places in which Americans live, work, and play is striking. Some big-city residents live in high-rise apartment buildings with hundreds of neighbors, many of whom they wouldn't recognize on the street. Others live in areas so remote that a grocery store is an hour's drive. The variation in the political issues that American communities face is no less pronounced. To city dwellers, questions about charter schools or congestion pricing on roadways might loom large; to rural residents, broadband access or grazing rights might be front and center (Cramer Walsh 2012;

Cramer 2016). Even within physical distances as short as a few dozen yards, the challenges people face can vary sharply. As Rae (2003) explains in reflecting on New Haven, Connecticut, "I remember noticing in my days in city government that crime and other key features of urban life showed remarkable respect for invisible boundaries. Thus, for example, violent crime was a daily event on one side of Prospect Street, yet a single incident on the other side was a startling phenomenon" (xvii). It is not just susceptibility to crime. The schools one can attend, the jobs one can apply for, the taxes one pays, even the quality of the air one breathes—all are strongly related to where one lives (Sampson 2012).

Given that variation, it is unsurprising that political and social scientists have long studied local contextual effects (Zorbaugh 1929; Key 1949; Blalock 1967; Sampson, Morenoff, and Gannon-Rowley 2002; Sampson 2012). In this vein of scholarship, the core question is about the conditions under which people's places of residence influence their attitudes and behavior. For example, V. O. Key's canonical 1949 research on the American South concludes that "the presence of large numbers of Negroes is associated with intense political consciousness" (517). In the pre–World War II American South, African Americans tended to be concentrated in the areas where the soil could sustain plantation agriculture and slavery, meaning that there were certainly socioeconomic differences between the whites living near African Americans and those living elsewhere in the South. But according to Key, there was an independent effect of racial context on whites above and beyond those individual-level differences (see also Acharya et al. 2016).

More generally, the example of Key's work on the South clarifies how aggregation effects are distinct from contextual effects. Both types of effects seek to account for why politics differs across places. The former— aggregation effects—implies that the community-level political differences we observe stem from the aggregation of individual-level differences, whether in income, education, race, ethnicity, gender, religion, or a variety of other factors. By contrast, the latter imply what Key inferred—a causal impact of living in a particular locale above and beyond individual-level factors.

To date, research on nationalized political behavior and research on contextual effects have proceeded almost entirely on separate tracks. Still, they address related questions and so merit joint consideration. As defined in chapter 2, one of nationalization's core elements is that national political divisions animate state and local politics. Of course, even in a nationalized polity, people's political attitudes and behavior will vary sharply depending on who they are—on individual-level attributes. Wealthier people and more religious people tend to be Republicans, for example (Fiorina, Abrams, and Pope 2005; McCarty, Poole, and Rosenthal 2006; Gelman et al. 2008), while people of color and women lean Democratic (Dawson 1994; Hajnal and Lee 2011; Gillion, Ladd, and Meredith, forthcoming). The distribution of these individual-level attributes varies by place, so political attitudes and behaviors do as well (Rodden 2013). But because those attitudes and behaviors are formed in reaction to the same set of national figures, parties, policies, and symbols, their relationship to individual-level characteristics should vary relatively little by place (see also Feller, Gelman, and Shor 2012). In a nationalized polity, the relationship between demographics and attitudes is similar across space. Demographically similar towns should have similar political attitudes.

Following Key, many studies have examined the relationship between the ethnic and racial demographics of communities and their residents' attitudes on related social and political questions, both inside and outside the United States.[3] Although less numerous, other studies have considered contextual attributes beyond racial and ethnic demographics, from how communities are designed and developed (Gainsborough 2001; Oliver 2001; Hopkins and Williamson 2012; Nall 2015) to local economic conditions (Books and Prysby 1999; Ansolabehere, Meredith, and Snowberg 2011; Reeves and Gimpel 2012; Newman 2016), wartime casualties (Kriner and Shen 2007), local religious affiliations (Campbell 2006), and abnormal weather patterns (Egan and Mullin 2012).

Still, as many contextual studies frankly acknowledge, there are important challenges to studying the causal effects of living in specific places. Empirically, researchers typically study contextual effects by using statistics to account for several individual- and context-level variables and then assuming that there are no omitted variables. In other words, researchers assume that aside from the factors included in the statistical model, there are no other relevant factors that are related to the outcome as well as the contextual factor of interest.[4] This assumption is a very strong one in the face of residential selection and other factors that might jointly influence where people live and what they think politically. People's choices about where to live reflect their resources and values, making it difficult to disentangle the causal effect of where someone lives from the various factors leading people to live in certain communities in the first place (King 1996; Bishop 2009; Tam Cho, Gimpel, and Hui 2013; Nall and Mummolo 2016).[5] Additionally, researchers studying contextual effects are often forced by data availability to use an administrative geographic unit, such as the

census tract, ZIP code, or county. In fact, community boundaries as measured through the US census or other data sources can differ sharply from
the communities that people themselves perceive and experience (Wong
2007; Wong et al. 2012; Hjorth, Dinesen, and Sonderskov 2016). Another
wrinkle comes from the fact that where people live is only one of several
contexts they experience on a daily basis (e.g., Baybeck and Huckfeldt
2002; Moore and Reeves 2017). Community influences might also vary in
strength over one's lifetime, meaning that the present-day context is but
one of several relevant contextual variables (Goldman and Hopkins 2016).
In short, this line of research has formidable intuitions behind it but also
formidable empirical challenges before it.

   In rare instances, scholars have been able to conduct randomized experiments on local contexts, either by providing incentives to relocate (de
Souza Briggs, Popkin, and Goering 2010; Gay 2012; Chetty, Hendren, and
Katz 2015) or by varying aspects of people's day-to-day environments experimentally (Enos 2014; Sands 2016). Enos (2014), for example, enlisted
Spanish-speaking confederates—undercover researchers, essentially—to
wait for trains at select Boston-area stations. The result was an uptick in
anti-immigration attitudes. Researchers can also harness existing, as-if-
random variation in people's contexts: Egan and Mullin (2012) use devia-
tions in weather patterns to show that those changes can move perceptions
about the evidence for climate change. In still other instances, scholars have
examined large-scale relocations that were exogenous—that is, that took
place for reasons external and unrelated to the people affected—to get
leverage on contextual influence (e.g., Hopkins 2012; Enos 2015). Jointly,
these studies strongly suggest an effect of racial and ethnic contexts on attitudes. Yet insights about the influence of racial and ethnic contexts might
not hold for other types of local contexts or for other political issues. After
all, racial and ethnic differences are among the most divisive questions in
American politics (e.g., Carmines and Stimson 1989; Kinder and Sanders
1996; Schickler 2016; Tesler 2016), and they continue to have a profound
effect on where Americans choose to live (Gould 2000). Racial and ethnic
contexts might prove the exception, not the rule.

Politicized Places

To be sure, there is some reason to think that local contextual effects should
be common in political life and should not be limited to racial or ethnic

contexts. At the psychological level, the importance of space in human cognition is evident in how we talk (Lakoff and Johnson 1980): from saying we are "feeling down" or "down and out" to "moving on up," English is littered with spatial metaphors. What's more, many political questions have disparate spatial impacts (e.g., Kriner and Reeves 2012, 2015a, 2015b), impacts that candidates and elected officials have incentives to publicize (e.g., Grimmer, Messing, and Westwood 2012; Grimmer, Westwood, and Messing 2014). Political issues that are spatially proximate might also be more tangible, salient, and personally meaningful than those that are not, increasing their resonance and influence with the public (Crano 1995).

Social interactions might generate distinctive opinions in different places as well. As Cho and Gimpel (2012) note, "It is not hard to imagine circumstances under which colleagues and neighbors would be influential in the formation and expression of political beliefs" (445; see also Huckfeldt and Sprague 1990, 1995; Huckfeldt, Johnson, and Sprague 2004; Cho and Rudolph 2008; Sinclair 2012). Such processes of contextual influence are fully compatible with substantial residential sorting that is correlated with people's political views (Bishop 2009; Cho, Gimpel, and Hui 2012; Nall 2015; Nall and Mummolo 2016). Differences in opinion that were initially a by-product of people's moving decisions might subsequently be reinforced by their interactions with friends and neighbors. At the same time, people with minority views in a given place might fall into silence (Noelle-Neumann 1993). That dynamic was captured in an op-ed by an Alabama Democrat, who said that "as blue dots in a red state . . . my family can shut up, leave town, or speak up" (Hoffman 2016). Places of residence might also subject people to differing campaign activity and so shape their attitudes and behavior through that channel (e.g., Johnston, Hagen, and Jamieson 2004; Huber and Arceneaux 2007; Cho and Gimpel 2010). According to this line of reasoning, contextual effects should be common across a range of issue areas. Similar people should think about politics differently in different places.

Yet it is also plausible that geographic contexts have little independent effect on political attitudes, especially in a nationalized political moment. Geographic mobility and the contemporary communications technologies that will be addressed in later chapters might mean that place is not a primary source of identity for most Americans (Abrams and Fiorina 2012). Additionally, scholarship on public opinion suggests that personal experiences often remain separate from politics in voters' minds (Lane 1961; Citrin and Green 1990; Sears and Funk 1991; Mutz 1992, 1994). In the words of political scientist Robert Lane, many experiences in daily life are "mor-selized" in voters' minds, meaning that they are compartmentalized and not connected to broader standpoints or ideologies (see also Converse 1964). One might notice the rising price of gas or the "for rent" signs in neighboring buildings without connecting those observations to questions of politics and public policy. If so, people might approach political issues by using their partisanship and other long-standing predispositions (Sears 1993; Green, Palmquist, and Schickler 2002)—predispositions developed in reaction to national politics (Sniderman and Stiglitz 2012). As a consequence, they might not reason based on elements of local geography or demography.

Still another possibility—dubbed "politicized places" (e.g., Hopkins 2010, 2011b, 2012)—steers a middle course between these two views. Rarely do geographic facts or other observations from daily life have obvious political implications. In the course of a single day, people are likely to be barraged with thousands of pieces of information that have potential political relevance: they may observe the condition of local roads, "going out of business" signs in storefronts, a nearby nuclear reactor, or the weather, not to mention people of varying class and ethnic/racial backgrounds in different places. That said, there are multiple steps needed to connect an observation in daily life with views about public policy or partisan preferences. People need to acquire the novel information and to integrate it with their political attitudes—and neither step is automatic. In fact, despite making thousands of observations about the local environment in a single day, an individual is likely to be highly selective in processing that information. So, the uptake of information from the local environment cannot be assumed, it must instead be explained.

One potent catalyst for the acquisition of new information is a sense of threat. People tend to be especially sensitive to and concerned about negative outcomes (Kahneman and Tversky 1979; Rozin and Royzman 2001; Miller and Krosnick 2004). In the face of potential loss, they often respond by becoming anxious and seeking out new information (Brader, Valentino, and Suhay 2008; Gadarian 2010; Gadarian and Albertson 2014; Albertson and Gadarian 2015). Local demographic changes seem to be especially likely to attract attention, as they are sometimes destabilizing (Green, Strolovitch, and Wong 1998; Hopkins 2009, 2010; Newman 2012; Enos 2014). Eulau notes that "the most significant factor in the environment of a person is another person" (as quoted in Cho and Gimpel 2012, 447), an observation that is compatible with the contextual effects researchers commonly identify for living in diverse ethnic or racial environments. Stated more generally, it is plausible that local demographics are an especially salient feature of people's environments and thus that demographic features and especially demographic changes are likely to be noticed.

Let's say that people do pay attention to a particular aspect of their local environments—what then? Even if a person notices an aspect of the local environment, she might not draw any political implications from it. It would be unusual to hear someone say "Traffic was bad today" and then to immediately blame the incumbent president. One catalyst for connecting contextual information with politics is news media coverage, which has the capacity to frame specific observations in ways that link them with more general political trends and personalities (Iyengar and Kinder 1987; Mutz 1994; Winter 2008). News coverage can associate specific facts or events with general trends and can give the public some sense of who is responsible (Iyengar 1991). It is plausible, then, that local conditions and the news media interact to encourage people to acquire information and to connect it with their political predispositions.

This "politicized places" hypothesis does not assume that facts of local geography or demography are inherently political (see also Hopkins 2010, 2011b), but it does provide an explanation for which aspects of local geography and demography are most likely to be politicized: those that can attract attention and that relate to issues salient in the news media. Racial and ethnic contexts meet both criteria and so are cases where we would be likely to see contextual effects. And, in fact, there is already evidence that local racial and ethnic demographics can influence attitudes in precisely the way suggested by the politicized places hypothesis. For instance, Hopkins (2010) finds that native-born white and black Americans adopt more anti-immigration views in response to an influx of immigrants only when immigration is a nationally salient issue. That research also uses panel data to show that Americans' immigration attitudes became more closely related to their local contexts in the wake of the 9/11 attacks. Hopkins (2011b) identifies a similar pattern in Britain's 2005 election, when immigration was a prominent issue. At the same time, Hopkins (2012) shows that differing coverage of evacuees from Hurricane Katrina led to differing responses among residents of Houston, Texas, and Baton Rouge, Louisiana. To date, however, the politicized places hypothesis has been tested exclusively on ethnic and racial contexts. Whether it applies to other types of contextual influence is an open question.

Cases and Data

Past research generates competing expectations about the extent to which local contexts influence political attitudes and about the issues on which such contextual influences are more or less likely. Here, we detail ten separate tests of local contextual effects, describing the rationale for each as well as the specific survey data and contextual measures employed. These tests are drawn from a variety of issues and conceptions of local contexts. Some, such as the immigration case, hue closely to the archetypical example of people living in more ethnically or racially diverse communities. But many others do not. One advantage of some of the less typical cases is that they might reduce the threat of selection bias as an alternative explanation for any findings. Given the central role of racial and ethnic demographics in explaining who lives where (Gould 2000), it is hard to separate out the effect of living in a diverse community from the factors that lead people to live in diverse communities in the first place. But there are other cases where the contextual factor of interest—say, proximity to a coastline or to wolves—might be less central in people's moving decisions. As a consequence, selection bias could be less pronounced.

Given the centrality of salient frames and the corresponding cognitive accessibility to the "politicized places" hypothesis, we first present high-salience cases. Put differently, these are cases in which the core political issue at stake is prominent in politicians' rhetoric and voters' thinking. That salience should facilitate connections between observations in daily life and political attitudes. Still, these cases were chosen to vary in other ways as well, such as whether the contextual attribute is demographic or geographic and whether its valence is unambiguously negative. Where possible, we make use of dependent variables measuring different local perceptions of context (e.g., are crime rates higher in your community?) alongside more obviously political attitudes about preferred public policies. Doing so will help us isolate whether the absence of contextual effects is rooted primarily in different perceptions of local contexts or in the different political preferences that might stem from those contextual realities.

Table 5.1 summarizes the full list of cases and data sources. In this section, we describe the cases in turn, using the example of proximity to the 9/11 sites to explain the specific estimation strategy in detail. We then report the results when applying the same strategy to the other examples. Readers interested in more details about the data analysis should see the online appendix.

TABLE 5.1 **Summary of cases**

Example	Year(s)	Contextual measure	Dependent variable	Data source	Valence
High-salience cases					
(1) Terrorism	2004	Distance to NYC, DC	Antiterror spending	NES	–
(2) Crime	1993–2000	County crime rate	Anticrime spending	GSS	–
(3) Economy	2006	County unemployment	National economic conditions	Pew	
Low-salience cases					
(4) Air pollution	1994–2000	Level of ozone	Environmental spending	GSS	–
(5) Climate change	2006–2010	Proximity to coast	Warming is important	Pew	–
(6) Nuclear power	2009	Distance to nuclear plant	Favor nuclear power	Pew	–
(7) Wolves	2012	Distance to wolf pack	Support hunting	Survey module	–
(8) Federal power	2006	Proximity to federal land	Federal is preferred government	SCCBS	
(9) Defense	2000–2004	Distance to nearest base	Defense spending	NES	+
(10) Income inequality	2004	Tract Gini	Tax policy	NES	

As outlined above, research on contextual effects faces unavoidable and significant challenges of research design. Even so, prior scholarship has focused primarily on ethnic/racial contexts and so has made little use of the leverage that exists by comparing various political issues and types of contextual variation. If we observe a pattern repeatedly across different empirical tests, with different conceptions of local context and different outcomes, our confidence in the pattern's robustness grows. Residential sorting stands as a compelling alternative explanation for any given correlation between place and attitudes, but it seems unlikely to operate in similar ways for spatial factors as varied as proximity to crime, military installations, nuclear power plants, and wolves. In some cases, we can get added empirical leverage by examining whether the correlation between a contextual factor and a political attitude changes over time. If a correlation between an element of people's contexts and their attitudes increases after the contextual factor becomes more meaningful—because of a terrorist attack, for example—our confidence that the underlying relationship could be causal grows (see also Hopkins 2011b).

9/11 Targets and Terrorism

As our first example, we discuss proximity to the targets of the 9/11 attacks and support for antiterrorism spending in detail, and we then apply the same techniques to the other examples. Across each of our ten examples, the dependent variables and the contextual measures vary, but the empirical strategy employed is highly similar, and the results are presented in the same format.

Few events transformed American politics so dramatically and immediately as the September 11, 2001, terrorist attacks on the World Trade Center, the Pentagon, and Shanksville, Pennsylvania. Within hours in late summer of 2001, terrorism became a dominant public concern. But given that the attacks targeted two cities on the eastern seaboard, it is plausible that they had a particular effect on people living in those metropolitan areas. For one thing, their residents were much more likely to know someone who died in the attacks than were people elsewhere, giving the attacks a very personal meaning (Hersh 2013). In New York, even those without a personal connection to the attacks saw countless "missing person" posters covering subway station walls and tasted the charred air for days following the attacks. And, of course, fears about future attacks focused on New York and Washington, DC.

Were people living at or near the 9/11 sites especially affected by the attacks and especially concerned about preventing future terrorism (see also Huddy et al. 2002; Hersh 2013)? To assess that possibility, we turn to the 2000–2004 American National Election Study (ANES) panel, an in-person political survey that asked about respondents' views on spending on the war on terrorism in 2004. As a measure of proximity to the 9/11 targets, we estimate the distance in miles between each respondent's census tract and the closer of either lower Manhattan or Arlington, Virginia. Using tract-level geographic identifiers for the 840 respondents to the 2004 wave of the panel, we link respondents to other contextual measures of interest as well. The panel also asked about respondents' views on defense spending in 2000.[6] This question can serve as a placebo test for the terrorism analyses, meaning that it can allow us to test whether the specific cause we identify is plausibly at work. In general, attitudes toward antiterror spending and defense spending are highly correlated. For that reason, the availability of a question about defense spending prior to the 9/11 attacks allows us to see if living near New York City or Washington, DC, was correlated with defense-related attitudes even prior to the attacks, providing a benchmark against which to compare the correlation visible afterward.

We seek to distinguish contextual effects from aggregation effects, so our analyses should account for individual-level differences that might explain why people living in different places have different attitudes on a given issue. To study attitudes on antiterrorism spending, and in all subsequent cases, we fit three separate regression models that adjust for factors that might be correlated with both the contextual attribute and the attitude of interest.[7] In doing so, our goal is to identify which results are robust to different modeling approaches. The most parsimonious model[8] includes individual-level measures of education, gender, race, and Hispanic ethnicity as indicator variables.[9] Certainly, if respondents differ in their proximity to the 9/11 sites, they might also differ in other community-level attributes, from the wealth of their neighborhood to its racial demographics. Accordingly, the basic statistical models also include seven contextual covariates derived from the 1990 or 2000 US census, measured at the lowest level of aggregation available: income inequality measured using a Gini coefficient, logged median household income, the percentage who are black, the percentage who are foreign-born, the percentage with a bachelor's degree, the percentage who have remained in the same home over the prior five years, and the population density.[10] The results of any one example depend on the usual assumption of ignorability—that there are no unmeasured variables that influence both the contextual factor and the attitude of interest. But as we build a pattern of results across a wide variety of cases, each with different potential biases, the evidence should grow more compelling.

When modeling an outcome, we want to be sure that our statistical models include no variables that could be consequences of the outcome, as doing so would induce bias. Partisan identification is an attitudinal measure, and so in theory, it has the potential to be influenced by features of one's local context (Huckfeldt and Sprague 1995; Sinclair 2012). That would weigh against its inclusion. Yet it is also a stable identity (Green, Palmquist, and Schickler 2002), especially after adolescence (Niemi and Jennings 1991; Sears and Levy 2003), making it more plausible that partisanship would shape Americans' responses to context than the reverse. It is also highly relevant here, since we are interested precisely in any effects we can detect above and beyond those due to people's alignment with the national parties. Accordingly, our second model includes the covariates detailed above along with partisan identification, measured as a series of indicator variables. It is this second model that we use to generate the primary results for each case, although the results are always substantively similar to those from the first model omitting partisan identification. They are also consistently similar to results from a third model that adds indicator variables for each category of ideology alongside partisan identification. These models should do a successively better job of accounting for where respondents fall on the national left–right dimension.

Scholars of contextual effects also face challenging questions of measurement, as they must decide whether to focus on subjective or objective measures of contexts (Wong 2007; Hjorth, Dinesen, and Sonderskov 2016) as well as addressing the modifiable areal unit problem—the question of the level at which context should be measured (Wong et al. 2012). Here, our focus is on objective indicators of context, as our theoretical interest is in the extent to which such objective differences translate into differences in political attitudes across communities.[11]

After the 9/11 attacks, terrorism was highly salient, and proximity to would-be targets had a clear negative valence. We fit each of the three linear models described above to the 840 respondents in the 2004 ANES panel, with the dependent variable being the four-category measure of antiterrorism spending preferences. The complete results are available in appendix table 1. In all three models, there is a statistically significant negative relationship between the logged distance from the nearest 9/11 target and support for antiterrorism spending: those who live closer to New York City or Washington, DC, are more supportive of antiterror spending. That correlation holds true both with and without conditioning on partisan identification. It also persists when we vary the threshold distance at which we declare a respondent to live near the 9/11 sites, as the appendix details.

We next take our baseline model throughout this chapter—one that conditions on political partisanship and a host of demographic and contextual factors—and add a measure of proximity to a 9/11 target: 1 for anyone living within fifty-seven miles of lower Manhattan or Arlington, Virginia, and 0 otherwise. On the left side of figure 5.1, we report the ex-

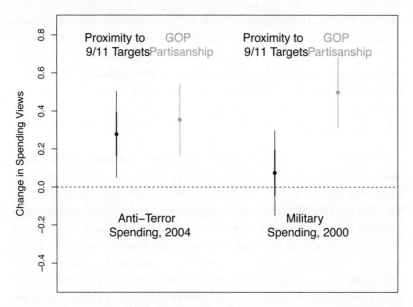

FIGURE 5.1. Proximity to terrorist attacks and attitudes toward antiterrorism and military spending

On the left, this figure illustrates the expected change in support for antiterrorism spending in 2004 among people living within fifty-seven miles of a 9/11 target. On the right, it shows the same relationship for military spending attitudes in 2000.

Source: 2000–2004 ANES Panel.

pected increase in support for antiterror spending among those living close to a 9/11 target using this model. The effect of living within this distance is 0.28, or 42 percent of the dependent variable's standard deviation. This conditional correlation is nearly as large as that for moving from being a strong Democrat to a strong Republican (0.34), as the second vertical line on the left side of figure 5.1 shows. In keeping with the politicized places approach, proximity to the 9/11 targets is a powerful predictor of antiterrorism attitudes.

But is such a relationship causal? The generally Democratic tilt of the Washington, DC, and New York metropolitan areas suggests that we wouldn't have expected that relationship ex ante. Still, to be more systematic, we next exploit the fact that these respondents took part in multiple surveys by looking for the same spatial pattern prior to the 9/11 attacks. If the same respondents' 2000 attitudes toward defense spending were structured similarly, we would conclude that the pattern observed for antiterrorism spending is likely spurious: an event in 2001 cannot shape attitudes elicited in 2000. But as the right side of figure 5.1 demonstrates, that is not the case. There is no strong evidence that people living near the 9/11 sites were more supportive of military spending back in 2000. That finding makes it more likely that the 2004 finding reflects a genuine response to 9/11 among those who lived closest.

Local Crime Rates

Having introduced the paper's approach to estimating contextual effects using the example of proximity to the 9/11 attacks, we now consider the remaining nine examples, all of which employ parallel empirical strategies. We next turn to crime, another issue that poses a concrete threat to people's safety and that varies markedly across space. Crime and policing have been prominent political issues nationally since crime rates began rising in the 1960s (Weaver 2007; Hopkins 2011a) and remained salient during the period in question (1993–2000), with a median of 22 percent of Gallup respondents naming crime the nation's most important problem (Baumgartner and Jones 2013). But crime also has very particular spatial impacts: in some communities, crime is routine, while in others, it is exceedingly rare. In 2014, Baltimore's murder rate of 33.8 people per 100,000 residents was more than nineteen times that of nearby Bowie, Maryland (US Department of Justice 2014). Even within Baltimore, the danger of crime varies dramatically from neighborhoods like Canton to neighborhoods like Sandtown-Winchester, tracking racial and class divisions closely (e.g., Sampson, Raudenbush, and Earls 1997). Crime can fundamentally transform neighborhoods, driving parents to keep their children inside at all times and making even routine trips perilous (Wilson 1996; Wilson and Taub 2007). If there are attributes of people's local contexts that they are aware of and responsive to, crime should surely appear on that list.

To measure county-level crime rates for each year, we use the Federal Bureau of Investigation's Uniform Crime Reports (UCR), summing the number of instances of eight categories of crime: homicide, rape, robbery, aggravated assault, burglary, larceny, vehicle theft, and arson. We then divide the total number of crimes by the county's population and merge these measures to General Social Survey (GSS) respondents between 1993 and 2000 using county-level information on the respondents' locations. The resulting crime rate measure varies from 0.00 to 0.16 total crimes per capita, with a median of 0.045 and a standard deviation of 0.025. Two GSS

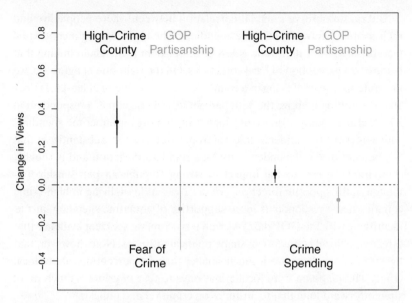

FIGURE 5.2. Local crime rates, fear of crime, and support for anticrime spending

Source: GSS, 1993–2000.

questions are of particular interest as dependent variables. The first is a question about local perceptions of safety: "Is there any area right around here—that is, within a mile—where you would be afraid to walk alone at night?" The second instead addresses national policy, asking about preferred levels of spending on "the police and law enforcement."[12]

We employ a statistical model with similar independent variables to those above, including respondents' partisanship and a series of individual- and county-level demographics. The results are straightforward: GSS respondents in high-crime counties above that threshold are more likely to report a fear of crime than those in low-crime counties. As the appendix details, for essentially any threshold in the crime rate, the difference is almost always substantively and statistically significant. Consider residents whose county crime rates are in the top quartile, meaning that the crime rate is over 6,211 per 100,000 people. As the left side of figure 5.2 illustrates, people in higher-crime counties on average are 0.33 higher than others in terms of their concerns about local crime. That effect is massive, accounting for two-thirds of the dependent variable's standard deviation (0.49). People living in high-crime communities know it.

But do we observe a similar correlation between where people live and their attitudes toward anticrime spending? The chain linking a contextual feature to a political attitude is less clear-cut than is the chain linking that feature to a perception of local conditions. On the right side of figure 5.2, we illustrate the effect of living in a county with a crime rate of at least 6,211 per 100,000, putting it above the 74th percentile. All else equal, a respondent in a high-crime county scores 0.057 higher in support for anticrime spending, with a 95 percent confidence interval from 0.013 to 0.101. Substantively, that is 9 percent of the dependent variable's standard deviation and is roughly comparable in size to the impact of strong Republican partisanship (although in the opposite direction). In the 1990s at least, living in high-crime counties made respondents more supportive of anticrime spending, just as identifying with the GOP did.[13] As with terrorism, we see clear evidence that threatening local contexts can shape political attitudes. Note, however, that the substantive effect size is much smaller than for perceptions about local crime. The mapping from local crime rates to fear of crime is much more straightforward than that to attitudes on crime-related policies.

Local Economic Conditions

So far, we have seen evidence of contextual effects for two high-salience political issues. But both terrorism and crime involve threats to personal safety and so they may be especially easy tests of contextual influence and politicized places. We now turn to an issue that is perpetually salient but that does not involve threats to safety: local economic conditions. Economic conditions vary widely across the United States and provide pronounced advantages and disadvantages across space as a result. What is more, the state of the national economy is a perpetual political issue (Vavreck 2009)—in 2006, the median share of Gallup respondents citing it as the nation's most important problem was 14 percent. Local economic conditions also influence various elements of daily life, from the ease of finding a job to the prices in local stores. Prior scholarship has shown that local economic conditions can influence Americans' perceptions and their voting behavior (Books and Prysby 1999; Gay 2006; Ansolabehere, Meredith, and Snowberg 2011; Reeves and Gimpel 2012; Newman 2016).

On the weekend prior to the 2006 midterm elections, the Pew Research Center surveyed 2,912 respondents by phone about their views of the economy and vote intentions. Using self-reported ZIP codes,[14] we merge those survey responses with 2005 and 2006 Bureau of Labor Statistics

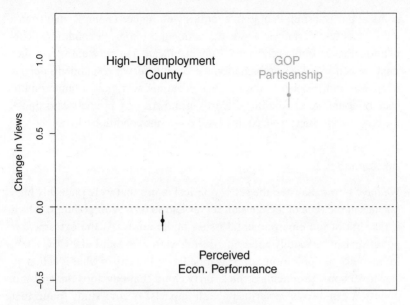

FIGURE 5.3. Local economic conditions and perceptions

Source: Pew 2006 Survey.

data on county-level unemployment. County-level unemployment varied from a first quartile of 3.8 percent to a third quartile of 5.3 percent, with the median respondent living in a county with an unemployment rate of 4.6 percent. The model specification includes the standard six contextual variables, measured at the ZIP-code level. The dependent variable is perceptions of national economic performance.[15]

In figure 5.3, we examine whether our core models detect a correlation between the county-level unemployment rate and perceptions of national economic performance in 2006, just prior to the November midterm elections. In 2006, Republicans controlled the presidency and both chambers of Congress, so it is unsurprising that Republicans are much more optimistic about the nation's economic condition (see also Gerber and Huber 2010). In fact, strong Republicans score 0.76 higher on the 1–4 scale than do strong Democrats, which is 88 percent of the dependent variable's standard deviation. By contrast, when we divide respondents at the median county-level unemployment rate of 4.6 percent, we find that those in counties with high unemployment perceive the economy to be worse by just –0.09, with a 95 percent confidence interval from –0.16 to –0.03. The coefficient for the county-level unemployment measure is just one-tenth as large as the coefficient for political partisanship. People in counties with higher unemployment rates are slightly less optimistic about the national economy, a conditional correlation that is frequently statistically significant but substantively rather small. When asked about the national economy, survey respondents appear to answer with respect to the national economy, with only a limited influence of county-level conditions. Partisanship strongly predicts who thinks the economy is doing well; county-level economic conditions do not.

Air Pollution

We have now exhausted the set of political issues that were plausibly high salience at the time of the relevant survey and so turn to air pollution, which is the first of the environmental issues under study. At the extreme, air pollution can be readily apparent: during winters in Salt Lake City, Utah, for instance, air pollution can be trapped over the city in what is called an "air inversion," producing a thick, dirty cloud that envelops the city. Air pollution can also have serious health impacts. A 2011 study found that the removal of tollbooths and the concomitant traffic congestion demonstrably reduced premature births by mothers living nearby (Currie and Walker 2011). Still, the issue is not highly salient. At no time from 1994 to 2010 were environmental issues named by more than 3 percent of Gallup respondents as the nation's most important problem, and the median value over that time span was 1 percent. Air pollution is concentrated in certain places. Are concerns about air pollution concentrated as well?

Tailpipe emissions from cars are a primary source of ozone pollution, which is in turn one of the most dangerous forms of air pollution. Via the Environmental Protection Agency, we have data on ozone levels from measurement stations in between 301 and 363 separate US counties depending on the year, while for the remaining counties, we use the measurement from the nearest station for the month of the survey. Across US counties, the median such distance is 21.3 miles in 1996, with a standard deviation of 33.5.[16] The measurement stations are concentrated in counties with larger populations, so 42 percent of GSS respondents live in such counties. Given that ozone is positively related to sunlight, we also merged in monthly temperature data from the nearest of approximately 140 weather stations. The geographic distribution of ozone for 1998 is mapped in figure 5.4.

To measure pollution-related perceptions and political attitudes, the analysis focuses on two GSS questions. The first asks about the perception that pollution caused by cars is dangerous to the respondent's family, with

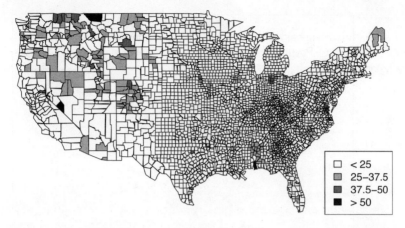

FIGURE 5.4. Ozone pollution across the United States, 1998

Source: Environmental Protection Agency.

the response options varying from "extremely dangerous" to "not danger-ous."[17] The second asks about whether spending on "improving and pro-tecting the environment" should be increased, left as it is, or decreased.[18]

In our analyses, we turn first to the question about the perceived threat of air pollution to the respondent and her family, as illustrated on the left side of figure 5.5. For example, if we define more heavily polluted counties to be those respondents whose counties' ozone levels are at or above the 75th percentile, the effect is a precisely estimated zero (−0.005, SE = 0.04). By contrast, Republicans are a striking −0.39 less likely to see pollution from cars as dangerous. And given those results, it is not surprising that people living in areas with more ozone pollution are indistinguishable from those living elsewhere in terms of their preferred levels of environmental spend-ing at any threshold, as shown on the right side of figure 5.5.[19] Back in 1971, political scientist Matthew Crenson wrote about how air pollution was de-politicized in Gary, Indiana: due to the power of the steel industry, the city's low air quality did not produce any political movement aimed at mitigation (Crenson 1971). Four decades later, air pollution remains depoliticized.

Climate Change and Proximity to Coasts

On October 29, 2012, the storm surge associated with Hurricane Sandy flooded New York City, the New Jersey shores, and other parts of the

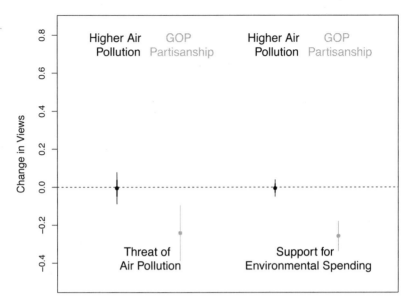

FIGURE 5.5. Ozone pollution, perceptions of danger, and support for environmental spending

Source: GSS 1994, 1996, 2000.

northeastern coastline. For some politicians, the storm brought the risks from climate change into sharp relief. Days later, New York mayor Michael Bloomberg made a surprise endorsement of Barack Obama, noting that "the devastation that Hurricane Sandy brought to New York City and much of the Northeast—in lost lives, lost homes and lost business—brought the stakes of next Tuesday's presidential election into sharp relief." He added that "our climate is changing" (Hernandez 2012). We saw above that in the wake of the 9/11 attacks, those Americans living closest to the targets became more supportive of antiterror spending. Is there a similar link between people who are especially vulnerable to rising sea levels or other consequences of climate change and related attitudes?

The issue of climate change shares some basic features with the air pollution example. It is also an environmental issue, one that poses a differential threat based on geography. Here, we focus specifically on ocean coastlines, as residents in such communities might be worried about their communities' long-term prospects in the face of rising sea levels (for evidence from New Zealand, see Milfont et al. 2014). Unlike air pollution, this threat is primarily in the future, not the present, and so is associated with increased uncertainty. For a sizable subset of Americans who chose their communities before the 1990s, climate change was unlikely to have been a consideration in that choice, limiting concerns about selection bias. Still, while climate change has never been among the top issues for American voters, it has received media attention in recent years.

In six surveys between June 2006 and October 2010, the Pew Research Center asked a total of 10,810 respondents about important political issues, including global warming.[20] Using ZIP-code centroids, we then measure each respondent's minimum distance to an ocean coastline. The interquartile range varies from 4.7 to 387.2 miles, with a median of 127.5 miles.

Figure 5.6 depicts the results when predicting Americans' attitudes about the importance of climate change as an issue. The key measure of the distance to a coastline is those within two miles, a figure that covers 20 percent of the US population. The effect of living near an ocean coast is 0.06 (SE = 0.03) and is borderline significant.[21] Still, it is small in substantive terms. By way of comparison, strong Republicans are on average 0.88 lower in their perceptions of climate change's importance. That is 84 percent of the dependent variable's standard deviation. If the goal is to

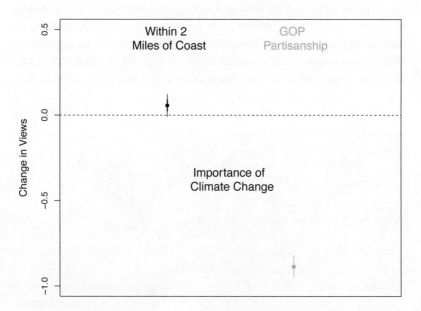

FIGURE 5.6. Proximity to coasts and importance of climate change

Source: Six Pew Surveys, 2006–2010.

accurately predict which respondents think climate change is important, it is far more valuable to know a respondent's partisan identification than her place of residence.

Nuclear Power Plants

From Three Mile Island to the Fukushima nuclear crisis in Japan in March 2011, periodic crises call our attention to another space-based threat: the possibility of radioactive discharges from nuclear power plants (Baumgartner and Jones 1993). Such threats are obviously spatial, as those nearest to nuclear power plants are at the greatest risk. Indeed, the US federal government identifies two zones of increased risk for those living near nuclear power plants, one within ten miles and a second within fifty miles.

To measure the potential influence of proximity to nuclear power plants, we identified the ZIP code of the sixty-five nuclear power plants currently operating in the United States. Using ZIP-code centroids for the 2,001 respondents to the Pew Research Center's April 2009 General Public Science Survey, we then calculated each respondent's proximity to the nearest nuclear power plant. Here, the first quartile is 33 miles, while the median is 58 miles and the third quartile is 103 miles. Figure 5.7 shows the geographic distribution of both nuclear power plants and respondents to that nationally representative survey by ZIP code. Here, the dependent variable is whether the respondent favors or opposes "building more nuclear power plants to generate electricity."

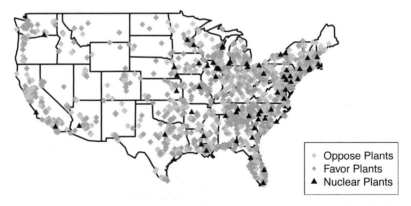

- Oppose Plants
- Favor Plants
- ▲ Nuclear Plants

FIGURE 5.7. Nuclear power plants in the United States

Source: Pew 2009 Survey.

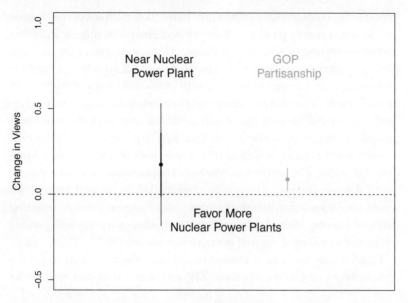

FIGURE 5.8. Proximity to nuclear power plants and support for nuclear power

Source: Pew 2009 Survey.

In figure 5.8, we use a 2009 Pew survey to examine how proximity to a nuclear power plant correlates with support for building new power plants. Within twenty-one miles of a nuclear power plant—a distance that includes 10 percent of our survey respondents—the effect is 0.17 with a standard error of 0.18.[22] Here, the estimated effect of partisanship is smaller (0.09) but much more precisely estimated: while it is clear that Republicans are more likely to favor more nuclear power plants, it is not clear whether living near one moves attitudes in a pro- or antinuclear direction. At least when it comes to supporting additional nuclear power plants, proximity to existing plants is not a powerful correlate. And there is no evidence that living near a nuclear power plant makes nuclear power more threatening in general.

Proximity to Wolves

The reintroduction of wolves into Yellowstone National Park and Idaho in 1995, and the resulting spike in wolf populations, led officials in Idaho, Montana, and Wyoming to legalize wolf hunting. Here, too, we see elements that might induce a contextual effect: the issue is potentially most important to those who live in the range of the wolves. Much of the rhetoric on the issue concerns protecting livestock, and also protecting elk and other animal populations for hunting by people. Here, we augment the standard models by including indicator variables for respondents who are ranchers or hunters to avoid conflating space with individual-level self-interest. To examine the relationship between people's proximity to wolves and their attitudes about wolf hunting, the researcher added several questions to a live-interviewer telephone survey of four hundred respondents in Idaho's First Congressional District as well as fifty respondents in three western Montana ZIP codes. The survey was conducted between April 6 and April 13, 2012.[23] The dependent variable is respondents' views on wolf hunting, assessed via a question with four response categories ranging from believing that wolf hunting "should stop immediately" to believing that wolf hunting "should continue until the wolf population is eliminated."[24]

Figure 5.9 uses a map to present one view of the data, with survey respondents located based on their ZIP code's centroid and wolf packs

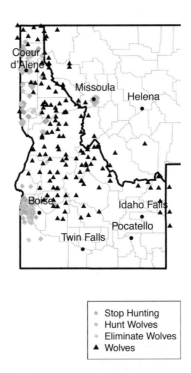

FIGURE 5.9. Map of wolves and survey respondents

Source: 2012 Survey Module.

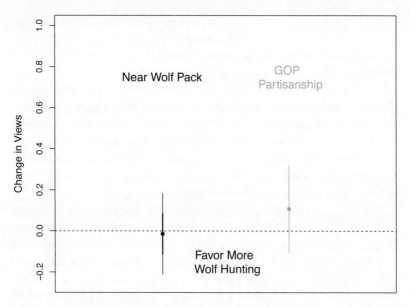

FIGURE 5.10. Proximity to wolves and attitudes toward wolf hunting

Source: 2012 Survey Module.

located based on the 2011 Idaho Wolf Monitoring Progress Report. The
survey respondents are clustered in three areas: those who live in the
southwestern part of the state near Boise, those who live in the state's
panhandle, and the Montana sample in and near Missoula. The map uses
shading to show the 17 percent of respondents who want to end wolf hunting, the 57 percent who wish to see it continue, and the 26 percent who
want to see the wolf population eliminated entirely. The median distance
to the nearest wolf pack is 27.2 miles, with an interquartile range from
14.8 to 34.1 miles. The geographic clustering is evident in the bottom
panel of appendix figure 20, as the share of respondents within a given
threshold spikes at several places.

This survey has the smallest sample size of those examined. But even
so, as figure 5.10 illustrates, we can rule out a strong, threatening effect of
proximity to wolves. Twenty-seven percent of the respondents live in ZIP
codes within 15 miles of a wolf pack, and at that threshold, the estimated
coefficient for distance is −0.02, with a 95 percent confidence interval from
−0.21 to 0.18. In other words, it is quite close to 0, especially given that the
dependent variable's standard deviation is 0.65. To the extent that wolves
are threatening, that threat does not appear concentrated among those living nearby. Not all potentially threatening contexts are influential, it seems.

Federal Land

As the Bundy family with whom we opened this chapter reminds us, in western US states, federal control of large swaths of land has been a periodic political issue (e.g., Cawley 1993). The wolf issue is part of a broader issue that has been a theme of state and local politics, especially in western states, for decades: federal control over land and resources. The issue might well be most acute for those living closest to large federal land holdings. Yet this issue rarely breaches the national political agenda, making it an interesting test case for the hypothesis linking contextual effects to national salience and attitudinal accessibility.

Here, we use a similar procedure to identify the proximity to federal lands not administered by the Department of Defense (DOD) for each of the 2,741 national respondents to the 2006 Social Capital Community Benchmark Survey (SCCBS). For non-DOD land, the median distance is 39 miles, with an interquartile range from 27 miles to 52 miles. To measure attitudes related to the federal government, we used a question about respondents' preferred level of government: "From what level of government do you feel you get the most for your money?" The response options were: "local," "state," and "federal/national." Cliven Bundy's expectation—and ours as well—is that those who live near federal land will have a more negative perception of the federal government relative to their state and local governments.

In figure 5.11, we consider whether proximity to federal lands (excluding military bases) influences 2006 SCCBS respondents' relative preference for the federal government over their state and local governments. In that year, the federal government was controlled by Republicans, which explains the sizable positive coefficient for strong Republicans (0.075). Consider the 9 percent of Americans within sixteen miles of federal land: they are no more or less likely to prefer the federal government, as the estimated effect is 0.010 with a standard error of 0.025.[25] Here, too, the appropriate conclusion is that proximity to federal land does not correlate with attitudes as expected. Federal lands have the potential to bring funding, jobs, and tourism, facts that might help explain these inconclusive results.

Proximity to Military Bases

Mike Turner was first elected to the US Congress from a Dayton, Ohio-area district in 2002. As of January 2016, the first issue on his website was a

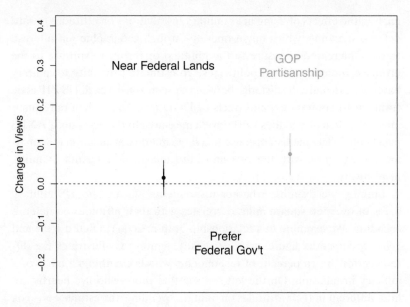

FIGURE 5.11. Proximity to federal lands and attitudes toward US government

Source: 2006 SCCBS.

national one: jobs and the economy. But just below it was "Wright-Patterson
Air Force Base," which is located within the district (Turner 2016). The base
also plays a substantial role in Representative Turner's professional biogra-
phy, which notes that "prior to Congressman Turner's election, there was
no advocate for Wright-Patterson Air Force Base on the important House
Armed Services Committee. Congressman Turner filled that void and
throughout his time in Congress, Wright-Patt has successfully added approximately 10,000 jobs and remains the largest single-site employer in the
state of Ohio" (Turner 2016).

Turner's example is far from unusual. Defense spending is itself a major budget item and perennial political question. America's 440 military
bases are often major employers (National Park Service 2016), and so
protecting them is a central commitment for many members of Congress.
Given the popularity of the US military, and given its role in creating jobs
and bolstering local economies, it seems possible that having a military
base nearby could influence attitudes on defense spending.

Here, we examine that question. We do so by returning to the 2000–
2004 ANES panel employed above. Its 840 respondents enable us to

analyze the effects of living near military installations on attitudes toward
defense spending, which might operate through geographic self-interest,
through increased exposure to the military, or through exposure to the
pro-base rhetoric of local politicians. To estimate proximity to military
bases, we calculate the distance between the centroid of each US ZIP code
(using 2010 boundaries) and tracts of DOD land larger than ten square
miles. We then merge these ZIP-based measures to the 2000–2004 ANES
panel data.[26] The median distance to a large military installation is approximately 23 miles, with the first and third quartiles at 13 and 41 miles,
respectively.

Initially, we examine whether respondents' distance to US military
bases of over ten square miles correlates with their attitudes on defense
spending. We examine this relationship both in 2000 (in figure 5.12) and
2004 (in appendix figure 23). Specifically, figure 5.12 illustrates the difference for the 10 percent of respondents who live within 7.2 miles of a
military installation. On the left, we see that those who live nearby are
little different in their attitudes on military spending: the estimate is −0.05
with a standard error of 0.08. On the right, we see by contrast that strong

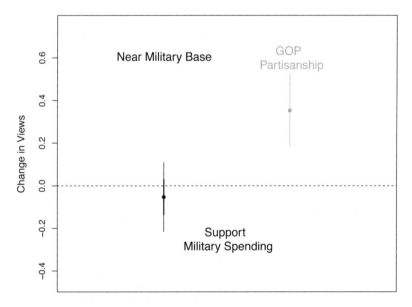

FIGURE 5.12. Proximity to military bases and attitudes toward defense spending, 2000

Source: 2000–2004 ANES Panel.

Republicans are staunchly more supportive of military spending, with an estimated coefficient of 0.35. This pattern is especially interesting in light of potential selection biases: those living near military bases are likely to include active-duty members of the military and their families as well as veterans. Yet neither that selection bias nor any effect of living near military bases is sufficient to shift attitudes on defense spending, at least in 2000 and 2004. It is plausible that a concrete threat—say, a move to close a base—could induce a political response among nearby residents. But on its own, mere proximity to a base does not.

Local Income Inequality

Local income inequality is our final empirical example. In recent years, both actual income inequality and public and scholarly attention to the issue have risen sharply (e.g., Piketty and Saez 2003; McCarty, Poole, and Rosenthal 2006; Bartels 2008; Page and Jacobs 2009). In 2014, incoming New York City mayor Bill DeBlasio made the issue a centerpiece of his inaugural address, declaring that "we are called to put an end to economic and social inequalities that threaten to unravel the city we love" (DeBlasio 2014).

Some scholarship suggests that income inequality has local consequences, as people struggle to "keep up with the Joneses" by increasing their expenditures (Frank 1985; Bertrand and Morse 2013). Others have linked local income inequality to stress levels and public health (e.g., Kawachi et al. 1997). Income inequality should be visible locally (Newman 2016; Newman, Johnston, and Lown 2015), as it might affect local consumption patterns or home prices. At the same time, concerns about the appropriate definition of "context" (e.g., Wong et al. 2012) are especially pronounced in this case, as people might well compare themselves to family members, friends, or coworkers who are not their immediate neighbors. The contextual variable in question relates to people, not proximity, enabling us to test Eulau's claim about the role of demographic contexts outside the arena of racial and ethnic distinction.

Here, we evaluate that possibility by again employing the 2000–2004 ANES and its tract-level identifiers. Specifically, for each respondent, we use 2000 census data to estimate a tract-level Gini coefficient for household income inequality. This variable ranges from a first quartile of 0.35 to a third quartile of 0.42; the higher the coefficient, the more inequality. As a dependent variable, we first consider a perceptual question asked in

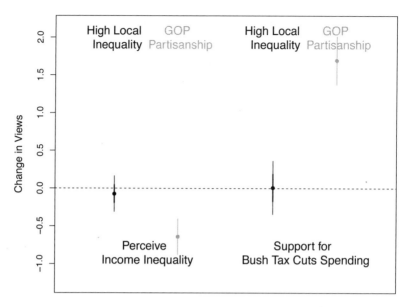

FIGURE 5.13. Local income inequality, salience of inequality, and attitudes on tax cuts

Source: ANES 2004.

2004: "Do you think the difference in incomes between rich people and poor people in the United States today is larger, smaller, or about the same as it was 20 years ago?" Notice that this question asks about the United States, not about the respondent's community. We then consider a second dependent variable that is more explicitly political: "As you may recall, [Congress passed/President Bush signed] a big tax cut a few years ago. Did you favor or oppose the tax cut, or is this something you haven't thought about?"

Using the 2004 respondents to the ANES panel, we first consider the relationship between income inequality in one's census tract and perceptions of rising income inequality nationally. On the left side of figure 5.13, we see that strong Republican identifiers are substantially less likely to perceive rising income inequality, with a coefficient of 0.64 for a dependent variable with a standard deviation of 0.90. That coefficient dwarfs the median coefficient for being in a neighborhood whose inequality is higher than the 90th percentile (−0.07)—and as appendix figure 24 illustrates, there is no threshold at which respondents in high-inequality tracts are more likely to perceive rising inequality nationally. In this case at least,

people either do not recognize tract-level inequality or else do not connect it with national conditions. Given these null results with respect to
perceptions of inequality, and given the parade of null results documented
above for low-salience political issues, it is thoroughly unsurprising that
people in high-inequality tracts are no more or less supportive of the 2001
Bush tax cuts, as the right side of figure 5.13 shows. At least in 2004, people in more unequal contexts were no more likely to notice inequality or
to oppose tax cuts targeting wealthier Americans. Here, too, the contrast
with partisanship is stark, as Republicans are substantially more likely to
support the Bush tax cuts.

Conclusion

Before the 2016 Oregon standoff was the 2014 Nevada standoff. In it, a
long-standing dispute over payment for grazing on federal lands came to
a head in an armed confrontation between Bundy and his supporters and
government officials. But if the spark was thoroughly local, the reaction
was anything but. Bundy's standoff garnered extensive media coverage
from Fox News and other national media outlets. It also drew initially ap-
proving statements from Republican political figures ranging from Kentucky senator Rand Paul to Texas governor Rick Perry. Texas senator Ted
Cruz linked the standoff to the president, noting that it was the "unfor-
tunate and tragic culmination of the path that President Obama has set
the federal government upon" (Noble 2016). In both Oregon and Nevada,
seemingly local issues quickly became linked to a central national question: the role of the federal government in day-to-day life. In fact, in the
Oregon case, the father and son whose incarceration prompted the Oregon standoff dissociated themselves from it, and residents of the Oregon
community were reported to want the Bundys and their allies to leave
(Heim 2016). The Oregon standoff was not an indigenous protest but an
opportunity seized by out-of-state activists.

In a similar vein, this chapter has considered ten separate cases of potential contextual effects that vary on numerous dimensions, including
their potential to induce threat and their salience in national politics. One
such case was proximity to federal land. But on the Bundy family's sig-
nature issue and on several others, we find little evidence that people's
political attitudes are consistently correlated with attributes of their daily
environments. Table 5.2 summarizes the overall results, dichotomizing

TABLE 5.2 **Summary of results from analyses of ten local contextual effects**

Example	Survey year(s)	National salience	Demographic factor	Clear threat	Contextual correlation
(1) Terrorism	2004	Y	N	Y	Y
(2) Crime	1992–2000	Y	N	Y	Y
(3) Economy	2006	Y	N	N	Y
(4) Air pollution	1993–2000	N	N	Y	N
(5) Climate change	2006–2010	N	N	N	N
(6) Nuclear power	2009	N	N	Y	N
(7) Wolves	2012	N	N	Y	N
(8) Federal land	2006	N	N	Y	N
(9) Defense/ bases	2000	N	N	N	N
(10) Economic inequality	2004	N	Y	N	N

both national salience and the strength of contextual correlations in the name of simplicity. Contextual correlations are deemed meaningful based not only on statistical significance but also on their substantive magnitude, relative to both the relationship for partisanship and the dependent variable's standard deviation.

Early in the chapter, we outlined a variety of hypotheses about contextual effects, including those emphasizing that particular contextual features might shape attitudes. Perhaps contextual features that pose a threat are especially likely to shape attitudes, we speculated. Or maybe demographic features—features of the people nearby—might be more influential than geographic features like shorelines. But these hypotheses fail to make sense of the results in at least one example. For instance, the strength of threats and of negatively charged contextual attributes might explain the contextual correlations identified for terrorism and crime, but they cannot explain the null effects for nuclear power or proximity to wolves. If demographic contexts are especially influential, why does local income inequality have essentially no relationship with people's perceptions of inequality or tax policy preferences?

The "politicized places" hypothesis provides another set of expectations about when people's contexts shape their attitudes. It contends that aspects of people's local contexts are not inherently noticed or connected to their political attitudes, but that under the right conditions they can be politicized. Coverage in the news media is especially potent in providing people with frameworks that facilitate connections between day-to-day life and broader political questions. As table 5.2 demonstrates, the "politicized places" hypothesis explains the observed pattern well. Those issues that are especially salient in national politics—and that are likely to be especially accessible in the minds of American survey respondents—are more likely to generate substantively meaningful contextual correlations.

If local politics can sustain political divisions that are distinctive from those in national politics, one implication is that we should be able to find cases where people's political attitudes vary systematically based on their exposure to the issue. Here, we considered a range of issues that had the potential to generate such local contextual effects. But while each example has its idiosyncrasies, and while the fit between concept and measurement is better in some cases than in others, the overall pattern is harder to explain away on such bases. Local contextual effects appear to be more the exception than the rule. What is more, contextual effects are more likely on issues that are already prominent in national political debates. Local issues appear more to be extensions of national issues than alternatives to them.

CHAPTER SIX

Explaining Nationalization

A lberta is an oil-rich province in western Canada. But in political and economic terms, some Americans dub it "Canada's Texas." Just as Texas is a solidly Republican state and home to the most recent Republican ex-president, Alberta is a bastion of the federal Conservative Party and the home base of former Conservative leader Stephen Harper. In fact, even in the 2015 election that ended Harper's nine-year tenure as prime minister, Alberta returned a higher share of Conservative members of Parliament than any other province.

Yet when we peer into subnational politics, the similarities melt. The state of Texas has been under unified Republican control since 2002 and has had consecutive GOP governors for twenty-two years since George W. Bush won in 1994. But after a long period of Conservative government, Alberta has seen significant volatility in its provincial politics. In 2012, the upstart Wildrose Party—a party that does not contest federal elections—took 34 percent of the provincial vote by challenging the governing Conservative Party from the right. Three years later, the left-leaning New Democratic Party broke through in provincial elections, taking control of the provincial government with 41 percent of the vote. The party system in Alberta is quite different than the federal party system in Canada, a fact true of other Canadian provinces, including British Columbia and Quebec. The Texas Republican Party is essentially hegemonic; the Alberta Conservative Party is not.

What explains the volatility of Alberta's politics when compared to the stability of Texas's politics? To ask that question is to ask about the causes of nationalization in the United States. In chapter 2, we distinguished between two facets of nationalized political behavior. The first is the nationalization of political divisions, and it is evident in the increasing alignment of vote choice across the levels of government (chapter 3) as well as in the paucity of local contextual effects (chapter 5). The second is the nationalization of voter engagement, which we see in voter turnout and a wide range of other participatory acts (chapter 4). This distinction is important partly because the two facets of nationalization need not move in tandem. One can imagine state or local elections that see *higher* engagement because they are nationalized, as in the 1960–1961 campaign to recall an Anaheim, California, school board member that was motivated by anticommunism (McGirr 2001).

The first four chapters of the book were primarily descriptive: their goal was to demonstrate the extent of nationalized political behavior. In voting patterns, in participation, and even in attitudes on local issues, we find levels of nationalization that powerfully undercut the assumptions about state-level primacy built into the US Constitution (Levy 2006, 2007). In this chapter and those that follow, we lay the foundation for separate explanations for the two facets of nationalized political behavior, explanations we then test empirically in chapters 7, 8, and 9.

This chapter first provides a brief overview of its explanations for each facet of nationalization. But to fully understand those explanations and the key alternatives to them, it then considers the explanations offered by prior research. Although this book's novel evidence comes from the fifty American states, its concepts need not. So, in search of potential explanations, this chapter surveys the more extensive literature on nationalization beyond the US. Scholarship on the origins of nationalism—a separate but related phenomenon—focuses on the role of information technology in enabling political communities as large as nations to exist. Research on political nationalization within existing nation-states instead emphasizes factors internal to the political system and identifies political competition and the division of state authority as prime nationalizing forces. Comparative research also reinforces the importance of national and ethnic identities in shaping the course and extent of nationalization. In short, the key ingredients of this book's ultimate explanation of nationalization—political parties, identities, and media sources—lie within different strands of prior research. At the same time, the accumulated evidence is frequently circumstantial, as it is often drawn from loose associations in trends over time.

To be sure, past work and intuition suggest a variety of other potential explanations for nationalization, from economic shifts and changing geographic mobility to the end of the one-party South and the centralization of governmental authority in Washington, DC. How can we sort through the various competing explanations? In recent decades, social scientists' standards for calling a relationship "causal" have grown stricter, and social science research has enjoyed improved credibility as a result. Even so, the workhorse approaches to causal inference are derived from randomized experiments, and more generally from situations in which well-defined causes act at a single point in time on randomly selected subsets of the population of interest. Such approaches are difficult to apply in the case of nationalization, as the main explanations advanced in prior work are broad, macrosocial phenomena likely to act over time. Certainly, many of the specific causal links proposed here lend themselves to experiments or other tests that are credibly causal, and we employ those tests where possible. But the book's overarching explanations necessarily rely on looser, more subjective standards similar to the "preponderance of the evidence" employed in some courtrooms.[1] Throughout, the book aims to distinguish claims that are causal in the strict sense of the term from those that are more speculative and more dependent on synthesizing patterns across a range of studies.

In short, this chapter has a few intertwined goals. After summarizing its explanations of nationalized political behavior, it proceeds to detail prior research on nationalization and related phenomena, including nationalism and political polarization. This chapter then outlines several seemingly plausible explanations of nationalization, some of which turn out not to fit the existing evidence well. As we saw in chapter 3, the nationalization of vote choice has waxed and waned since the New Deal, making it amenable to tests with time-varying data. Political engagement, on the other hand, has become steadily more nationally oriented over decades, meaning that tests with over-time data will be less decisive. Accordingly, this chapter focuses primarily on explanations of nationalized vote choice, leaving for chapters 8 and 9 the challenge of explaining nationalized political engagement. As this chapter unfolds, its over-time evidence will lead us to focus on political parties and discount several alternative explanations of nationalized political behavior.

Overview of the Core Explanations

This book offers separate explanations for the two facets of nationalization. The first focuses on political parties. In democratic political systems, parties play a key role as an intermediary between voters and governments. They simplify the task of voting by developing well-known reputations that can help voters make informed choices without knowing much about specific candidates (Popkin 1994; Sniderman and Stiglitz 2012). It stands to reason that contemporary voters might not distinguish between voting at the state and federal levels because the major parties no longer differ at those levels to the extent that they used to. Like customers choosing between Burger King and McDonald's, voters today are faced with very similar choices irrespective of where they live.

What's more, a party-centered account is better tailored to explain the first face of nationalization—the growing similarity in presidential and gubernatorial voting—than the declining state and local political engagement that is nationalization's second face. To explain today's nationalized patterns of political engagement, this book instead points to changes in American media markets. It is hard to mobilize voters around elections for which they lack information. And shifts in American media markets in recent years are likely to have had a profound impact on the information Americans get about politics at different levels of the federal system. Cable news and online news are two growing sources of political information, and they both heavily emphasize national politics. As national media outlets on cable television and the Internet take over audience bandwidth that was previously devoted to print newspapers and local television, news audiences are learning less about state and local politics.

As the opening paragraphs of this chapter suggest, examples like Canada and also the United Kingdom loom as shadow cases throughout these chapters. But both countries offer a cautionary note about assuming that changing media markets alone can produce nationalized political behavior. While those countries have undergone similar changes in their media markets, they have not experienced concomitant nationalization. One important difference between the United States and those nations is the role of enduring political attachments within the country, whether to Quebec or Scotland and Northern Ireland (Levy 2007). While changes in the media market can shape the political information that people receive, they do not do so in a vacuum: media outlets choose content based on their perceptions of audience interest (Gentzkow and Shapiro 2010). In fact, as choices among media outlets proliferate, citizens' interests and identities become increasingly important in shaping the news media they consume (Prior 2007). Media markets can facilitate nationalization's second face but only when there are not strong subnational identities serving as a counterweight.

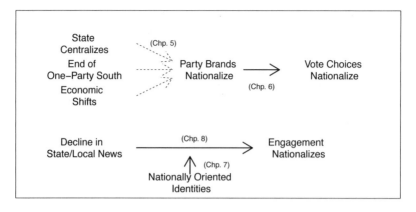

FIGURE 6.1. Explanations of nationalized political behavior
This figure summarizes the explanation for each facet of nationalized political behavior.

Those pathways, in brief, are the two tracks of this book's explanation of nationalized political behavior. Figure 6.1 illustrates each, with solid arrows showing the central explanations advanced in this book. Shifts in the political parties play a prominent role in nationalizing voters' choices, as chapter 7 documents empirically. At the same time, chapters 8 and 9 illustrate how Americans' nationally oriented political identities work in tandem with changing media markets to dampen engagement in state and local politics.

To lay the groundwork for these explanations, this chapter details prior explanations of nationalization and related phenomena. Some factors, including residential mobility, turn out to be ill suited as straightforward explanations of nationalized voting patterns. Another group of factors— highlighted by the dashed arrows in figure 6.1—are likely to have influenced vote choice only indirectly, acting through their impacts on the political parties. Three such factors merit particular attention. The state parties might have nationalized in response to the increasing centralization of governmental authority at the federal level, as Chhibber and Kollman (2004) contend. The decline of the one-party South is a second potentially influential factor (Glaser 1998; Ware 2006; Black and Black 2009; Mickey 2015; Schickler 2016). Within the South, the end of Democratic hegemony was in itself an example of nationalization, as voters' state-level party preferences came into line with their national voting. But the beginning of real two-party competition throughout the South also

had implications beyond its borders, homogenizing the parties ideologically and ushering in an era of fierce competition nationwide (see also
Caramani 2004). The third possibility holds that party brands nationalized because of economic transformations that have reduced local and
regional distinctiveness (Bensel 1984; Porter 2003). The underlying idea
is that agricultural or industrial economies of prior eras had the potential to generate more disparate interests across space than does today's
service economy (see also Hopkins 2017). As we will see, the time trends
for these factors are such that none is likely to have led directly to nationalized voting, at least outside the South. None can make sense of why
nationalized voting patterns declined in the 1960s and 1970s. But all three
may have nationalized the political parties over the long run and shaped
vote choices nationwide through that channel.

Prior Explanations of Nationalization

Much of the research on nationalization has focused on party systems and
countries outside the United States, so we turn first to that scholarship
in search of hypotheses about its potential causes. We consider both research on nation formation and nationalism and research on the separate
but related question of nationalization within established nation-states.
While some of the earliest work on nation building emphasized the role
of communications technologies, more recent research on comparative
nationalization points to factors internal to the political system, such as
party competition and the centralization of governmental authority.

   Nationalizing trends predate and in fact made possible the modern
nation-state. To explain its rise, social scientists, including Ernest Gellner
(1983) and Benedict Anderson (1991), emphasize the importance of print
media and education. With the spread of literacy and written material
in vernacular languages between the seventeenth and nineteenth centuries, people could increasingly conceive of themselves as part of a national
community that was at once beyond their daily experience and yet politically meaningful. The initial appearance of the nation-state was partly a
product of changes in communication technologies that made it possible
to imagine far more expansive communities.

   Still, the fit between a nation's self-conception and the political boundaries of the associated state is often imperfect, providing the potential for
conflict. The relationship between Quebec and the rest of Canada is one

example; the relationship among Scotland, Wales, Northern Ireland, and England is another. There is no guarantee that people within a political system will share the same conception of the nation. The organization of the political parties might well reflect those differences, with parties competing only in specific parts of the polity or appealing to ethnic or religious loyalties. In work like Caramani (2004), party systems are considered nationalized to the extent that the same parties compete in different constituencies within a polity.

What, then, explains the extent to which party systems are nationalized? Caramani (2004) offers perhaps the most comprehensive account of the nationalization of party systems in Europe. In his view, nationalization is largely unidirectional: the "results presented in this work attest to a general process of national political integration, that is, an evolution toward the nationalization or homogenization of politics" (5). From studies of seventeen countries, he demonstrates that nationalization "took place 'early' in the electoral and political history of Europe," (78) frequently before World War I. That timing is consequential, as the nationalization of party systems largely preceded the widespread adoption of proportional representation, the political incorporation of working-class voters, and the growth of social democratic parties. It also preceded the diffusion of broadcast communication technologies, such as radio and television.

While Caramani considers various potential causes of nationalization, his research emphasizes the supremacy of the left–right cleavage as well as the effects of electoral competition. To win power, parties needed to win seats, so the logic of electoral competition led them to adopt platforms that made them competitive across a broad swath of territory. That said, nationalization has proceeded unevenly in different countries, with regional parties persisting in some parts of Europe. Notice, however, that such conceptions have trouble distinguishing between regional differences that are the product of the uneven distribution of individual-level characteristics and those that are the product of differing political competition or behavior across space.[2]

By focusing on the federal systems of Canada, Great Britain, India, and the United States, Chhibber and Kollman (2004) reach a related but distinctive conclusion about the central causes of nationalization. In their words, "as governments centralize authority, taking powers away from or imposing new conditions on lower levels of government, voters will naturally have more incentives to try to influence politics at higher levels" (78). According to Chhibber and Kollman, the New Deal in the United States was an important breakpoint, as it concentrated power in

Washington, DC, and made control of the federal government the central prize of US politics. It's the same impulse that led Lyndon Baines Johnson to tell a longtime friend he was making a mistake by leaving Washington, DC, to run for governor of Texas when "here's where the power is" (Caro 2012, 93). Evidence from Squire (2014) reinforces the claim that the New Deal was a watershed moment in American federalism: fewer members of Congress were leaving to assume state-level positions during the New Deal than at any point before or since, as the federal government was where the action was. LBJ was not the only politician to be lured to seek federal office during the New Deal. Still, one important feature of Chhibber and Kollman's view is that it is not unidirectional. In their view, nationalization can wane, as it did in Britain in the wake of decentralization in the 1990s.[3]

Before the New Deal, many politicians were content with control over state or local governments. In the opening decades of the twentieth century, for instance, southern Democrats were unlikely to be part of a winning presidential coalition, as only one Democratic presidential candidate— Woodrow Wilson—won office between 1897 and 1932. Yet the southern Democrats' state-level hegemony was unchallenged and provided substantial control over policy and patronage, as Huey Long knew well. One pre–New Deal observer of American politics was Walter Lippmann— and for Lippmann, "the real alignments were local, and the national alignments 'mere coalitions which create, not parties of principle, but governing majorities.' The parties served to unite factions which might otherwise be irreconcilable. Thus it was, he maintained, that the 'very absence of consistent national principle in either party is fundamental to the domestic peace of the United States'" (Steel 1980, 249). This description nicely illustrates the pre–New Deal parties. In decentralized political systems, politicians can work together in national politics while being grounded in quite disparate local policies or goals. One's national affiliation does not determine one's local views, as the parties contain substantial internal divisions (see also Noel 2013).

As an explanation of parties as organizations, Chhibber and Kollman (2004) fits well (see especially Hopkins and Schickler 2016). But as an explanation of the nationalization of Americans' vote choices, it runs into substantial challenges. One is the Great Society. As president from 1963 to 1968, Lyndon Johnson oversaw a period of significant expansion in federal authority, as new laws and programs expanded the federal government's role in everything from public education and health care to welfare and voting rights. However, as we saw in figure 3.2 in chapter 3, the

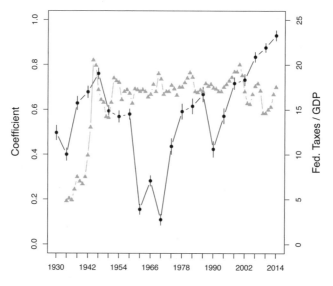

FIGURE 6.2. Nationalization and governmental authority
This figure depicts the relationship between gubernatorial and presidential voting using black
dots, reproducing figure 3.2 from chapter 3. Federal tax receipts as a share of GDP are represented by gray triangles.

1960s and 1970s were precisely the years when federal and state-level vote
choices were becoming decoupled. Certainly, it remains plausible that in
the long term, political parties organize themselves to capture power at the
level where it is concentrated within a federal system. But the fact that
the 1960s saw an expansion of federal authority as well as a sharp drop in
nationalized voting suggests that there must be a more proximate explanation of voting patterns—voters do not appear to respond directly to the
distribution of authority.

As another way to test this possibility, consider figure 6.2. The figure
reproduces figure 3.2 by using black dots to illustrate the correlation between county-level gubernatorial and presidential vote choice in midterm
elections outside the South. Alongside that metric of nationalized vote
choice, we show with gray triangles federal tax receipts as a share of GDP.[4]
As figure 6.2 demonstrates, there is no clear relationship between nationalized voting and this measure of federal governmental authority. In the
1930s and 1940s, the share of GDP going to the federal government grew
dramatically with the New Deal and World War II. It then remained relatively stable, with brief spikes during the 1960s, the late 1970s, and the late

1990s. Vote choices—and also relative engagement in federal politics—rapidly grew more nationalized after around 1980, at a time when Ronald Reagan's New Federalism and tax cuts were ostensibly pushing authority away from the federal government. Nationalized voting rose dramatically at a time when the distribution of governmental authority remained relatively static, making it hard for the latter to be a consistent or direct cause of the former. What is more, in chapter 4, we saw survey evidence that further undercuts the claim that Americans respond directly to the migration of governmental authority. Americans report paying disproportionate attention to the presidency even while acknowledging the substantial impact of mayors and governors on their day-to-day lives. Shifts in governmental authority remain a compelling explanation for why parties as organizations have nationalized. But they cannot directly explain the patterns in either vote choice or participation.

Polarization and the Political Parties

As we saw just above, federal authority is a poor fit as a direct explanation of nationalized voting behavior. But perhaps political polarization—and the concomitant increase in the parties' distinctiveness—is better suited to explain the ebbs and flows of nationalization's first face.

In important respects, today's partisanship differs from that of the 1950s. At the elite level, federal politicians from the two major parties take increasingly distinctive positions across party lines and similar positions within them, a phenomenon known as "polarization" (McCarty, Poole, and Rosenthal 2006; Levendusky 2009; Noel 2013). Whereas it was common in the 1950s and 1960s to find conservative Democrats and liberal Republicans within the halls of Congress, the Obama administration saw essentially no overlap in the average policy positions adopted by congressional Democrats and Republicans (Poole and Rosenthal 2016). Moreover, the 1950s and 1960s saw congressional voting that was defined by at least two different dimensions of disagreement, as some members who were liberal on issues related to government spending were conservative on issues related to race (e.g., Carmines and Stimson 1989; Poole and Rosenthal 1997). Today, the policy preferences of the two parties are more easily characterized along a single dimension (Poole and Rosenthal 1997; McCarty, Poole, and Rosenthal 2006; Jochim and Jones 2013; Noel 2013; but also see Karol 2009). That means that the two major parties have been sending voters increasingly clear, consistent, and distinctive signals about their policy preferences.

Scholarship disagrees about the extent to which the public itself has followed suit and polarized. Some point to the centrism of public opinion as evidence that polarization is primarily an elite-level phenomenon (e.g., Fiorina, Abrams, and Pope 2005). Others contend that mass-level polarization has increased dramatically since the 1970s (Abramowitz and Saunders 2008) and point out that recent years have seen a marked increase in partisan voting as well as a stronger relationship between partisanship and Americans' opinions on specific issues (Bartels 2002; Bafumi and Shapiro 2009). Yet there is widespread agreement that voters are now more sorted by ideology than in prior decades, with conservatives overwhelmingly defining themselves as Republicans and liberals as Democrats (Bafumi and Shapiro 2009; Levendusky 2009; Noel 2013). In federal politics, increased elite-level polarization makes the two parties more distinctive, and mass-level sorting and polarization reduce the parties' capacity to win support from voters who identify with the other party.

In recent years, questions related to political polarization have spawned an extensive body of research. To date, however, scholars and pundits alike have largely ignored the impact of polarization in state and local politics. There, too, the impact of polarization is likely substantial. Former president Dwight Eisenhower quipped that "there is not one Republican party, there are forty-eight state Republican parties" (Bernstein 2000, 171). During Eisenhower's presidency in the 1950s, there were meaningful differences across the state parties in their organizational strength and platforms (Mayhew 1986; Paddock 2005).[5] To understand state politics, one needed detailed knowledge about state history and about the idiosyncrasies of its groups and parties: social groups that were mainstays of the Democratic Party in some places might tend toward the Republican Party elsewhere (e.g., Phillips 1969). That was especially true of the one-party South (e.g., Key 1949; Mickey 2015), but it was by no means unique to it. Ambitious individuals might opt to join a party or run for office under its banner based more on the strength of its local organization or the resulting job prospects than on ideological alignment. But ideological polarization has important implications for that local texture. As the parties become more distinctive and ideological at the national level, the room for state-level variation in the parties' platforms may shrink considerably.

To provide preliminary evidence of the connection between polarization and nationalized vote choice, consider figure 6.3. Using black dots, it again presents the correlation between presidential and midterm gubernatorial voting at the county level outside the South. The gray triangles

FIGURE 6.3. Political polarization and nationalization
This figure illustrates the correlation between presidential and gubernatorial voting in mid-terms (*black dots*) and political polarization measured via DW-NOMINATE (*gray triangles*).

represent the level of polarization in the US House, as estimated via DW-NOMINATE (Poole and Rosenthal 1997).[6] As the figure makes plain, trends in political polarization match those in nationalized vote choice surprisingly well for the second part of the time series. Polarization began to rise sharply in the late 1970s, at precisely the time that midterm voting became more nationalized. Of the time series that we have examined, only political polarization seems to match the observed trends in nationalized voting closely.

To be clear, nationalization and polarization are distinct phenomena. Polarization is a process in which elected officials from the two major political parties adopt increasingly divergent policy positions, one that has heightened ideological sorting and reduced partisan defections at the ballot box. Nationalization is a multifaceted, mass-level process through which voters care less about state and local politics and use the same criteria to pick candidates across the federal system. Still, the two processes are closely related and potentially reinforcing. When the parties adopt clear and divergent ideological positions, voters may be increasingly likely to see state and local candidates through the lens of their national loyalties. So polarization may well foster nationalized voting patterns. The causal arrow might run in the opposite direction, too. In a nationalized polity, elected officials are focused primarily on differences between left and right and can't be won over by appeals to their constituents' local interests. Given the connection between polarization and nationalization, it is worth considering polarization as a would-be cause of nationalization. It is worth considering some of the explanations put forward for polarization as explanations of nationalization, too.

The End of the Solid South

As we saw in chapters 3, 4, and 5, both elements of nationalization have been on the rise since around 1980, and those changes are evident in a wide range of attitudes and behaviors. That suggests that nationalization's causes are themselves likely to be broad, durable, and long acting—they must be capable of shaping attitudes and behavior in many places over long periods of time. We should focus, then, on the broader explanations of political polarization. Changes that are specific to one house of Congress or to particular state governments, to cite two examples, are unlikely to explain why political behavior has nationalized.

That said, the realignment of many white southern voters and politicians from the Democrats to the Republicans in the second half of the twentieth century is one distinct possibility. After the end of Reconstruction in 1876, much of the American South fell under one-party Democratic rule for more or less the following century (Key 1949; Black and Black 2009; Mickey 2015). The Democrats' near monopoly on southern congressional seats and Electoral College votes had important implications outside the South, as it shaped the balance of power in Washington, DC, while making the Democrats an ideologically broad majority coalition (Noel 2013). But by the 1960s, the Democratic lock on the South was beginning to crack. GOP presidential nominee Barry Goldwater lost the 1964 presidential election by historic margins, but after opposing the 1964 Civil Rights Act, he also managed to win several Deep South states that had not gone Republican since Reconstruction (Carmines and Stimson 1989). Those victories were a harbinger of the coming realignment, as GOP presidential candidates today can now count on a swath of southern states from South Carolina to Louisiana (Phillips 1969). To be sure, it took the Republicans another generation to build their party organizations in the South and contest state, local, and congressional races with the same success. But by 1994, they held a majority of House of Representatives seats from the eleven states of the former Confederacy. And as of 2016, every one of those eleven states had Republican-controlled legislatures, and all but two had Republican governors.

Within the South, this shift to two-party competition with a pronounced GOP advantage was itself an example of nationalization's first face. From the 1970s to the 2010s, southerners increasingly brought their voting for state, local, and congressional races into alignment with their presidential voting. Southern white voters first warmed to GOP presidential candidates, with voting at other levels and eventually partisan identities following behind (Green, Palmquist, and Schickler 2002; Burden and Kimball 2002). For instance, Rick Perry was a Republican governor of Texas from 2000 to 2015, but he only left the Democratic Party in 1989. This fact pattern suggests the importance of the parties' structures and organizations in channeling vote choices as well as the durability of partisan loyalties.

Still, the end of the Solid South had critical implications for nationalization beyond the region's borders, too. In Congress, many southern Democrats were among the most conservative members of the party, so the replacement of those conservative Democrats by conservative Republicans made the Democratic Party far more homogeneously liberal. With less ideological diversity, the Democrats adopted more consistently liberal platforms, giving the party a clearer ideological hue. On the Republican side, the party's movement south led to an increased emphasis on social and cultural issues as well as a far more ideological party (Barber and McCarty 2013; Grossmann and Hopkins 2015; Hopkins 2017). Changes in voting in one region can foster polarization nationwide.

The shift of most white southerners from the Democratic to the Republican Party has also heightened electoral competition, as it ushered in an era of fierce competition for congressional control (Lee 2016). For Republicans, the end of the Solid South put presidential and congressional majorities in reach; for Democrats, it forced the party to make up its losses in seats and support elsewhere. Even so, as Barber and McCarty (2013) point out, Republican senators and representatives have become more conservative even outside the South in recent decades, meaning that southern realignment is not the only explanation for polarization. Moreover, the end of the one-party South was unlikely to directly factor into voters' decision making outside the region. Instead, the most likely channel through which it was likely to affect vote choices elsewhere was through its impacts on the parties and their brands. In short, within the South, the end of the Solid

South *was* an element of nationalization. But elsewhere, it was a potential *explanation* of nationalization.

Alternative Explanations

We turn now to other, nonpolitical explanations that are sufficiently broad so as to be credible explanations of nationalization. McCarty, Poole, and Rosenthal (2006) note the strong correlation between rising income inequality and political polarization, positing that increasing income differences lead to diverging policy preferences among voters and then their representatives (see also Gelman et al. 2008). Some scholarship has also linked political polarization with shifts in campaign finance. As we saw in chapter 4, since around 1990, there has been a sharp rise in candidates' reliance on individual donors and on out-of-district campaign contributions, both of which are likely to be more ideologically motivated than alternative sources (Barber and McCarty 2013; La Raja and Schaffner 2015; Fontana, forthcoming).

Still other scholarship on polarization points to the increasingly fragmented media environment and the rise of avowedly ideological news outlets (Prior 2006; Levendusky 2013a, 2013b; Hopkins and Ladd 2014), a set of explanations we take up in chapter 9. For now, it is worth noting that while both changes in campaign contributions and in the availability of ideological news may well have accelerated nationalization, the nationalizing trends in voting behavior were visible as early as the 1980s. In short, they predate key changes in both campaign finance and media consumption.

Residential Mobility

It is also possible that the nationalization of American political behavior might be driven by more general social phenomena not previously linked to polarization, such as changes in residential mobility or transformations in the American economy. In theory, increasing residential mobility is one straightforward explanation for more nationalized political behavior. Americans who are born in one state, educated in a second state, and newly resident in a third are less likely to be very knowledgeable about or attentive to their home state. From Frederick Jackson Turner's "frontier thesis" forward, Americans' self-understanding has been as a mobile people ready to pursue the next opportunity. In 2012, just 36 percent of

Florida residents were born in Florida (Aisch and Gebeloff 2014), for example, meaning that many Florida voters have not been learning about Florida's history and politics since birth.

That said, Florida is more the exception than the rule. In the median US state, 59 percent of 2012 residents were born in the state (Aisch and Gebeloff 2014). More to the point, the over-time trend in mobility is downward, not upward. After large-scale migrations like the Great Migration and the flight from the Dust Bowl, Americans have settled down somewhat. The percentage of Americans who moved across county lines is down slightly from the 1950s and 1960s (Fischer 2002). According to Frey (2009), in 2007–2008, overall US migration reached its lowest point since World War II. In fact, only 1.6 percent of Americans made an interstate move in 2008–2009. On its own, residential mobility seems unlikely to explain either facet of nationalized political behavior, as the trends do not match up.

Although it is beyond the scope of this book, one could still imagine that changing patterns of mobility among specific socioeconomic groups do influence party nationalization. For instance, if socioeconomic elites are now more likely to attend college or to settle in places far from their hometown, that could shape their social networks and perceptions. It could contribute, for instance, to the single nationalized network of party staffers and activists observed by Bernstein (2000). It could also make sense of the marked decline in senators representing the state in which they were born, as appendix figure 26 illustrates. One route to elite-level nationalization is if many political candidates are drawn from and adopt the perspective of a nationalized socioeconomic elite (see also Carnes 2013).

Economic Shifts

If Americans' moves are not driving nationalization, perhaps the economy is shifting in consequential ways around them. Many accounts of political conflict stress underlying economic divisions, whether over questions of taxes, government spending, or trade (Beard 1913; McCarty, Poole, and Rosenthal 2006; Gelman et al. 2008). One prime example is Bensel (1984), which contends that American political divisions between 1880 and 1980 can be understood as an ongoing conflict rooted in regions' differing economic imperatives. Divisions between the agricultural South and the industrializing Northeast are one archetypal example. Whereas southerners in the late nineteenth century sought open markets for their agricultural products, northeastern industrialists sought trade barriers to protect their growing industries. Those differences were closely linked to the political parties, with the Republicans representing the northeastern industrialists and the Democrats the southern planters.

If earlier economic conflicts were a central source of political division— and of regional political differentiation—perhaps those conflicts have become more muted in recent decades. Bensel, describing his study of voting in Congress, notes that "the average level of sectional stress on competitive roll calls has generally declined over the last century" (52). Today, regions of the United States are less identified with specific sectors of the economy than in prior eras (Caselli and Coleman 2001; Duranton and Puga 2005). As one example, cars are still made in Michigan, but they are also made in Tennessee and Kentucky. The growth of the service sector may undercut regional differences as well, as one can find Walmart stores, McDonald's restaurants, and hospitals throughout the country.

Regions in the United States once had vastly different income levels, as the American South was much poorer than other parts of the country. But that no longer holds true (Barro et al. 1991; Caselli and Coleman 2001; Cowie 2001). The rise of a consumer-oriented economy also means that Americans are exposed to similar brands and marketing across the country (Cohen 2004; Ritzer 2011). These transformations, in turn, may well mean that economic interests no longer follow straightforwardly from one's state or region of residence. To be sure, economic questions may well remain an important political division—but they now seem to divide metropolitan areas from more rural areas rather than dividing states or regions (Desmet and Fafchamps 2005; Cramer Walsh 2012; Rodden 2013; Sellers et al. 2013; Cramer 2016). The political interests of urban dwellers in Seattle may now look more like those of New Yorkers than those of residents of eastern Washington. Put differently, economic divisions may divide people within states rather than dividing people across states (Mc-Carty, Poole, and Rosenthal 2006; Gelman et al. 2008). Transformations of the American economy, in short, have the potential to influence the nationalization of political behavior.

Like several of the other factors considered in this chapter, these economic trends are largely monotonic. In other words, they have unfolded slowly and trended in the same direction over decades. Kim (1998), for instance, shows that regional specialization by economic sector has declined steadily since around 1900. Given that, neither economic transformations nor changes in federal authority are well suited to explain the first face of nationalized political behavior directly, as the trends do not match well. Nationalized voting has not inexorably risen. Instead, it has waxed and waned at various points in the last half-century, with its most recent spike starting around 1980. That's not to say that these other factors are irrelevant, though. Over time, they could influence the ways in which the two major political parties organize conflicts into American politics and could shape voting behavior indirectly.

Ex ante, there were various plausible explanations for why Americans' vote choices have nationalized. But after examining temporal trends, we can set aside several. Of the factors examined here, only political polarization appears to track patterns of nationalized voting closely, a fact that suggests that changes in the political parties may be central in explaining today's nationalized political behavior. Still, correlation does not imply causation. On their own, time-series analyses often rely on impossibly strict assumptions ruling out omitted variables. Rising political polarization was hardly the only politically relevant factor that changed around 1980. So, in the next chapter, we turn to a more detailed analysis of the connection between the parties' brands and voting behavior, one that draws on cross-sectional as well as over-time variation.

CHAPTER SEVEN

E Pluribus Duo

John F. Kennedy took the State of West Virginia by storm. It's now history. However, what people should remember is that it was a presidential race that was bought and paid for—cold cash for nearly every voter. The Kennedys were well aware of our brand of politics. I guess it was their brand, too. —Raymond Chafin, Democratic County Chairman, Logan County, West Virginia[1]

The year was 1960, and Raymond Chafin was the Democratic Party's chairman in Logan County, West Virginia. A coal-producing county in the southern part of the state, Logan was known then as a place where votes could be bought and sold (Loughry 2006). And John F. Kennedy, who found himself fighting Hubert Humphrey in that state's primary, needed votes. Days before the May 10 primary, Chafin reports getting a call from Kennedy allies asking how much money Chafin would need. His answer: "About thirty-five," meaning $3,500. But when Chafin met the airplane at a local airstrip as instructed, he found that it had not $3,500 but $35,000, money he claimed bought votes for Kennedy (Loughry 2006). Kennedy won the West Virginia primary, with impressive margins in Logan and the neighboring counties (Loughry 2006). His victory demonstrated to party bosses elsewhere that Kennedy could win Protestant voters, effectively sidelining opponents such as Senate majority leader Lyndon Johnson (Caro 2012).

Allegations of vote buying in a presidential primary are undeniably important. But for our purposes, more important is the idea that West Virginia had its own brand of politics, one in which candidates competed by providing tangible rewards to voters. From Key (1949) to Hero (1998), from Phillips (1969) to Mayhew (1986), and from Elazar (1966) to Gimpel (1996), scholars have shown repeatedly that states did have their own brands of politics, and they have set out to explain why. Why did a figure like Huey Long emerge in Louisiana in the late 1920s, exercising virtually dictatorial powers over a twentieth-century American state (Key 1949; Williams 1981; White 2006)? Why did traditional, patronage-seeking parties dominate states like Connecticut and Illinois while failing to take root in neighboring states like Massachusetts and Wisconsin (Mayhew 1986)? To understand both voting and policy making in a specific state, detailed knowledge of that state's political history was essential (Key 1949; Phillips 1969; Mayhew 1986; Gimpel 1996).

Still, many of the most striking examples of interstate differences are now decades if not centuries old. Back in chapter 3, we charted the increasingly tight relationship between presidential and gubernatorial voting since approximately 1980, and we took it to be strong evidence that the divisions between the two national parties increasingly animate gubernatorial campaigns. In chapter 6, we saw that political polarization accelerated at about the same time as nationalized voting patterns, suggesting a potential relationship. Here, we develop and test that possibility by tracing changes in state political parties and voters' perceptions of them. The core claim: that today's state parties increasingly follow their national patrons by offering voters clear ideological choices. What's more, voters don't seem to perceive even the modest differences across state parties that remain. Like McDonald's, today's major parties are thoroughly nationalized brands. They are thought to offer voters highly similar choices in disparate parts of the country—and voters respond accordingly.

In the United States, political parties are widely reviled. James Madison famously denounced "mischiefs of faction" in "Federalist 10" (Hamilton, Madison, and Jay 1788). Yet political scientists are a rare exception. As a group, they often appreciate the benefits parties bring, including their role in simplifying the choices before voters (Banfield 1961; Key and Cummings 1966; Popkin 1994; Aldrich 1995; Fiorina, Abrams, and Pope 2005; Sniderman and Stiglitz 2012). This chapter first briefly outlines that pro-party line of thinking.

Still, our conceptions of the relationship between parties and voters come chiefly from federal politics (e.g., Jessee 2012)—whether and to what extent those same models work across the levels of government is less clear (but see Tausanovitch and Warshaw 2014; Caughey 2015; Einstein and Kogan 2015). Accordingly, this chapter then considers spatial models in which state parties have varying capacities to adjust to state-level opinions. In some cases, the state parties are free to shift their platforms in keeping with their state's voters; in others, they are tethered to their national party brands. Even though reality undeniably lies between

those two theoretical poles, these models help illustrate how tighter perceived connections between state and national parties can align state and
national voting even when citizens' preferences remain the same. They
show a mechanism through which elite-level polarization in national politics can have state-level impacts on voters.

It is important, then, to characterize the state parties' positions and priorities relative to each other over time. Beyond anecdotes, is there empirical
evidence that state parties are in fact more integrated with and more similar
to their counterparts in other states than in the past? To develop an answer,
we first turn to prior research on state parties. In earlier eras, patronage was
often a critical goal of winning elections, a fact that gave some state-level
parties powerful incentives to moderate their platforms. Raymond Chafin's
commitment to JFK doesn't seem to have been grounded in ideological af-
finity. But the changing goals of party elites and activists, accompanied by
changes in campaign finance and party organization, seem to have altered
the calculus decisively.

Reinforcing this story, existing data on voting in state legislatures indicate that on balance, the state-level parties are indeed polarizing in ways
that parallel national trends (Shor and McCarty 2011). To be sure, there
is still variation in the ideological positions of different state legislative
caucuses: northeastern Republican legislators are more liberal than those
elsewhere, and southern Democratic legislators are likewise more conservative. Nonetheless, like their national counterparts, the state parties are
increasingly distinctive in the policies they support.

Yet due to data limitations, analyses of state legislative voting behavior
can take us back only to the mid-1990s, and the actions of state legislators
might not have much impact on how voters perceive state parties anyway (see
especially Rogers 2016). To broaden our time frame and evidentiary base,
the chapter next turns to extensive analyses of more than sixteen hundred
state party platforms dating back to 1918. Using tools from automated text
analysis, we can identify forty topics that have been prevalent in state party
platforms and then trace the attention to them across parties and over time.
These analyses demonstrate that the state parties are increasingly homogeneous: whereas the platforms in earlier eras focused more on state-specific
topics, they now emphasize whatever topics dominate the national agenda.

Just because the state parties are increasingly similar nationwide does
not necessarily mean that voters perceive them as such. To consider that
question, the chapter then turns to the empirical evidence on voters themselves, documenting that virtually no voters have different partisan identifications at the state or local levels. What's more, voters do in fact per-

ceive today's state parties in largely the same ways that they perceive the national parties. And even those state-level differences in positioning that remain are not reflected in contemporary voting for governor.

When making sense of state-level voting behavior, earlier generations of observers needed to consider each state and its idiosyncrasies separately to appreciate the distinctive choices on offer there (Key 1949; McCormick 1973; Phillips 1969; Mayhew 1986; Gimpel 1996). A state-by-state approach is less necessary today (see also Hatch 2016; Rogers 2017). This chapter's core finding is of nationalizing parties and of highly nationalized perceptions of the parties. By using a variety of different sources of data, this chapter is able to trace the pathway from party positions and priorities to voter perceptions. Its results reinforce the speculative conclusion of chapter 6 that polarization and associated changes in the political parties have induced more nationalized voting patterns.

Political Parties in State and Nation

In the United States, political parties are not exactly popular. In part, that might be due to the long history of transactions like those Raymond Chafin described above. But it is also because being a partisan has a decidedly negative connotation in contemporary America, as if being a political partisan were the opposite of being a deliberative democratic citizen (Keith et al. 1992; Rosenblum 2008; Klar and Krupnikov 2016). Few Americans say that their political loyalties are important to their identity, as we'll see in chapter 8. What's more, roughly one-third of Americans conceal their party attachments under the label of "Independent." For many, to acknowledge one's partisanship risks being identified as an unreflective hack and a subpar citizen.

There is a notable exception to this antiparty tradition: even as most Americans view the parties and their most fervent supporters negatively, political scientists see parties as indispensable to mass-level democracy (Rosenblum 2008). Parties provide a cognitive shortcut—a heuristic— with which time-pressed voters can infer a variety of facts about a candidate based on a single label (Popkin 1994). Voters do not need to know the candidates' stances on a newly emerging issue if they can infer them from the parties' overall reputations (Sniderman and Stiglitz 2012). But if partisan identification is a key heuristic, is it primarily national in orientation and meaning? And if so, why, and with what consequences? Those are among the questions that animate this chapter.

Schattschneider defined political parties as "an organized effort to gain political power" (1942, cf. Noel 2014). But it is critical to follow another political scientist of the same generation, V. O. Key, by distinguishing between three different meanings of the word "party": parties in government, parties as organizations, and parties in the electorate (1964). Note that strength in one form does not necessarily mean strength in another. Parties can be strong as organizations but scarcely recognized by the electorate, or the reverse. One goal of this chapter is to characterize variation in the political parties across states, a question focused on parties as organizations and parties in government. To answer that question, we first need to consider other definitions of "parties."

In what is perhaps a reflection of the parties' contemporary nationalization, research on political parties in recent decades has focused overwhelmingly on the national parties. Canonical scholarship considers parties to be teams of elected officials (Aldrich 1995). In this view, parties manage electoral competition and coordinate actions within government and so play a critical role in advancing politicians' goals. This approach is compatible with politicians who seek office for the spoils as well as those who seek to influence policy. But the primacy it places on politicians themselves dovetails nicely with politics that are oriented around distributing jobs and other material perks: it is elected officials who typically control and divvy up the spoils of governing.

A more recent strain of scholarship gives increased emphasis to the loosely affiliated thinkers and interest groups who join the parties' coalitions to pursue their policy goals (Cohen et al. 2009; Karol 2009; Masket 2009; Noel 2013). In this view of parties, the key actors are not exclusively or even primarily candidates for office. To an important extent, they are the interest groups, activists, and opinion leaders who work to shape what the party stands for. Notice that these actors are thought to be pursuing policy primarily, not patronage. It is instructive that a more recent conceptualization of parties emphasizes policy and ideology over jobs, contracts, and direct material benefits. Now armed with a basic understanding of political parties and their capacity to structure voters' choices, we turn to conceptual models of state-level party positioning.

A Conceptual Model of State and National Positioning

In chapter 2, we considered spatial models of politics to develop definitions of nationalization. The core claim was that we can identify the first face of nationalization based on the political issues that divide people at the different levels of government. Politics are nationalized when the dimensions of political conflict are similar across the levels of government—when the issues that animate national politics, whether they are health care or labor unions, also animate state and local politics. And when very different issues divide people in state or local politics, such a polity is not considered nationalized.

Still, even in a state or locality that is nationalized by that definition, subnational politics might remain distinctive from jurisdiction to jurisdiction (Gimpel 1996). Consider a state where the parties and voters are divided on the same issues that divide them nationally, but also one where the backing for the two national parties is decidedly uneven. Whether you call such a place "Utah" or "Massachusetts," the critical question then becomes the capacity of the disadvantaged subnational party to become competitive by giving voters a reason to prefer it. One possibility is to compete along another dimension, for instance by trying to be the party of local service, experience, or incumbency. Another is for the state party to remain competitive on ideology by adopting a more moderate stance than its national copartisans.

Figure 7.1 depicts this question graphically. The left panel shows the ideological placement of the parties and voters nationally. Following Downs (1957), it shows a centrist distribution of voters, although it departs from Downs in showing two parties that maintain distinctive positions. Here, we assume that the parties are not single-minded seekers of votes but instead balance competing imperatives to win and to implement a specific platform. Let's also assume that there are shocks from election to election—scandals, recessions, and so on—that advantage one party or the other, giving parties further from the median voter some chance of winning. In this first hypothetical scenario, the two national parties are equally far from the median voter, making this scenario a competitive one.

But, of course, states and localities vary in their distributions of national political allegiances. Given that variation, what happens in subnational politics hinges on the capacity of the state or local parties to adjust accordingly. In the middle panel of figure 7.1, we see a right-skewed distribution of preferences: in national politics, this is a solidly Republican state in the mold of contemporary Utah or Wyoming. In this example, the parties adapt by both moving right. Such a movement allows the state Democratic Party to remain competitive, while permitting the GOP to take a more conservative stance. It also introduces important heterogeneity across states, as state parties shift to reflect the relative liberalism or

Nat'l Politics, Nat'l Platforms	State Politics, State Platforms	State Politics, Nat'l Platforms

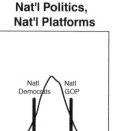 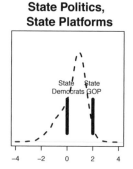 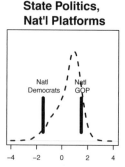

FIGURE 7.1. Possible configurations of state parties and voters
This figure shows three theoretical configurations of voter preferences and party positions.

conservatism of their state (see also Erikson, Wright, and McIver 1993). The same issues occupy national and state politics, but there is ideological daylight between the state and national parties. Now consider the right panel in figure 7.1. Here, we have the skewed distribution of state preferences but parties that are wedded to their national platforms. Although competitive nationally, the Democratic Party's national platform is well to the left of most voters in this state, making it uncompetitive. By contrast, the Republican Party's national platform is quite close to the state's median voter. In this scenario, we might see something close to one-party rule of the governor's mansion, with the Democrats taking over only when a crisis, scandal, or an especially weak candidate (Hall 2015) makes voters willing to overlook their out-of-step stance. In December 2015, voters of solidly Republican Louisiana backed Democratic gubernatorial candidate John Bel Edwards over Republican David Vitter after the latter had been weakened by having solicited a prostitute. So, scandals can cost even dominant parties the governor's chair. But such cases are surely the exception: of the other states in the Republican-leaning South, only Virginia had a sitting Democratic governor as of 2016.

The inability of the parties to escape their national reputations affords one party a consistent advantage, reducing electoral competitiveness and its by-products. In most elections, the advantaged party will have more votes than it needs—and as a result, it can sacrifice some voter support, whether through its candidate choices, its tolerance for corruption, its pursuit of unpopular policies, or other behaviors that could cost it votes. The trade-offs inherent in these two scenarios are nicely summarized by Paddock (2005), who writes, "A decentralized party system allows for the articulation of a variety of particularistic interests, but has a harder time integrating those interests into a coherent whole. Nationalized parties, on the other hand, are more effective at integrating interests and representing a national majority, but less able to reflect the nation's inherent heterogeneity" (35).

This discussion encourages us to ask a few related but distinct empirical questions. First, to what extent do the parties differ in the positions they take across states—and how have those differences been changing over time? Also, irrespective of the actual positions taken by the parties, do voters *perceive* the parties to vary in meaningful ways across the states, and if so, how? The state parties' actual positions are of course consequential for governing and are potentially related to voters' perceptions. But voters do not necessarily perceive those positions clearly, making it important to consider both the actual parties and perceptions of those parties to the extent we are able. We do both in the sections to come.

The Changing Landscape of State Political Parties as Organizations

Mayhew (1986) endeavors to explain variation in parties as organizations across the American states, focusing on the extent to which states have a traditional party organized around obtaining and protecting jobs and other material resources. Such traditional party organizations are evident only among the oldest states, Mayhew finds, and show impressive continuity over time in the states where they do emerge (see also Shefter 1994; Trounstine 2008). In such states, the primacy of patronage has important implications. Certainly, it means that winning elections consistently is paramount—if the party needs to advance policies that differ from what its members most prefer, it still might well do so to protect its hold on power and the resources that come with it (Epstein 1986). What's more, a politics organized around patronage is one with room—at least in theory—for significant state-level differences in party platforms. After all, for parties that are organized to capture jobs at the state level, the party's national ideology is less important than its capacity to win elections and provide jobs and other resources. Raymond Chafin, the vote-buying party chairman we met at the outset of the chapter, had originally backed Kennedy's opponent, Hubert Humphrey.

At the turn of the twentieth century, patronage politics was firmly established in some states and largely absent in others. Yet as Lunch (1987) shows, even those states where it was established saw a series of related shifts by the middle decades of the twentieth century. Civil services laws reduced the already-limited supply of patronage jobs available at the same time that rising affluence reduced demand for them (see also Erie 1988). Older generations of party activists motivated by patronage gave way to a newer generation of activists with explicitly ideological goals (Wilson 1962; Wildavsky 1965; Perlstein 2009; Noel 2013). Unstated but important is the fact that these ideological goals were usually national in orientation. Whether the underlying issue was anti-communism, civil rights, social welfare, or something else, it was frequently national in motivation and orientation. When coupled with the changes in the structure of civic participation and interest groups detailed in Putnam (2000), Skocpol (2003), and chapter 1, these shifts laid the groundwork for an increasingly nationalized activist core at the heart of both national parties. These activists could and did shift their activities across the levels of government with little difficulty, pursuing political opportunities locally with an eye toward national debates (McGirr 2001). They were also bolstered by national organizations such as the American Legislative Exchange Council, which sought allies in advancing a unified program in various statehouses (Hertel-Fernandez 2014, 2016; Garlick 2015).

As Paddock (2005) documents, there were institutional changes that had a nationalizing influence on state party organizations as well. Many traditional parties organized around patronage had extensive social connections to voters. Those social networks were an important asset, as they provided a way to mobilize voters on behalf of party-backed candidates come election day. As patronage declined, so too did one source of field workers. That does not mean state parties drifted off into the sunset—instead, they became more professionalized in the 1960s and 1970s (Cotter et al. 1984). As with other organizations, state parties shifted their tactics, becoming clearinghouses for data on their state's voters (Hatch 2015; Hersh 2015). That reliance gave them newfound relevance in service to candidates (Aldrich 1995) while putting them into closer contact with the national party (Paddock 2005)—and reducing their direct contact with voters.

Similarly, shifts in campaign finance provided state parties with a role that was at once new and yet dependent in important ways on the national parties. The post-Watergate campaign finance regime created strong incentives for the national parties to funnel money through the state parties. This fact gave the state parties increased resources (La Raja 2003). As Paddock (2005) notes, "This intra-party integration and growing state party professionalism, however, came at a price. The state parties lost a lot of autonomy they traditionally enjoyed in a decentralized system" (55). State parties appear to have grown stronger even as they have become less distinctive from state to state. Back in chapter 6, we mentioned President Dwight Eisenhower's quip that "there is not one Republican party, there are forty-eight state Republican parties" (Bernstein 2000, 171). That comment seems outdated today, and not just because of the addition of two more states to the union.

Polarization in State Legislatures

Even in national politics, voters do not typically follow roll-call votes within the legislature closely, and they are certainly not likely to follow state legislation closely, either (Rogers 2016). There is thus no presumption here that voters respond directly to the policy positions taken by state parties. Nonetheless, those positions provide a starting point in understanding how state parties in government have changed in recent years. Specifically, our aim is to measure state parties' political positioning, both relative to their counterparts across the aisle and to the parties in other states. Do state parties appear to be bound to the mast of the national parties, or are they able to craft positions that are responsive to the specific conditions they face? In this section, we consider two different types of data that speak to that question. We begin with existing evidence on voting in state legislatures and then provide novel evidence from state party platforms.

To measure state parties' positioning, recent work by Shor and McCarty (2011) provides an unparalleled resource. Using surveys of state legislators along with a model of roll-call voting, they are able to provide one-dimensional scores that indicate where individual state legislators fall on a continuum. These ideal points appear to be reasonable approximations of individual-level ideology as expressed through legislative voting, and they allow Shor and McCarty (2011) to calculate ideological scores for each party in each state legislative chamber. To be sure, state legislators are but one element of the state party. But they are a crucial and comparatively stable element, and their over-time policy making should serve to shape their state party's reputation even when they do not control the governor's mansion.

Figure 7.2 depicts the average ideal points for each state party's caucus in the lower chamber of the state house between 1996 and 2014. Note that these individual-level measures are time invariant. They assume that legislators have a single ideology throughout their careers and so will only detect

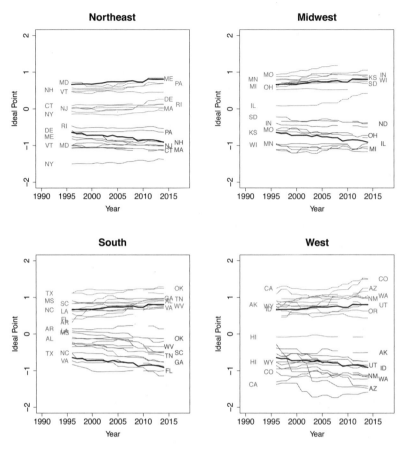

FIGURE 7.2. Ideological differences in state legislatures
This figure shows the ideal points for each state party estimated by Shor and McCarty (2011) for states in the Northeast, Midwest, South, and West. The top, dotted lines depict the Republican ideal points for each state's lower chamber, while the bottom, solid thin lines depict the same for the Democrats. The solid heavy lines indicate the median ideal point within the party across states.

changes that stem from turnover among legislators. Nonetheless, it is clear that there is, even in recent years, significant state-to-state variation, as prior research, including Gimpel (1996), Paddock (2005), and Coffey (2014), reports. For example, consider the Republican parties of the Northeast: they are essentially all estimated to be more liberal (lower) than the national median for state Republican parties, which is depicted with a solid black line. Similarly, in the South, virtually all of the Democratic parties are more conservative (higher) than the median state Democratic party in the country.

Simply put, state parties do differ, and they generally differ in the ways that a model of state-level adaptation would lead us to expect: more conservative states have more conservative parties on both sides of the aisle (Paddock 2005; Shor and McCarty 2011; Coffey 2014). This observation is in keeping with Paddock's (2005) conclusion that "there are clear differences in tone and substance between more ideological state parties . . . and their more moderate counterparts" (132).[2]

Yet it is also evident that, on balance, the state parties have been polarizing (Shor and McCarty 2011), as the party's medians grow apart even over this eighteen-year time span. Only three states' lower chambers were more polarized in 1996 than in 2014, while thirty-eight were more polarized in 2014. For upper chambers, the comparable figures are only slightly more even, with ten states showing more polarization in 1996 and thirty in 2014. And in some states, the polarization has been substantial—consider the growing liberalism of the California Democratic Party or the increased conservatism of the Colorado Republican Party. On balance, the state parties are following their national counterparts by polarizing: they are opening larger ideological gulfs between them, making the choices facing voters starker. And they are doing so in ways that are frequently at odds with their collective electoral incentives. The California Republican Party is among the most conservative despite being in a solidly Democratic state, and the Arizona Democratic Party is quite liberal for a state that leans toward the GOP.

Declining Heterogeneity in State Party Platforms

The data from Shor and McCarty (2011) allow an unparalleled understanding of the actual positions taken by individual state legislators and state legislative caucuses after 1995. Yet if the election return data detailed in chapter 3 are any indication, nationalizing trends were back under way by the 1980s, making it valuable to consider state parties' priorities over a longer time frame. Here, we do so using a sample of state party platforms dating back to 1918, when Woodrow Wilson was president. To be sure, these platforms are for the most part not widely read, and they generally track activist opinions rather than those of state voters (Coffey 2007). But that is precisely the point: the process of developing the platforms itself forces activists to hammer out their views—and in so doing, express something approaching the emergent views of the state party (Paddock 2005; Hatch 2016). Thus, when the state party simply adopts the national party platform as its own, as the Alabama GOP did between 2000 and

2004 and the Kansas GOP did between 1992 and 2004, that is not simply a time-saving shortcut. It is partly an expression of agreement with the national party and hence evidence of the first face of nationalization.

We begin with the extensive collection of party platforms detailed in Feinstein and Schickler (2008) and Paddock (2005) and made available by their respective authors. Focusing on states included in those two collections, we then contacted various state archives and libraries and used web searches to identify additional platforms.[3] For these analyses, we focus on forty-seven states for which we have at least four platforms. Due to the challenges of finding platforms for earlier years, our collection underrepresents southern states while overrepresenting midwestern states. In all, we have a collection of 1,579 state party platforms from one of the two major political parties between 1918 and 2014. The median platform is from 1968, but the coverage is actually weaker in the 1970s than in decades before or since. We have almost equal numbers of Democratic (820) and Republican (759) platforms.

To better understand the types of issues addressed by these platforms and how those issues vary by time, state, and party, we turn to unsupervised, automated content analysis. Put simply, we use a computer algorithm to identify topics of interest within the platforms. The specific approach we employ is Latent Dirichlet Allocation (LDA; Blei, Ng, and Jordan 2003), a statistical model with a long track record of recovering substantively meaningful topics from various collections of text (Chang et al. 2009).[4] Topic models like LDA begin with a user-defined number of topics and then estimate a model that characterizes each topic or cluster as a distribution over words. Put differently, these models identify clusters of words that tend to co-occur within documents. After some experimentation, we chose forty topics as a useful representation of the set of documents.[5]

As an example of the information LDA returns, figure 7.3 presents one of the forty topics recovered. As the labels at the top make clear, platform segments using this topic disproportionately include words stems such as "right," "equal," "civil," and "discrimin," meaning that this topic covers civil rights. In the top panel, we present the raw share of each platform that is estimated to fall into this particular topic, with gray dots showing Republican platforms and black triangles showing Democratic platforms. In the bottom panel, we fit a smoothing line for each party to illustrate the broader trends. As we might expect, there is an uptick in attention to civil rights after World War II (see especially Schickler 2016), one that is initially led by Republican platforms. But in succeeding decades, the topic comes to be used more heavily in Democratic platforms.

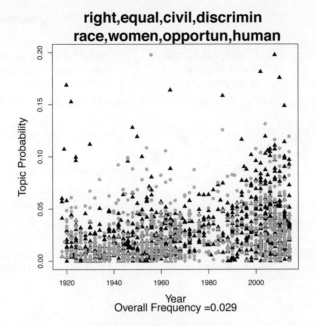

**right,equal,civil,discrimin
race,women,opportun,human**

Year
Overall Frequency =0.029

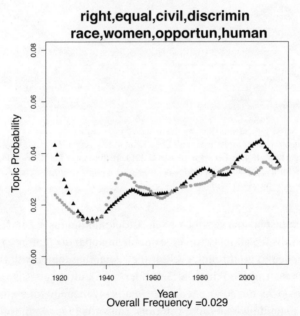

**right,equal,civil,discrimin
race,women,opportun,human**

Year
Overall Frequency =0.029

FIGURE 7.3. One topic from LDA model of state party platforms
This figure presents one of the forty topics recovered by fitting LDA to 37,092 platform segments from 1,579 state party platforms. The top panel presents the share of each individual
platform estimated to fall in this topic, with gray circles showing Republican platforms and
black triangles showing Democratic platforms. The bottom panel applies a smoothing line
over time for each party.

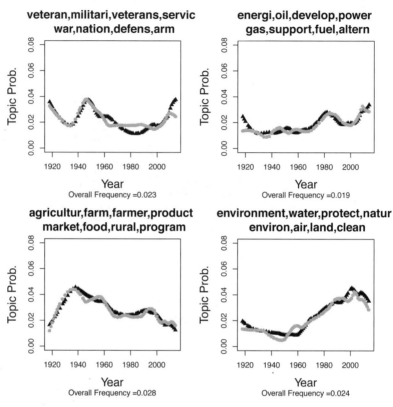

FIGURE 7.4. Select topics from LDA model of state party platforms
This figure depicts select topics from an LDA model fit to a corpus of 37,092 segments from 1,579 state party platforms between 1918 and 2014. It illustrates the distribution of topic probabilities for each state party platform for select topics. Each topic is labeled with the eight highest-scoring words in that topic.

We next display the results for select topics in figures 7.4 and 7.5, with the full results for all forty topics available in appendix figures 27–36. We lack the space to go through each of the remaining topics with the same detail (see instead Hopkins and Schickler 2016), although it is clear that the vast majority are coherent and substantively meaningful. Some topics cover long-standing issues like veterans' concerns (figure 7.4, top left) or agriculture (figure 7.4, bottom left). Others address more recent concerns, from energy (figure 7.4, top right) and the environment (figure 7.4, bottom right) to crime (figure 7.5, top left), immigration (figure 7.5, bottom left), and health care (figure 7.5, top right). A few topics are used more heavily by one side of the political aisle. Notice, for example, that the topic of abortion (figure 7.5, bottom right) is employed more by contemporary Republican platforms. This upward trend is indicative of the increasing role of abortion and social issues generally in dividing the two political parties (Moen 1992; Adams 1997; Lacy 2009; Wilcox and Robinson 2010; Putnam and Campbell 2012; Schlozman 2015; Hopkins 2017). It is consistent with Coffey's 2014 finding that state parties sometimes downplay issues on which their national copartisans are out of step with the state electorate. Overall, though, the two parties' attention to specific issues tends to track closely, with only occasional cases where there is a sharp

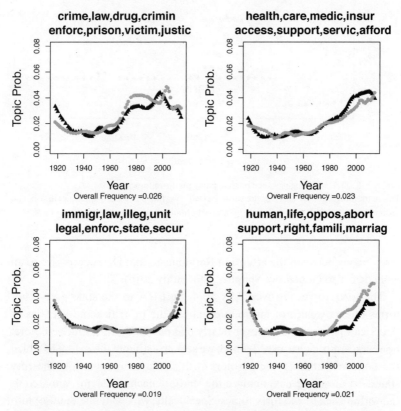

FIGURE 7.5 Select topics from LDA model of state party platforms

This figure depicts select topics from an LDA model fit to a corpus of 37,092 segments from 1,579 state party platforms between 1918 and 2014. It illustrates the distribution of topic probabilities for each state party platform for select topics. Each topic is labeled with the eight highest-scoring words in that topic.

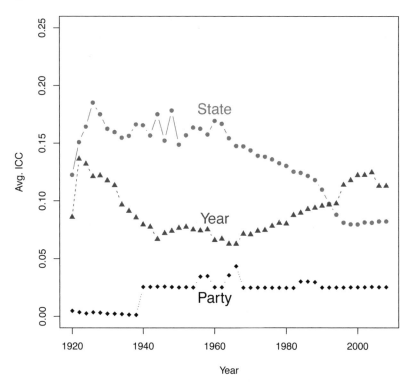

FIGURE 7.6. Decomposing variance of state party platform topics
This figure illustrates the share of the variance (ICC) in state party platform topics that can be
explained by the platform's year (*triangles*), party (*diamonds*), and state (*circles*).

discrepancy between the attention Republicans and Democrats give to an
issue (see also Gentzkow, Shapiro, and Taddy 2016).

The forty topics uncovered by applying LDA to the state party platforms offer a wealth of information about the priorities and agendas of
America's political parties over nearly one hundred years. Our goal here,
however, is more narrowly defined: we seek to estimate the extent to which
the political parties present voters with similar choices across the fifty
states. To do so, we next analyze the share of each platform estimated to
fall within each of the forty topics. Specifically, we divide the data set into
successive eight-year increments and then fit a multilevel model with year,
party, and state-level clusters for each topic and window of time. Those
models, in turn, allow us to estimate the share of the overall variation in
the usage of each topic that can be accounted for by knowing the platform's year, the party that wrote it, and the state in which it was written.[6]

Figure 7.6 illustrates the results of this decomposition of the variance in topic usage. It presents three fractions: the average share of variance across topics explained by the state, year, and party. (Technically, these statistics are known as intraclass correlations or ICCs.) We see a slow and limited uptick in the share of the variance explained by party, which is consistent with evidence elsewhere that the parties diverge primarily in how they talk about issues (Gentzkow, Shapiro, and Taddy 2016). The trend for state-level variation is much more pronounced. Until around 1960, knowing what state a platform came from was critical in knowing the topics it was likely to highlight. The ICCs for clusters by state were typically around 15 percent to 17 percent and dwarfed those associated with knowing the platform's year or party. But those ICCs for state-level clusters then began to decline sharply, stabilizing in recent years at around 8 percent. By contrast, year-to-year swings in attention to different topics grew over the same period, indicating that there is increasingly a single national agenda to which the various state parties are responding. Far more than in the past, the state parties now shift their gaze in unison, from education to terrorism or gay marriage as national politics dictate. Both of these trends are evidence, in short, that the state parties are increasingly talking about the same issues nationwide.

State-Level Identification

As seen through legislative voting patterns and state party platforms, the state parties have been polarizing and homogenizing—the Republicans and Democrats take increasingly divergent positions within states and talk about similar issues across states. But do voters continue to perceive the state-level parties as distinctive? The sections to come consider various pieces of evidence on that question.

Observers have long been struck by split-ticket voting (Burden and Kimball 1998, 2002). Even in 2016, states from Massachusetts and Maryland to Illinois and Louisiana were uncompetitive in presidential races but had governors from the opposite party. Given the skewed distribution of party attachments in many states and localities, it is quite plausible that people who find themselves in the center of national politics could be on the left or the right of a particular locality. One potential explanation is that voters actually have different patterns of identification at the different levels of government—and that some people who are Democrats nationally might not lean Democratic at the state level. One study from the 1980s advanced precisely this point. Niemi, Wright, and Powell (1987)

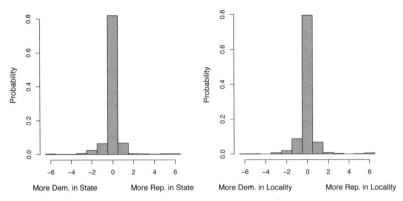

FIGURE 7.7. Party identification across levels of government
This figure depicts the distribution of national versus state (*left*) and national versus local (*right*)
partisan identification. It shows the difference between partisan identification measured via a
seven-point scale in state/local politics subtracted from the same measure of national partisan
identification. As the figure makes clear, those who term themselves "Republicans" or "Democrats" are highly likely to apply the same identification across the levels of the federal system.

Source: September 2013 SSI survey. *n* = 760.

contend that multiple identifiers—people who identify with a different
party at the state and national levels—risk contaminating the traditional
measure of partisan identification. They show that in the 1958 American
National Election Study, 5 percent of respondents were "multiple identifiers," meaning that their partisan identification differed in state and
national politics. By 1970, with the realignment in southern politics well
under way, that figure had risen to 14 percent. On the other hand, Green,
Palmquist, and Schickler (2002) find little evidence of multiple identifiers and contend that "despite the marked differences between state and
national voting patterns, the distribution of American partisanship does
not change appreciably when attention is focused on state rather than national political parties" (44). To what extent do contemporary Americans
identify with different parties at the state and national levels?

To answer that question, our 2013 Survey Sampling International (SSI)
survey included measures of partisan identification at the national, state,
and local levels. In all cases, we asked respondents to place themselves on
the traditional seven-point scale, from strong Democrats (1) to strong Republicans (7). Consider the left panel of figure 7.7, which illustrates the difference between the state and national measures. As it shows, 81 percent of
respondents give exactly the same answer to both questions, and 95 percent

of respondents are no more than one category different, perhaps dropping from "strong Democrats" to "weak Democrats" but not more. When we consider respondents within two categories, the figure rises to 98 percent. More surprisingly, the results are highly similar when we look at the difference between national and local identification, as the right panel of figure 7.7 shows. Simply put, people's partisan identification varies little across the levels of government.

Not a Dime's Worth of Difference: Perceptions of the Parties

Still, Americans might differ in their perceptions of the state versus national parties if not in their partisan identities. To examine that possibility, we included a pair of open-ended questions in our 2014 GfK survey. By allowing respondents to use their own words, open-ended questions provide an opportunity to see what respondents associate with the two parties—and whether those assessments differ when thinking about the state parties versus the national parties. Specifically, 251 respondents were asked to assess one of the major parties in their state, while another 250 were asked to assess one of the two major parties nationally.[7]

The responses were highly informative. Without any prompting, some respondents actually identified the similarity between the state-level parties and their national counterparts. For instance, one person asked to describe the Maryland Republican Party replied, "The party tends to have a more rural focus and to follow national party trends." Another indicated that the North Carolina GOP was "not fighting Obama tactics enough."

Certainly, responses that blur the boundaries between the state and national parties are informative—but so, too, are responses that reflect a single undifferentiated perception that covers the national- and state-level party. For instance, this assessment of the New York Republicans as "a bunch of old white men with old money" has commonalities with an assessment of the national GOP as "old white fuddy duddies who don't want to give black people more government money to not work." We thus coded each response on a variety of dimensions, such as whether it mentioned the party's ideology, policies, or candidates. We also recorded whether the assessment made reference to a visible social group (such as black people in the response just above) or to corruption. We further recorded positive and negative adjectives as well as any mentions of the relative strength of the two parties.

TABLE 7.1 **Descriptions of state and national parties**

	State Democrats	National Democrats	p-value	State Republicans	National Republicans	p-value
Ideology	0.124	0.194	0.137	0.130	0.132	0.966
Policy	0.053	0.109	0.112	0.058	0.107	0.154
Candidates	0.035	0.008	0.150	0.007	0.017	0.499
Social groups	0.088	0.116	0.477	0.109	0.157	0.257
Corruption	0.035	0.039	0.891	0.029	0.083	0.065
Positive adjective	0.142	0.194	0.278	0.138	0.083	0.156
Negative adjective	0.283	0.349	0.274	0.399	0.413	0.811
Relative strength	0.142	0.023	0.001	0.101	0.025	0.010

Note: This table summarizes the coding of open-ended responses from the January 2014 GfK survey asking respondents about their state or national Democratic or Republican parties. In each case, the first, second, fourth, and fifth columns indicate the share of open-ended responses earning each (nonexclusive) categorization. The p-values report the results of t-tests indicating a difference in means between the state and national parties.

Table 7.1 reports the results for each national and state party. We consider a description of the Colorado Democrats as "progressive" to indicate ideology—and as table 7.1 shows, 12.4 percent of descriptions of state-level Democrats and 19.4 percent of descriptions of national Democrats have ideological content. This difference doesn't quite meet the traditional threshold for statistical significance, as the table's third column indicates. But it is nonetheless instructive, especially when compared with the fact that the state and national GOPs each received ideological descriptions 13 percent of the time (see also Grossman and Hopkins 2015).

Overall, the similarities between the descriptions employed by those asked about the state parties and those asked about the national parties are striking. References to policies are a bit more likely when describing the national parties, with around 11 percent of the national descriptions but just 5–6 percent of the state descriptions mentioning concrete policies. One person termed the national Democrats "tax lovers," while another policy-oriented response described them as a "liberal party focused on progressive policies and providing assistance to those who cannot afford it." Still, some assessments of state parties did have policy content, such as the view of the Missouri GOP: "They are strong 2nd amendment."

Research on partisanship and political attitudes has repeatedly emphasized the importance of social groups (Conover and Feldman 1984). In Green, Palmquist, and Schickler's 2002 view, partisan identities are to an important extent answers to the question, "Which social groups are associated with which parties?" If wealthy white voters are associated with the GOP, a working-class black voter is unlikely to identify with them. Given that, we measure the extent to which our respondents made reference to social groups as they described one of the political parties. In keeping with Green and coauthors' work, social groups like the wealthy, the middle class, blacks, Latinos, women, LGBTQ identifiers, city dwellers, and rural residents come up in between 9 percent and 16 percent of responses. For instance, when asked about the national Democrats, one respondent noted, "Since our president is black—naturally every black voter wants to keep him in office so they can continue to keep getting everything for free and not hold a job, when they are supported while not working." With respect to our primary goal—assessing whether perceptions of the parties differ at the state and national levels—the open-ended responses make it clear that the same groups are associated with the same parties across levels. For one thing, the difference between the probabilities that a respondent mentions a social group at the state or national level is just 3–4 percentage points. What's more, the specific groups mentioned do not vary across levels, as one New Jersey resident's assessment that the state GOP "favors the rich" attests. One close call comes from Nevada, where a resident explained that the state Democratic Party "relies mostly on the Hispanic vote." Another comes from Wisconsin, where a respondent described the state GOP as "a group of politicians that are trying to level the field for all employees as far as what the government is providing them. RE: making teachers & other governmental & union employees more responsible for paying there [sic] own insurance" (see also Cramer 2016). Such associations do reflect the groups and agendas of state politics. But both would be expected to hold in various states and are unsurprising given the role of Latinos and public-sector unions in the national Democratic coalition. Indeed, of the 251 respondents who provided a view of a state party, not one linked the party to a social group in a way that would be unexpected given the parties' national coalitions.

What about corruption? It seems possible that some state parties might be perceived as especially corrupt. In fact, corruption is mentioned relatively infrequently by our respondents, except in reference to the national GOP, where it comes up 8 percent of the time. But a plurality of the responses were brief responses that used just one or two descriptive words. Between 8 percent and 19 percent of the responses used positive adjectives, such as the description of the Massachusetts Democrats as "caring" or that of the Colorado Republicans as "awesome." But negative descriptions were far more common, like the respondent who termed the Michigan GOP "lame" or the one who wrote of the national Democrats the word "yuk!!" Even here, there is little difference between the share of negative descriptions provided at the state and national levels. Twenty-eight percent of respondents described their state Democratic parties in negative terms while 35 percent did the same for the national Democratic Party. With a p-value of 0.27, that difference does not approach statistical significance, but it still offers a hint that there could be daylight between the perceptions of the state Democratic parties and those of the national Democrats. Yet on the Republican side, the division was almost identical, with 40 percent using negative descriptions at the state level while 41 percent did so nationally. Clearly, the use of negative adjectives dwarfs the use of positive adjectives, a result we might have expected given the low regard in which political parties are held.

While the parties are relatively evenly matched nationally, they are less so in specific states, and that, too, is reflected in the responses: 14 percent of responses about state-level Democrats and 10 percent of responses about state-level Republicans make reference to their relative political strength or weakness. One respondent went so far as to explain, "Seattle is really liberal so we're mostly Democrat-controlled. Can't really say I know much of what the Republican Party does." Another described the California Democrats with a single word: "hegemony." A Michigan resident noted that the Democrats were "the underdog in our area," while a Massachusetts resident explained that "the Republican Party in my state is tenacious yet struggles to make strides based on demographics."

Our respondents do differentiate between the state and national parties but principally on the strategic question of whether a given state party is dominant. The overall impression is of similarity across the levels, with hints of state-national differences only among the Democrats. And even that might reflect perceptions formed in an earlier era. As one respondent noted about the Florida Democrats, "Some moderates remain but the more liberal national party continues to gain influence." George Wallace famously said that there's "not a dime's worth of difference" between the two major parties during his third-party bid for the presidency in 1968. Today, that description is more apt when it comes to the national parties and their state-level subsidiaries.

State Parties and Gubernatorial Voting

In the world of state parties described by politicians like Dwight Eisenhower, strategists like Kevin Phillips, and political scientists like V. O. Key, the various state parties had very different reputations among voters. To be a Republican in New York meant something very different than in Virginia, Nebraska, or Arizona. Those reputations, in turn, were likely to have influenced voters' perceptions. But in a highly nationalized polity, the national party brands shape voters' perceptions, even in state-level elections. As a consequence, once we account for individual-level differences across voters, knowing factors about their state parties should not add much to our ability to predict their gubernatorial voting.

To examine this issue empirically, we now consider voting in gubernatorial elections as observed in 1998, 2002, 2006, and 2010 national exit poll data. Even after removing respondents with missing data, we are left with 12,401 observations in those four years from states that held a midterm gubernatorial election. To measure state party positions, we turn back to the state legislative ideal points estimated by Shor and McCarty (2011) for 1998, 2002, 2006, and 2010 as an approximation of state-level party positions. The core assumption: the median state legislator should typically reflect the state party's ideology. The party ideal points within each state and year turn out to be highly correlated, meaning that they provide a reasonable measure of the degree to which a state party's legislators are on the right, on the left, or in the center.

To compute measures of state-level party positioning, we then average across the two chambers to create a composite score for each state in each of the three years under consideration. For Democratic legislators, the average score is –0.66, while for Republicans it is a symmetric 0.66.[8] These resulting averaged ideal points match our conceptions of state-level party positioning well. As we saw earlier, the Democratic parties with the lowest scores are California, Connecticut, New York, and New Hampshire, while the Republican parties with the highest scores are those in Alabama, Arkansas, Colorado, Montana, Oklahoma, and Texas. To be sure, these are not direct measures of the gubernatorial candidates' positions themselves. But they are arguably more useful as measures of state party brands, since they capture the overall positioning of each state party's legislators.[9]

We next fit multilevel models where voting for a Democratic governor is regressed on the average scores for Democrats and Republicans for the year of the exit poll.[10] As figure 7.8 illustrates, the position of the state's Democratic or Republican Party does not prove a strong predictor of gubernatorial voting in most cases.

In 1998, there is some hint that more right-leaning Republican parties increase the probability of supporting the Democratic gubernatorial

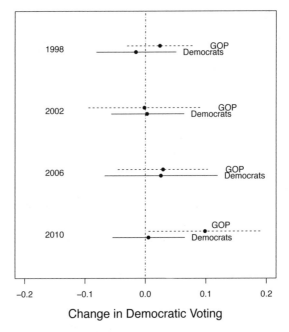

FIGURE 7.8. State legislators' ideology and gubernatorial voting
This figure illustrates the predicted change in Democratic voting associated with a one-standard-deviation shift rightward by either the state's Democratic or Republic legislators. The dots indicate mean effects while the lines indicate the associated 95 percent confidence intervals. The underlying model was a multilevel model with state-level random effects and various individual-level covariates fit to exit poll data from 1998, 2002, 2006, and 2010.

candidate. The linear coefficient is 0.092 with a standard error of 0.064, indicating that a one-standard-deviation move to the right end of the political spectrum by a Republican party is associated with a 3.1 percentage point increase in the probability of voting for the Democrat, all else equal. Findings in this direction are what we would expect if voters punish parties that stray from the center. Still, this effect is not reliably different than zero and is substantively small at any rate. What's more, the relationships for both parties for 2002 and 2006 are precisely estimated zeros. The Democratic coefficient is quite close in all four years, too. We detect a nonzero effect only in 2010 for Republicans: during the election that brought national attention to the Tea Party, as state Republican parties grew more conservative, their candidates lost support. Such a result might be driven by candidates like Colorado GOP gubernatorial contender Tom Tancredo. But for seven of the eight measures of interest, the effect of state party ideology is weak. In short, beyond basic individual-level factors like partisan identification and ethnicity, knowing the positioning of a state's political parties tells us virtually nothing about the likely gubernatorial voting of its residents for most recent elections. That finding is consistent with the claim that contemporary voters perceive the parties to offer more or less the same choice across states.

Conclusion

For two decades after Scott Brown's 1992 election as property assessor in Wrentham, Massachusetts, his career trajectory looked like that of many ambitious politicians. He combined effort and opportunity to move up the political ranks, shifting to town selectman and then to the Massachusetts statehouse. He surged onto the national stage in a January 2010 special election in which the Republican Brown managed to upset a heavily favored Democrat. The spoils of that victory were substantial: Brown took the US Senate seat formerly held by Democrat Ted Kennedy and ended the Democratic Party's filibuster-proof supermajority in the US Senate. In the 2012 general election for that same Senate seat, however, Brown's luck gave out. With turnout up by 42 percent in a presidential year, Brown lost to Democrat Elizabeth Warren by 7.5 percentage points.

In earlier decades, Brown's popularity and name recognition might have helped him contest the next Massachusetts governor's race, or else the other Massachusetts Senate seat, which was conveniently vacated soon after Brown's 2012 loss. But in a nationalized era, and with the control of the US Senate hinging on several 2014 races, Brown was instead recruited to run for US Senate in neighboring New Hampshire. Both the state and national Republican parties wanted to win the seat and didn't feel they needed a longtime resident of New Hampshire to do so. The fact that the New Hampshire GOP had no native sons or daughters able to keep Brown from winning the Republican nomination is instructive in and of itself. Brown lost the New Hampshire race to the Democratic incumbent—but the margin was less than 3 percentage points, making the race far closer than Brown's 2012 bid to keep his Massachusetts seat. Thanks to the national tides, Brown did better in a race in which his opponent was the incumbent and when he was running in a state he had called home for only eight months.

As this chapter has illustrated, Scott Brown's career is emblematic of shifts among both the political parties and the electorate. We saw that in prior eras, state parties were motivated to a significant extent by patron-age and so had incentives to tailor their platform to the contours of their state. Admittedly, even today, the Democratic Party remains competitive statewide in some states with GOP leanings nationally, with West Vir-ginia being one (increasingly lonely) example. Similarly, GOP governors can win in heavily Democratic states from Massachusetts to Maryland when national conditions are right. More generally, the parties' political positions continue to vary in meaningful ways across the states (Paddock 2005; Coffey 2007; Birkhead 2011; Shor and McCarty 2011). But the state parties are increasingly polarized, as analyses of voting in state legisla-tures demonstrate. They are also increasingly homogeneous in the issues they take up, as our analyses of state party platforms makes clear. In tan-dem, polarization and state party homogenization are likely to make ideo-logical differences more salient in voting. They are also likely to make it harder for state-level parties to distinguish themselves from their national copartisans through appeals to incumbency, local service, or the like.

When it comes to voting, though, polarization and nationalization are in the eyes of the beholder—and in this case, the beholders are the voters. Accordingly, this chapter also provided extensive evidence on contempo-rary Americans' partisan identities and their perceptions of the two parties. Those analyses confirm that voters today *perceive* the state parties as highly similar to their national affiliates. Perceptions of parties are grounded to an important extent in people's perceptions of social groups—and the social groups that Americans associate with the parties differ little at the state and national levels. Additionally, we see surprisingly little influence of state par-ties' ideologies on gubernatorial voting. At least when choosing a governor, voters typically give little weight to the state parties' ideological positioning.

Earlier chapters left us with a puzzle: what explains the first face of na-tionalization, the increasing alignment of voting patterns across the levels of government? By looking at state parties' goals, legislative voting be-havior, and platforms, this chapter has illustrated that they are polarizing and shedding their state-level idiosyncrasies. What is more, contemporary voters perceive the state and national parties in highly similar ways and vote accordingly. This evidence is all consistent with the claim that one key source of nationalized voting behavior is the increasingly salient ideo-logical differences between the parties. Scott Brown is a product of his times—and of a political world in which the parties offer clear, ideologi-cal choices to voters across the fifty states.

CHAPTER EIGHT

Sweet Home America

In the early years of the twenty-first century, the phrase "Sweet Home Alabama" has come to seem ubiquitous. It appears on Alabama license plates and roadside signs posted at the state's boundaries. In 2002, the phrase became the name of a feel-good romantic comedy starring Reese Witherspoon. Six years later, musician Kid Rock released a song about summertime romance set in northern Michigan where the couple sings "sweet home Alabama all summer long." Forty years after it was written, the song that made the phrase famous can still be heard—and sung along to—on radio stations around the country.

When Lynyrd Skynyrd originally released the song in 1974, though, it had a political edge that has been largely forgotten since. The lyrics announce, "In Birmingham they love the governor," a controversial line when that governor was the populist, prosegregation George Wallace. The song also explicitly repudiates singer Neil Young, who had criticized southern whites' response to the civil rights movement in his own song "Southern Man."

It's not just "Sweet Home Alabama." During the past forty years, the southern identity it sought to give voice to has changed as well. In a 1976 article, John Reed set out to map the South, not as defined by state boundaries but by locals' attachments. To do so, he went through phone books, measuring the use of the words "Southern" and "Dixie" in business names. Subsequent studies employed variants of the same method in later years (Alderman and Beavers 1999; Cooper and Knotts 2010). The term "Dixie" is overtly political, as it is closely connected to the Confederacy and the American Civil War. Its use declined notably between 1976 and 2008, as fewer businesses wanted to be associated with it (Alderman and Beavers 1999; Cooper and Knotts 2010). Over the same period, the evidence on the use of the term "southern" in business names is more mixed. Business owners appear to be abandoning a conception of the region that carries a divisive political connotation but not the more generic conception implied by the term "southern."

One cannot write about subnational loyalties in the United States without considering the American South. Yet, as this chapter will show, these descriptions apply not only to southern loyalties but to Americans' place-based identities more generally. Far from being exceptional, contemporary southern identity is emblematic. Americans have certainly not abandoned local or regional identities. Even today, "Where are you from?" is one of the first questions you will get in social situations where the answer is not clear. But as this chapter shows, Americans' place-based identities are typically weaker than other relevant identities. For one thing, Americans today identify far more strongly with their country and their families than with subnational units like their regions, states, or municipalities, something that wasn't always true. Moreover, of the place-based identities, the strongest are frequently directed toward Americans' neighborhoods, despite the absence of any corresponding political unit or government. As was the case with "Sweet Home Alabama," the contemporary content of today's place-based identities is not very political. The political edge that helped give the term "Dixie" its meaning has given way. By and large, Americans are not attached to their states or municipalities in ways likely to sustain meaningful political activity.

One goal of this chapter is simply to document the strength and content of various place-based identities—and add to the evidence from earlier chapters that today's American electorate is highly nationalized. At the same time, this chapter also helps to explain how identities fit into the book's explanation of nationalization. To be sure, identifying the causal role of identities is challenging, as the relationship between identities and nationalization is almost certainly endogenous. Put differently, place-based identities are likely to be affected by some aspects of nationalization as surely as they shape others, making it artificial to declare them straightforwardly either "cause" or "effect."

Still, place-based identities occupy a particular place in this book's broader account of citizens' declining engagement with state and local politics, the second face of nationalization. As this chapter's review of prior research on identities will document, identities are important partly because they shape people's attitudes and actions (e.g., Schildkraut 2014). One of those actions is information acquisition: people are more likely to seek out and acquire information that speaks to relevant identities than information that does not.

Now in some media environments, information about state and local politics is readily available, as it is bundled with national news and faces little competition for citizens' attention. In those environments, particular attachments or identities might not be strongly connected to the information people acquire. In the 1970s or 1980s, if one wanted to follow a local murder trial, a city council, a sports team, or the weather, local television news and newspaper coverage were two obvious choices. People who wanted information about any one of those subjects were likely to learn about the others as well. But the emergence of cable television and the Internet provided an array of new choices—and, crucially for our purposes, made people's attachments and identities more influential in their media consumption. As choices grow, so too do the influence of people's interests and identities on the information they seek out (see especially Prior 2007). For instance, when television networks devoted exclusively to sports launched, people's interest in sports and their attachments to sports teams came to shape their media consumption in a way that they hadn't previously. Chapter 9 examines the changing media environment and its implications for state and local news consumption. In this chapter, we focus on people's connections to their states and localities. But we do so partly to understand Americans' baseline motivation to seek out different types of political information when given the chance.

This chapter's goals are twofold. First, through a brief review of the burgeoning research on identities and their political impacts, this chapter illustrates that such identities are sufficiently stable and meaningful to be potential anchors for attitudes and behaviors. The chapter also considers the insights that emerge from the handful of studies that have addressed place-based identities explicitly as well as from community case studies that have addressed it more obliquely. Second, the chapter provides extensive new evidence on the strength and content of different place-based identities. It details the relative strength of various identities using the phrases found in books, online convenience samples, and nationally representative phone and Internet surveys. After illustrating the overall strength of various attachments, it also considers the question of who feels especially attached to place. The chapter then uses survey experiments as well as open-ended questions to better understand the content and political import of place-based identities.

Overall, the chapter's evidence is clear. Despite the American founders' assumptions to the contrary, contemporary Americans are far more connected to their nation than to their states or localities. National identity also has significantly more political content than do subnational identities.

Place-Based Identities: What Is Already Known?

In recent years, scholars from multiple social sciences have put considerable effort into understanding identity, but that work has sometimes defined the concept in ways that are domain specific or even incompatible. Indeed, one team of scholars diagnoses identity research as suffering from "definitional anarchy" (Abdelal et al. 2006, 695). Given that, it is critical to define what we mean by social identities generally and by geographically based social identities in particular.

Schildkraut (2014) provides a useful starting point, explaining that "group identities are largely considered to be social in nature, deriving their power from contexts and from the extent to which people consider their group-based memberships to be an important part of how they conceive of themselves as individuals" (443). A social identity is thus a relationship between an individual and a broader social group as it is understood by the individual. Schildkraut adds that "one's degree of attachment to the group and one's understanding of what it takes to be a member of that group are key factors that shape whether and how social identities affect attitudes" (443). For a social identity to be meaningful, people must conceive of themselves as belonging to some social group, whether it is as an American, a southerner, a Georgian, a resident of Atlanta, or a resident of the Poncey-Highland neighborhood.

Moreover, meaningful social identities delineate boundaries about who is or is not a member (Tajfel 1981; Wong 2010) as well as providing some understanding of what membership entails (Abdelal et al. 2006). To be sure, those boundaries and understandings differ across identities and may be malleable and contested even for a single identity. Consider American identity as an example. Not everyone agrees on who is an American or what it means to be American, and those disagreements are at the heart of debates over immigration policy (Schildkraut 2007, 2011, 2014; Theiss-Morse 2009; Wright and Citrin 2010; Wright, Citrin, and Wand 2012). Those boundaries have also shifted in important ways over time (Smith 1997): ethnoracial conceptions of who is American are far less acceptable today than they were a century ago. But those boundaries and understandings do provide a given social identity with contours that are widely recognized at a given point in time. Today, people do not agree on precisely who is or is not an American, but they certainly agree that there are Americans, that not everyone is an American, and that what it means to be American matters.

Social groups vary in the degree to which they engender attachments as well as in their content and the nature of their boundaries (Abdelal et al. 2006). Some identities have boundaries that are very permeable and where identification is voluntary; others have boundaries that are ascriptive and perhaps even inscribed in laws. Still, social identity strength varies across individuals: one group member may identify strongly with a given social identity while another may not. Social identities vary, too, in their content and their constitutive norms. To say that one is a loyal fan of the Atlanta Braves has very different implications for one's behavior than to say that one is a loyal Republican or a devout Christian.

The explosion of recent research on social identities has been highly productive but also uneven, with far more focus on some than on others. For instance, the argument of Green, Palmquist, and Schickler (2002) that political partisanship is a social identity has transformed its study, leading to a newfound appreciation for the stability of partisanship and the exceptional conditions under which it might change. To the extent that partisanship is a social identity, it follows that individuals' party loyalties shift primarily when the social groups associated with the parties are in flux. To take another example, as the political importance and demographic significance of immigration has grown, so too has research into American national identity and its political impacts (Schildkraut 2007, 2011, 2014; Theiss-Morse 2009; Wong 2010; Wright, Citrin, and Wand 2012). This body of research emphasizes that national identities are sufficiently stable so as to serve as explanations of policy attitudes.

Still, disparate strands of research on identities—both in the United States and elsewhere—also demonstrate that which identities are salient and politically meaningful hinges on the context (Posner 2004; Schildkraut 2014). Identities may be somewhat stable in the short run, but their political import can shift markedly as the situation does. For instance, when an African American family moves into a formerly all-white neighborhood in Detroit or Atlanta, and when white residents organize in response, racial identities can take on a local political importance that they previously lacked (Sugrue 1996; Kruse 2005; Lassiter 2006). As a result, political leaders sometimes have incentives to make certain identities salient or to downplay others. In doing so, they can divide people in ways that are politically advantageous and cement their own position as leader (Riker 1986; Kalin and Sambanis, forthcoming). In recent decades, we have seen that strategy in places as disparate as the former Yugoslavia (Gagnon 1994), the 1988 US presidential election (Mendelberg 2001), and black–white mayoral

elections (Hajnal 2007). While it is tempting to focus on the citizens holding a given identity, we cannot ignore the political actors who are working
to shift the identities through which people approach a situation.

That said, past scholarship tells us far less about the geographically
based identities—such as Americans' attachment to their neighborhoods,
municipalities, states, or regions—that are of interest here. In part, that
lack of knowledge might itself be a symptom of how nationalized contemporary American politics is. In a heavily nationalized polity, it makes less
sense to focus our attention on people's attachments to their towns, cities,
states, or regions. That's not to say that we know nothing about people's
attachments to place, though. Here, we consider research that focuses explicitly on local attachment and its political implications, much of it based
on surveys.

Prior Research on Place-Based Identities

To be sure, there is extant research on place-based identities. That research
has taken place in fields including political science and urban design, and it
finds that some Americans are attached to the places where they live.

There are several reasons that finding should not surprise us. For one
thing, small geographic units like neighborhoods shape people's social
networks, meaning that one's attachment to her neighborhood is likely
to be reinforced by day-to-day social encounters. According to the 2010
US census, 65 percent of America's homes are owner occupied, and those
homes are usually Americans' largest investments, providing many people with a significant financial stake in their communities as well (Fischel
2001). Moreover, a fair number of Americans are lifelong residents of
the same communities. In response to a 1996 question in the General Social Survey, 32 percent of respondents reported spending most of their
childhood in the same community where they were interviewed as adults,
while another 31 percent reported having grown up in another community within the same state. People who reported growing up in another
American state accounted for 30 percent, with those raised outside the
United States making up the remainder.

Demography provides added reasons why place-based identities might
be meaningful and might take on political import. American neighborhoods and even municipalities are often highly segregated in terms of race,
ethnicity, and socioeconomic status (Massey and Denton 1993; Fischer

2003), meaning that place-based identities might reinforce other politically meaningful social identities. Indeed, the phrase "inner city" nominally identifies a place but has clear racial overtones (Hurwitz and Peffley 2005); terms like "hillbilly" or "redneck" similarly convey not just a place but also race and socioeconomic status. Place-based identities overlap with other identities that are at once highly meaningful and politically charged, an overlap that might give them reduced complexity and enhanced political relevance (Roccas and Brewer 2002; Huddy, Mason, and Aarøe 2015; Cramer 2016).

Prior empirical tests have borne out these expectations about place-based identities, at least to some degree. One study that devotes significant attention to place-based identities is Wong (2010). Ex ante, one might expect that Americans would feel closest to geographic units that are the smallest and most proximate, just as the framers of the US Constitution did (Levy 2007). Yet by analyzing surveys from 1996, 2000, and 2003, Wong (2010) shows that Americans feel closer to their country than to smaller units like their states, cities, or neighborhoods. To improve their working or living conditions, a majority of Americans would be willing to move to another neighborhood or another locality within their state, and a sizable minority—44 percent—would be willing to move to another state. Americans do feel attached to the places where they live, but those attachments do not stop them from moving elsewhere. Even so, only 16 percent would be willing to leave the United States, providing initial evidence of the relative strength of American identity.

Importantly for our purposes, Wong (2010) also considers which groups of Americans feel especially close to their neighborhoods, cities, and states. It tends to be older Americans and longtime residents who feel closer to these subnational geographic units. In some surveys, less-educated Americans also feel more of a sense of community in their neighborhoods or cities. More-educated people are more engaged in politics (Wolfinger and Rosenstone 1980; Verba, Schlozman, and Brady 1995; Leighley and Nagler 2014), so that finding suggests a disconnect: those people who are more likely to be politically engaged are also less likely to feel a strong sense of place-based community.

Critically, identities can be personally and socially consequential without being politically consequential. One can identify strongly as a fan of a college football team without that identity entailing any particular political views or behaviors. It is thus critical to ask not just about the strength of certain identities but also about their content and political import.

Wong (2010), for instance, shows that Los Angeles County residents who identify with the county are more supportive of taxes for a variety of services than those who do not. Further evidence comes from Cramer Walsh (2012), who employs in-depth interviews with Wisconsin residents to explicate the meaning and political importance of rural identity. In that account, rural identity becomes politically meaningful in part because it overlaps with various other political and social identities.

Empirical Analyses of Place-Based Identities

To some degree, the political importance of Americans' attachment to their country, state, and locality hinges on the relative strength of those attachments. Americans are far more likely to move across local or even state boundaries than to move abroad, a fact that alone suggests that national identities might be stronger than state or local identities. Still, the early American Republic featured strong state-level identities, so much so that Hendrickson (2003) contends that the US Constitution was a sort of "peace pact" between states that might otherwise have gone to war. The relative attachments of contemporary Americans is an empirical matter, one we first address using collections of books written in American English. We then consider surveys of online convenience samples alongside two surveys drawn through nationally representative procedures.

Over-Time Evidence from Books

Measuring the strength of national and subnational identities from the early days of the American Republic is challenging, especially in the era before survey research (but see Merritt 1965). To provide one very rough approximation, we turn to Google's Ngram viewer[1] to analyze the relative uses of different phrases in its collection of books in American English. Certainly, authors are not a random sample of the American population, and who is able to be an author has undeniably changed over time. But authors are nonetheless an important indicator of sentiment among a highly educated subset. Specifically, we begin with uses of the phrase "I am American," which should give some indication of statements of American national identity.[2] For each year from 1800 to 2000, we then subtract the rate at which they occur from the joint occurrence of several similar state-level sentences

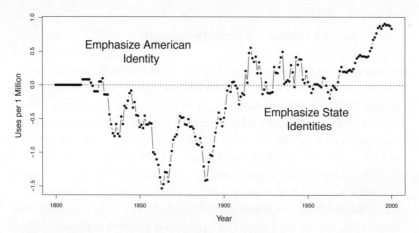

FIGURE 8.1. Rate of declarations of state and national identity in books
Using Google Books' collection of American English texts, this figure displays the relative
share of statements of American national identity ("I am American") compared with statements of various state-level identities.

in books in American English. We chose large, older states and identified
uses of the phrases "I am a Californian," "I am a Marylander," "I am a Mis-
sourian," "I am a New Yorker," "I am a Pennsylvanian," "I am a Texan," and
"I am a Virginian."

The resulting trends are illustrated in figure 8.1. To be sure, these
phrases are not at all common, especially in the early years of the data
set. In fact, there are no uses of any of these phrases until 1816. But in the
pre–Civil War period, we see more expressions of state-level identity than
of American national identity as we measure it, with the uses of state-level
identity reaching a relative maximum in 1863, during the height of the Civil
War. The metric then spikes downward again in the 1890s. The measure
becomes positive, indicating relatively more expressions of national identity, just before World War I, and it waxes and wanes in the early and middle of the twentieth century before becoming positive for good in 1968.
The metric peaks in 1996, almost at the end of the time series. Admittedly,
this is a single measure drawn from select books. But it tracks our expectations reasonably well and is consistent with the claim that expressions of
national-level identity are relatively more common today than in earlier
eras. State-level identities are likely to have peaked during the Civil War;
national identities have been peaking in recent years.

Survey-Based Evidence on Identity Strength

For a more fine-grained look at contemporary identities, we turn to survey data. In our September 2013 and March 2015 online surveys conducted through SSI, we assessed the strength of place-based identities relative to other social identities by telling respondents, "We'd like to know how important various things are to your sense of who you are. Please use your mouse to move the items below, so that the item at the top (1) is the most important to your sense of who you are and the item on the bottom (8) is the least important to your sense of who you are." With two surveys conducted on separate samples in separate years, we can be confident that any patterns are not the product of a particular moment in time.[3]

To be sure, these ranking exercises do not allow us to assess the overall strength of a given identity. Some people might be strongly identified with America, their church, and their job, while others might not be strongly identified with any of the options provided—and yet their rankings might be identical. But this exercise does illustrate the relative strength of different forms of identity. Each respondent was asked to rank eight of fifteen possible sources of identity, including "your job or occupation," "your racial or ethnic background," "your sexual orientation (e.g., straight, gay, etc.)," "your favorite sports team," and various others. Crucially, this approach allows us to ask about a variety of geographically defined identities. The items included several different geographic units of varying sizes, including "being American," "your region of the country (e.g., New England, South, etc.)," "the state where you live," "the town or city where you live," and "the neighborhood where you live."

Surveys record people's stated views, and survey respondents are not always accurate reporters of their own psychological processes. Put differently, we do not always know why we think a certain way, and we do not always want to tell a stranger even when we do. So as always with survey research, we need to be mindful of common biases, such as social desirability. People may be more likely to acknowledge some social identities than others—even an ardent fan of the University of Delaware's Blue Hens might rank other, more socially acceptable identities higher. The same might be said of a diehard Republican or Democrat (see also Klar and Krupnikov 2016). We also need to be aware of other biases likely to crop up here. The strength of reported identities is known to be asymmetric, with minority groups such as African Americans, immigrants, and LGBTQ identifiers

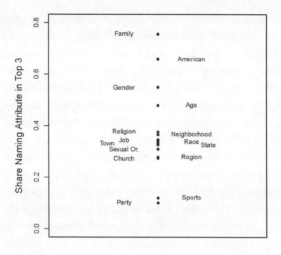

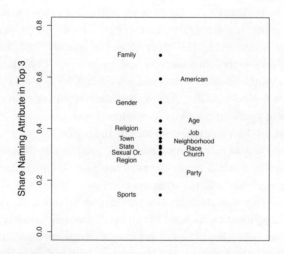

FIGURE 8.2. Identity rankings
This figure illustrates the share of respondents to 2013 (*top*) and 2015 (*bottom*) polls conducted by SSI indicating that each source of identity is among their top three.

reporting stronger connections to the related identities than do majority groups, such as non-Hispanic whites, the native-born, or straight people. To measure identity adherence, we accordingly calculated the share of all respondents who ranked each item in their top three and illustrate the results in figure 8.2.

The figure makes clear that some identities are very commonly ranked among the top three for these online respondents from across the United States, whether in 2013 or 2015. For example, family roles, such as being a parent, spouse, or child, topped the ranking, with 76 percent of respondents ranking that item in their top three if they saw it in 2013 and 69 percent doing the same in 2015.[4] Respondents' identities as Americans are also very important, with between 59 percent and 66 percent ranking American identity in their top three. Gender and age prove noteworthy as well, garnering shares of at least 50 percent and 43 percent, respectively.

With the exception of national identity, place-based identities have not frequently been asked about in prior surveys (but see Wong 2010), but the measures of them here tend to fall in the middle of the rankings. Thirty-five percent to 37 percent of respondents name their neighborhood among the top three, while 33 percent to 36 percent name their town and 33 percent name their state. Region falls lower, as it is named by only 28 percent in both surveys. There is no particular place-based identity that seems especially strong, either compared to the other place-based identities or compared to the other identities queried here in general. Critically, those places that correspond to political boundaries—that is, states and municipalities—engender a bit less loyalty than neighborhoods, which typically do not. Among the place-based identities, those at lower levels of aggregation, like the neighborhood, tend to be marginally more important than higher levels, such as the region.

As another way of measuring Americans' relative attachments to their state and nation, I asked respondents to the 2015 SSI survey to indicate whether six statements about their connection to their state or country were true or false. The statements were adapted from a scale commonly used to measure identity, such as "When I talk about my country, I usually say 'we' rather than 'they'" and "My state's successes are my successes."[5] Figure 8.3 shows the distribution of responses, with higher scores indicating a stronger attachment to the identity in question. Respondents asked about the United States typically report much higher levels of attachment than those asked about their state. Fifty-nine percent of respondents expressed the highest three levels of national identity; at the state level, the comparable figure was just 43 percent. This finding corroborates the pattern observed above—and flips the expectations of America's founders on their heads.

The advantage of online convenience samples like SSI's is that their affordability allows for extensive questionnaires, but the populations from

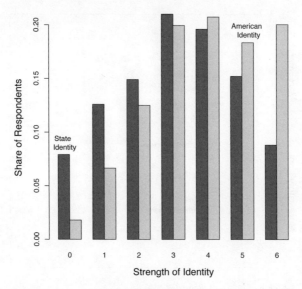

FIGURE 8.3. Strength of different identities, SSI

In the March 2015 SSI survey, respondents fielded six questions about their attachment to either their state or their country. This figure shows the distribution of the resulting measures of state and national attachment.

which they are drawn differ from the population of interest in meaningful ways. Given the potential for such biases, we now consider similar questions using the national sample of the 2006 Social Capital Community Benchmark Survey (SCCBS), a telephone survey conducted via random-digit dialing. Early in the survey, half of its 2,471 respondents were randomly selected to answer five questions about different aspects of identity.[6] Note that in this case, respondents are provided assessments on an absolute scale that runs from "not at all important" (0) to "very important" (3) rather than ranking these various sources of identity relative to each other.

Figure 8.4 demonstrates the mean results—and corroborates what we learned through the ranking exercise above. On average, respondents are most attached to their identity as Americans, with that identity garnering a 2.70 on a scale from 0 to 3, placing it closer to "very important" than to "moderately important." Respondents' religion, place of residence, and job are all tightly clustered between 2.19 and 2.24, indicating moderate importance. Racial and ethnic identity falls lower, at 1.81 (although for

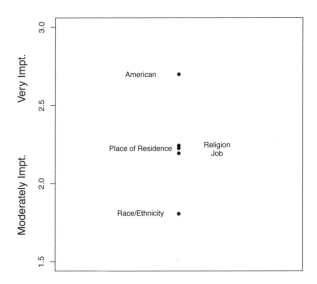

FIGURE 8.4. Strength of different identities, SCCBS
This figure reports the relative attachment to different sources of identity for 2,471 Americans surveyed as part of the 2006 SCCBS.

respondents who do not identify as white, it rises to 2.32). The results from the SSI ranking exercises above do not appear to be artifacts of the opt-in sample, the design of the questionnaire, or the context of the survey. American identity is far more important on average than are identities based on people's places of residence.

Evidence from a National Survey Experiment

Another way of assessing Americans' relative attachment to different places is to embed a question-wording experiment in a survey, which we did in our January 2014 GfK Knowledge Panel survey. The GfK survey has the advantage of a diverse sample, as it is drawn from online and off-line Americans through random-digit dialing and address-based sampling (see also Mutz 2011).

The strength of people's identities is commonly assessed using several survey items, one of which asks people, "When someone criticizes my (group), I take it as a personal insult." In the GfK survey, we asked all respondents this question but randomly varied whether the group in question was "my country," "my state," or "my city or town." Doing so provides one metric of Americans' relative attachment to different geographic units. Responses ranged from 0 ("strongly disagree") to 3 ("strongly agree").[7]

Figure 8.5 depicts the results of the experiment and makes it clear that the respondents are markedly more likely to take it as a personal insult when someone insults their country as opposed to their state or town. For those who were asked about their country, the mean score is 1.60, placing them closer to "somewhat agree" (2) than "somewhat disagree" (1). For state and town, however, the scores are 1.22 and 1.25, respectively, differences that are substantively meaningful as well as being highly statistically significant ($p < 0.001$). There is little difference between levels of attachment to respondents' states and to their localities—but they are far more attached to their country of more than three hundred million people than to their states or towns.[8] To the extent that politicians and political parties aim to mobilize support through appeals to various identities, appeals

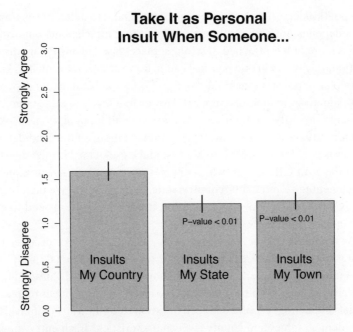

FIGURE 8.5. Insult experiment
In the January 2014 GfK survey, respondents were randomly assigned to be asked about whether they would take it as a personal insult if someone insulted their country, state, or town.

based on American identity are likely to resonate more powerfully than appeals based on a regional, state, or municipal identity.

To be sure, the experimental results do not imply that place-oriented identities are inconsequential, even when considered alongside the SSI and SCCBS results above. We know that racial and ethnic identities can be highly meaningful and that racial and ethnic divisions frequently structure national, state, and local politics (Carmines and Stimson 1989; Hero 1998; Kaufmann 2004; Hajnal 2007), even though they are ranked highly by a minority of the respondents here. Identities' political importance is not a simple reflection of self-reported attachment. To better understand the political implications of various identities, we need to probe their political content as well as their distribution across the electorate. So, we next turn to the question of which sorts of people are more or less likely to have strong place-based identities.

Who Identifies with the State or Municipality?

The political importance of Americans' attachment to different geographic units depends not only on the strength of those attachments but also on who is more or less attached. If stronger place-based identities are disproportionately found in one political camp, for example, they might take on particular importance, as candidates and other political actors appeal to those identities to mobilize support. However, if levels of attachment to a particular identity are relatively even throughout a population, invoking that identity only affords a strategic advantage if one of the candidates or parties is unable to do so. Here, we first make use of the "insult" question from the 2014 GfK survey, which enables us to glimpse the correlates of attachment to respondents' country, state, and city/town. We then turn to the SCCBS, which allows us to confirm the general patterns and to consider neighborhood-level attachment.

As a reminder, GfK respondents were asked to agree or disagree that "when someone criticizes my (group), I take it as a personal insult" and were randomly assigned to be asked about "my country," "my state," or "my city or town." Table 8.1 presents the results of three linear regression models predicting responses to each question using a variety of individual-level demographics and county-level characteristics.[9] Each entry shows a correlation coefficient, which is the change in the responses to the "insult" question given a one-unit change in the independent variable listed on the

TABLE 8.1 **Regression results, insult experiment**

	Country	State	City/town
Intercept	1.659*	2.426*	1.270*
	(0.474)	(0.556)	(0.462)
Education	−0.053*	−0.024	−0.016
	(0.024)	(0.023)	(0.023)
Income	−0.218	−0.067	−0.928
	(1.240)	(1.118)	(1.129)
Age	0.713	0.005	0.591
	(0.364)	(0.374)	(0.346)
Male	−0.086	−0.088	−0.026
	(0.105)	(0.102)	(0.099)
Black	−0.187	0.010	−0.152
	(0.211)	(0.195)	(0.196)
Hispanic	−0.318	−0.070	0.046
	(0.211)	(0.184)	(0.190)
Party ID	−0.017	0.030	−0.026
	(0.034)	(0.031)	(0.032)
Conservative ideology	0.148*	−0.038	0.014
	(0.048)	(0.045)	(0.043)
Has children	−0.283*	−0.034	0.079
	(0.120)	(0.126)	(0.122)
Married	0.015	−0.035	−0.078
	(0.120)	(0.116)	(0.119)
Homeowner	−0.109	−0.057	0.073
	(0.135)	(0.126)	(0.125)
County % black	−0.708	1.333*	−1.127
	(0.561)	(0.556)	(0.625)
County % Hispanic	−0.201	0.380	−1.138*
	(0.468)	(0.480)	(0.440)
County % with BA	−0.957	−0.003	−0.573
	(0.914)	(0.889)	(0.844)
County median household income	0.005	0.004	0.001
	(0.006)	(0.006)	(0.005)
County population density	0.001	0.002	0.016
	(0.009)	(0.007)	(0.012)
County total pop.	0.017	−0.073	0.056
	(0.049)	(0.049)	(0.047)
South	0.113	−0.298*	−0.023
	(0.130)	(0.139)	(0.136)
State % Obama		−0.012	
		(0.007)	
County % Obama			0.163
			(0.515)
R^2	0.170	0.041	0.063

Note: This table reports the results of OLS models fit to survey data from the 2014 GfK survey. The dependent variables are self-reported agreement that respondents take insults to their country, state, or town as a personal insult. *$p < 0.05$

row's left side. The numbers in parentheses give the associated standard errors, a measure of uncertainty about the correlation coefficient.

There are certain types of people who are especially likely to say that they are attached to their country and that they would take criticism of the country personally. Respondents who are less educated, are older, identify as conservative, and have no children under 18 are discernibly more likely to take a criticism of the country as a personal insult. Blacks and Hispanics report lower levels of attachment to the United States—and although those results are statistically insignificant here, Theiss-Morse (2009) finds and explains similar results in more detailed analyses.

When it comes to the state-level results reported in the middle column, however, there are only a few variables that appear to have strong or statistically significant predictive relationships. To at least the author's surprise, and possibly to all those who have sung "Sweet Home Alabama" at the top of their lungs, residents of southern states are less likely to take criticism of their state as a personal insult, although residents of heavily black counties—many of which are in the South—are more so.[10] Beyond that, we see that states where Obama performed more strongly in 2012 have somewhat lower levels of state-level attachment, at least by this metric. For example, when shifting 25 percentage points toward the GOP, which is roughly the equivalent of shifting from New York to Tennessee, we should expect the average score on the 0–3 scale to increase by 0.30. That is a sizable relationship for a dependent variable whose standard deviation is only 0.89. At the same time, we also need to acknowledge the weakness of most of the predictors in this model. As measured via the question about taking insults personally, attachment to one's state of residence has no strong individual-level correlates, which is what we would expect for survey questions that elicit little more than guesses in response.

At the municipal level, we do see a borderline-significant age effect. Older people are more likely to take criticisms of their city or town personally. Beyond that, the only strong predictors are not individual-level demographics but county-level characteristics: the county's percentage of black and Latino residents are both negatively associated with residents' attachment to their city or town, with respective p-values of 0.07 and 0.01. These results are in keeping with a long tradition of research on the so-called racial threat, and they reinforce the finding that racial and ethnic diversity might reduce attachment to one's city or town (e.g., Putnam 2007). Even so, it is equally important to note the weakness of individual-level predictors like partisanship, ideology, and homeownership in predicting attachment at the municipal or state levels. That weakness is the hallmark of attachments that are not very structured or relevant in dividing some voters from others.

Who Identifies with the Neighborhood?

Still, several community case studies give us reason to think that the neighborhood level might be different. Social identities at that level are buttressed by social networks and day-to-day encounters in a way that identities at higher levels are not. As documented in a variety of studies (Rieder 1987; Sugrue 1996; Gamm 1999; Self 2003; Kruse 2005; Lassiter 2006), the period between the 1950s and the 1980s saw large-scale political mobilizations in neighborhoods across the United States, largely in response to residential integration and black in-migration. The often-heated and defensive reactions to black families moving into previously white neighborhoods make it clear that many urban residents had strong commitments to the neighborhoods and communities they called home. Dahl (1961), for instance, provides the example of how a white working-class neighborhood in New Haven, Connecticut, organized quickly to prevent the development of cheap metal houses that would likely be home to African Americans. People's attachments to their neighborhoods might not be politically relevant in most circumstances, but they can certainly serve as the grounds for political mobilization if the neighborhood is thought to be threatened.

The 2006 SCCBS gives us an opportunity to understand what types of people are more or less likely to say that their place of residence is important to their sense of who they are. We thus used linear regression to consider which demographic and geographic variables correlate with identity strength at the national and neighborhood levels and present the results in table 8.2. In light of the evidence in Gamm (1999) on the importance of religion in shaping urban Americans' commitment to particular neighborhoods, we include indicator variables for Catholics and Protestants.[11]

We focus on two dependent variables: respondents' assessment of the importance of being American and of their place of residence to their sense of who they are. Both dependent variables range from 0 ("not at all important") to 3 ("very important"). As the ranking exercise above clarified, people are likely to think that being American is very important to their sense of identity. But even so, there is systematic variation in who is especially likely to think so. Again using statistical significance as a crude measure of association, we see that older people, those with lower levels of education, Republicans, conservatives, and longtime residents are especially likely to say that being American is very important. These patterns are similar to those above from the more recent survey. Each year of schooling reduces the assessed importance of being American by −0.018, so a high school graduate is predicted to be 0.072 higher on the 0–3 attachment scale than a college graduate.

Some of the same factors correlate with who reports that their place of residence is important, including having less education, being older, being Catholic or Protestant, and being a longtime resident. In fact, each year of education decreases the perceived importance of respondents' place of residence by −0.032, meaning that the same comparison between a high school graduate and a college graduate now yields an expected shift of 0.13. In some statistical models, Wong (2010) finds the same pattern. This correlation provides an explanation for why place-based identities might have a limited impact on political competition: they are felt more strongly by less-educated Americans who are less likely to be politically active (Wolfinger and Rosenstone 1980; Rosenstone and Hansen 1993; Verba, Schlozman, and Brady 1995).

At the same time, the correlates of attachment to one's place of residence differ in some informative ways from attachment to being American. In terms of American identity, African Americans and respondents with children at home are little different from others. Yet both groups report stronger attachments to their place of residence. So, too, do residents of dense communities and homeowners. And whereas Republicans report more attachment to American identity, Democrats report more attachment to their places of residence.

As we saw earlier, attachment to being American is substantially stronger than attachment to a particular neighborhood. Variation in people's attachment to being American is also more predictable than attachment to a particular place of residence, a fact that hints that it is more coherent. Both empirical observations suggest that for political actors looking for compelling arguments or motivating symbols, national identity provides far more powerful possibilities. There is certainly no modern-day equivalent of the late nineteenth-century GOP tactic of rekindling Civil War sectional loyalties by "waving the bloody shirt." Today, people from New England seem just as willing to "sing a song about the Southland," to quote Lynyrd Skynyrd.

TABLE 8.2 **Regression results, attachments to country or place of residence**

	Being American	Being from place of residence
Intercept	2.382*	1.742*
	(0.418)	(0.610)
Education	−0.018*	−0.032*
	(0.008)	(0.012)
Income	0.001	−0.001
	(0.001)	(0.001)
Age	0.008*	0.007*
	(0.002)	(0.002)
Male	−0.015	−0.083
	(0.043)	(0.062)
Black	0.129	0.426*
	(0.091)	(0.140)
Hispanic	−0.094	0.069
	(0.096)	(0.142)
Party ID	0.087*	−0.090*
	(0.029)	(0.043)
Conservative ideology	0.087*	0.030
	(0.021)	(0.031)
Has children	−0.010	0.165*
	(0.051)	(0.076)
Married	0.062	0.060
	(0.047)	(0.067)
Homeowner	0.024	0.139
	(0.060)	(0.085)
Time in community	0.034*	0.043
	(0.016)	(0.025)
Catholic	0.139*	0.176*
	(0.060)	(0.088)
Protestant	0.114*	0.137
	(0.051)	(0.075)
Tract % black	−0.123	−0.298
	(0.135)	(0.206)
Tract % Hispanic	0.025	0.244
	(0.158)	(0.227)
Tract % with BA	−0.302	−0.134
	(0.319)	(0.505)
Tract median household income	−0.001	0.000
	(0.002)	(0.002)
Tract population density	−0.001	0.007*
	(0.002)	(0.003)
Tract total population	−0.058	0.027
	(0.046)	(0.067)
R^2	0.138	0.080
N	1,093	1,038

Note: This table reports the results of OLS models in which the outcomes of interest are respondents' attachments to either America or their place of residence. The responses come from the 2006 Social Capital Community Benchmark Survey. *$p < 0.05$

Do Americans have attachments to various place-based identities? Yes, they do. At certain moments, usually under perceived threat, neighborhoods can and do mobilize as neighborhoods. Still, those neighborhood attachments are also a bit more predictable than people's attachment to their city or state. This is critical, as it suggests a disjoint between the geographies at which Americans identify and the political boundaries that shape their representation. And whether subnational identities have enough shared meaning and content that they can provide the basis for political mobilization is another question. The evidence presented here is not definitive, but on balance, it is discouraging.

The Political Impact of Attachment to Place

The results above characterize Americans' attachment to various geographic communities, from their neighborhoods and municipalities to their states and regions. Yet the political relevance of those attachments hinges not only on their strength or their strongest adherents but also on their content. Some identities may be strong but entail little or nothing about politics. Professional sports like baseball have little political content, so one can be an ardent supporter of the Minnesota Twins without that attachment having any bearing on one's political beliefs. Like sports-based loyalties, our SSI sample ranked partisan identities lower than most other identities we asked about (see also Abrams and Fiorina 2012). But because those attachments have very clear political implications, they prove profoundly influential in shaping political beliefs and behavior (Bartels 2002; Gerber and Huber 2010; Lenz 2013). The question here is whether place-based identities are more like attachments to sports teams or political parties. That is, do they have meaningful political content?

The Local Pride Experiment

One way to assess the political content of local attachments is to try to encourage them among some people and then observe if any politically relevant attitudes change. Specifically, during the September 2013 SSI survey, we told all respondents, "The congressional elections in November 2014 are a long way off." We then asked, "Thinking ahead, do you think you will vote for your current representative to the US House of Representatives, do you think you will vote for his or her opponent, or do you not expect to vote?" Responses were coded on a scale from 0 ("definitely vote for some-one else") to 4 ("definitely vote for current representative"). But there was an experimental twist. Of the 812 total respondents to the survey, 382 were randomly assigned to a question just beforehand designed to bring their lo-cal attachment to the forefront of their minds. Specifically, they were asked an open-ended question: "Thinking about the community where you live, what are you most proud of?"[12]

It seems plausible that voters might associate local politicians with the communities they represent. If so, by priming voters' local pride, we might also shape voters' views of those incumbents. But as it turns out, these respondents were unfazed by the exercise, as is evident in figure 8.6. For those whose local attachment was not primed, the mean score was 2.13, indicating a slight lean toward the incumbent. For those who first wrote what made them most proud of their community, the mean score was very

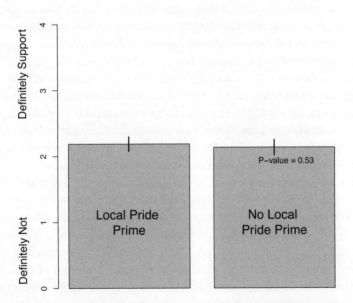

FIGURE 8.6. Local pride experiment
This figure illustrates the results of an experiment embedded in the September 2013 SSI sur-vey. Of the 812 respondents, 382 were randomly assigned to be asked what makes them most proud of their community, while the remainder were not. All respondents were then asked how likely they were to support their current US representative in the next general election, with responses ranging from 0 ("Definitely vote for someone else") to 4 ("Definitely vote for current representative").

marginally higher, at 2.19. A *t*-test returns a *p*-value of 0.52, meaning that such a small difference could easily result from chance alone. We replicated the experiment in the March 2015 SSI survey, with a highly similar result.[13] Being asked to think about what makes one most proud of her local community does little to change her assessment of her member of Congress, suggesting that local attachment and voting intentions are not very well integrated.

The Differing Content of National and State Identity

It is not simply that contemporary Americans identify more strongly with their nation than their respective states—the content of their identities differs across the two levels. To examine this, we now turn to the March 2015 SSI survey. One experiment within it asked respondents to explain in their own words either what they were most proud of about the United States or about their state.[14] Sixty-eight percent of respondents were willing to report something about the United States that they were proud of, whereas only 54 percent volunteered something about their state. The remainder chose an option labeled "nothing comes to mind." We classified the responses into nine overlapping categories and present the results in figure 8.7. The light bars illustrate the share of people who offer each type of response when asked about the nation, while the dark bars do the same for those asked about the state. The first thing to notice is that overall, people have a lot more to say about the nation than about their state, as the height of the bars indicates. Also, the types of things that people cite as sources of pride at the two levels are quite different. At the national level, people are quick to cite values such as freedom. In fact, 40 percent of all those asked about their pride nationally reply by mentioning American values. Thirty percent of the responses could also be termed "political," in that they mention politics, political values, or specific politicians. For instance, one individual responded, "that we elected a Black Man in my lifetime." Another explained he was proud of "how bush handled 9/11." Twelve percent of responses pointed to the national community by mentioning social networks, friends, or a sense of community, patriotism, or togetherness. Replies with the word "unity" fall in this category. When asked about the nation, no other response category garnered more than 4 percent of responses.

Responses about state-level sources of pride differed markedly. For instance, the single most common reply at the state level was to mention something about the state's landscape, weather, size, or natural resources.

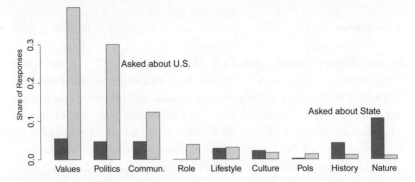

FIGURE 8.7. Pride in state and nation
This figure illustrates the distribution of responses to an open-ended survey question in the 2015 SSI survey about respondents' sources of pride in their state or country.

A Floridian singled out "the weather and the beaches," while a Washington State resident mentioned "our beautiful scenery and wildlife." Residents of eighteen states—Arizona, Arkansas, California, Hawaii, Idaho, Illinois, Kansas, Maine, Michigan, Minnesota, Missouri, New Jersey, North Carolina, Ohio, Tennessee, Texas, Virginia, and Wisconsin—all made related comments about the lakes, the fishing, the mountains, or other aspects of the landscape. Yet despite being the most common response category, only 11 percent of those asked about their state mentioned the landscape or natural beauty. Five percent of state-level responses fell into the "values," "politics," or "community" categories. One such community-oriented response noted, "It's not called the volunteer state for nothing. . . . Tennesseans always rally to aid their neighbors in times of trouble." In another, a Texan cited the state's friendliness.

In short, in the contemporary United States, American national identity differs from state identity in its content as well as its strength. National identity is quite relevant to politics: to an important extent, it is grounded in political values and choices, such as an enduring commitment to freedom in various spheres. The terms in which many Americans describe their pride in their country are the same terms found inscribed on many Washington, DC, monuments: freedom, opportunity, equality. By contrast, state-level identity is far less integrated with political values. When people think of their state, images from postcards seem to come to mind. These results thus reinforce the claim that when Americans think of their political community, they think nationally.

Conclusion

In 1936, William Faulkner published *Absalom, Absalom!* The novel brings back Quentin Compson, a key figure from Faulkner's earlier book *The Sound and the Fury*. In it, the Mississippi native tells his college roommate the tragedies that ensnared a cruel and ambitious slave owner named Thomas Sutpen and those around him, black and white. Sutpen had been killed shortly after the Civil War, but Quentin continues to wrestle with his legacy a decade into the twentieth century. In the book's final pages, after Quentin has brought the tragic story into the present, his Canadian roommate has one final question: "Why do you hate the South?" The book closes with Quentin's reply: " 'I dont hate it,' Quentin said, quickly, at once, immediately; 'I dont hate it,' he said. *I dont hate it* he thought, panting in the cold air, the iron New England dark: *I dont. I dont! I dont hate it! I dont hate it!*" (1936, 378).

One central question of *Absalom, Absalom!*—and of Faulkner's work generally—is the meaning of southern identity early in the twentieth century. As the novel's final words make clear, the question haunts Quentin, following him from Mississippi north to Harvard. To many contemporary readers, though, the depths of Quentin's emotions about the South may be hard to understand. Who today would get so worked up about her relationship to a region of the country? As this chapter has documented, regional, state, and local identities no longer have the strength or content to provoke such a question—or such an alarmed reaction. In the seminal 1980 book *Who Votes?*, Wolfinger and Rosenstone noted that in "turnout, as in so many other areas of political life, the South is likely to lose most of its distinctive character in the coming generation" (94). From this chapter's look at different subnational identities, they seem vindicated.

Primarily using surveys, this chapter has examined Americans' place-based identities. The evidence indicates that Americans do retain a connection to their neighborhoods, their localities, their states, and their regions. But when compared to their attachment to the nation as a whole, their place-based attachments are markedly weaker. What is more, the content of state-level identities is typically divorced from politics. They focus on beaches and bayous—on unique geographic features—rather than on the values or political traditions that could give rise to a meaningful, indigenous political culture. The authors of the US Constitution expected that Americans' primary attachments would be to their states and that those loyalties would be a vital counterweight to any centralizing tendencies in the new nation (Hamilton, Madison, and Jay 1788; Levy 2006, 2007; Young 2015). That assumption might have been quite reasonable in 1787, but evidence from the first two decades of the twenty-first century makes it seem badly outdated.

This chapter's look at Americans' place-based identities has identified yet more evidence of contemporary nationalization. Yet as we saw above, identities are worthy of study partly because, under certain circumstances, they can shape people's attitudes and actions. In the next chapter, we turn our attention to one such set of circumstances: those provided by America's shifting information environment. As we will see, recent changes in the media market have had the consequence of making Americans' interests, attachments, and identities more influential in the news they consume. In a low-choice environment, people are likely to watch whatever is on television, irrespective of their related identities (Prior 2007). If that includes local news, so be it. As media options proliferate, however, Americans' baseline attachments to different levels of government are likely to become more influential in the news media that they seek out—and in what they learn about politics. By showing in this chapter that Americans are not strongly attached to their states or localities, we are better positioned to understand why increased media choice has meant declining attention to state and local news in the next.

CHAPTER NINE

The Declining Audience for State and Local News and Its Impacts

Gentlemen, progress has never been a bargain. You've got to pay for it. Sometimes I think there's a man behind a counter who says, "All right, you can have a telephone; but you'll have to give up privacy, the charm of distance." —Jerome Lawrence and Robert Edwin Lee, *Inherit the Wind*

When political scientists like Donald Stokes and Philip Converse sought to explain the rising nationalization of American voting behavior they observed as of 1960, changes in the mass media seemed an obvious explanation. According to Stokes (1967), "In many ways the decline of these historical series can be linked to more general processes of nationalization in American society. Probably the most important has to do with the changing structure of mass communications" (196–97; see also Converse 1972).

From the vantage point of the 1960s, emphasizing mass communications was quite sensible. Over the 191 years between the Declaration of Independence and Stokes's essay, mass communications in the United States had undergone multiple revolutions. For more than a century, print media was the dominant mass medium, and the reach of newspapers extended alongside improvements in transportation, such as railroads. After 1884, old-style printing presses were replaced by linotype machines, allowing newspapers to grow beyond eight pages and carry substantially more information. In the 1920s and 1930s, radios proliferated, and the same information could be broadcast across the country in far less time than a stack of newspapers could be delivered. In the late 1940s and 1950s, radio was followed by broadcast television, which quickly supplanted earlier types of media as the central source of political news (Prior 2007; Song 2014).

The trend has gathered steam since Stokes's 1967 essay. In the 1980s, cable television took off, and it was followed by satellite television and the Internet. On balance, these changes served to speed the flow of information across space and enable media outlets to compete across ever larger swaths of territory. That is, they sharply increased the incentive among media outlets to provide information that appealed to people living in a variety of places. In theory, a medium that is able to provide information across great distances at low cost—the Internet being the archetypal example— might encourage a proliferation of information sources and a fragmentation of public attention. With such low production costs, even the smallest communities could afford to host their own online news outlets, and citizens might respond by fashioning eclectic, locally oriented media diets. In practice, however, the widespread availability of Internet access has had the opposite effect, concentrating attention on a handful of national outlets (Hindman 2009, 2011). Today's media market has become heavily winner-take-all, with outlets like the *New York Times* and Fox News thriving while local competitors like the *Rocky Mountain News* go out of business.

Given the magnitude of these changes, it is not surprising that scholars from various fields have considered their implications for national politics. Of late, researchers have been especially interested in how increased media choice and ideological diversity among news sources might contribute to political polarization. At the same time, there has been little attention to the differential impacts of those changes across the federal system. That absence is striking, as one of the most pronounced features of the recent changes has been the shift away from spatially bounded media sources like print newspapers. As this chapter illustrates, the media sources with growing audiences today are those that attract customers from around the country, from cable television outlets like CNN to websites like the Huffington Post and the *New York Times*. Those with shrinking audiences— most notably local newspapers but also local television news—tend to have audiences that are much more clearly delineated in space. In an era of intense competition among media outlets (Ladd 2012), those with content that is only of interest in specific places are at a disadvantage. Yet as Americans move from print newspapers to online sources, and as they move from broadcast television to cable television, they are exposed to less coverage of state and local politics.

Today's media market also gives a greater role to consumer demand. In earlier eras, information about national politics was commonly bundled with information about everything from local politics to sports and weather, whether in a single newspaper or an evening news program. People interested in one topic were likely to be exposed to the others. But as specialized media outlets proliferate, so too do opportunities for those without a strong interest in subnational politics to opt out altogether (Prior 2007). And as we saw in the prior chapter, few Americans have the strong attachments to their states or localities that would motivate them to seek out such information as media choices multiply. The links between information and political engagement, meanwhile, are well established: people who know more about politics are more likely to participate (Mondak 1995b; Verba, Schlozman, and Brady 1995; Delli Carpini and Keeter 1996; Prior 2007; Shaker 2014; Hayes and Lawless 2015). So, while earlier generations of scholars considered changes in the media as an explanation for the first face of nationalization, we focus on their role in shaping nationalization's second face, the declining relative engagement with subnational politics.

This chapter first reviews what prior research suggests about the nationalizing role of different media sources. It then brings several types of evidence to bear on its two core claims, claims that are separate but related. The first is that the American media market is transforming in ways likely to curtail Americans' exposure to state and local political news. The second is that this diminished exposure has demonstrable political consequences, as it has reduced Americans' knowledge about and engagement with subnational politics.

To chart the changing availability of state and local news, this chapter initially uses keyword searches and automated content analyses from two major newspapers—the *Chicago Tribune* and *Los Angeles Times*—to consider the attention given to the different levels of government from the 1930s to recent decades. Even in earlier eras, state-level politics received comparatively little attention, at least in the big-city papers studied here. Both national and local politics garnered more consistent attention, with state politics being the odd man out.

One might imagine that significant consolidation in media ownership and the reduction of newspaper staffing in recent years has dampened state and local coverage relative to national political coverage. In just the eleven years between 2003 and 2014, the number of full-time statehouse newspaper reporters dropped by 35 percent, to the point where just 29 percent of US newspapers have a statehouse reporter (Enda, Matsa, and Boyles 2014). But there are also competitive pressures in the other direction, with increased national competition encouraging some newspapers to emphasize the local content not available elsewhere (George and Waldfogel 2006). When studying the past twenty years, digital archives like *Newsbank* greatly expand our capacity to explore those questions by measuring newspapers' relative attention to national, state, and local politics. Across the fifty-one local newspapers examined here, we see no evidence of a consistent shift away from state and local content. The same is true for local television news, as measured through the transcripts of seventy TV stations in eleven states. These findings suggest that if nationalization is the product of the changing media environment, it is likely to stem from audience shifts *across* media types rather than content changes *within* media types. It is not that newspapers or local TV news have changed dramatically; instead, what people watch, listen to, and read have.

We next shift to the audience itself. There, this chapter uses contemporary survey data to illustrate that the media sources with declining audiences tend to be Americans' primary sources of information on local and state politics. Moreover, those declining audiences are the product of both generational replacement and individual-level changes in media consumption, as panel data from the same people in different years show. As the last chapter's findings on identity suggest, and as a population-based survey experiment presented in this chapter reinforces, contemporary Americans are at baseline more interested in national news. What is different is that they now find themselves in a media environment in which they can choose content to match their interests and identities.

Following that, the chapter turns to the political impacts of the changing information environment. It charts the relationship between Americans' media sources and their political knowledge. People whose primary news source covers state-level politics have more state-oriented knowledge than those whose primary news source does not. The chapter's final sections also show how the influence of media market boundaries has shifted over time in ways that demonstrate the declining influence of broadcast media markets on subnational political behavior. The effects of media market geography closely track the rise and fall of local TV news audiences. Those effects were much more pronounced in the 1970s and 1980s than they are today, indicating that today's political information is less spatially bounded—and more nationalized. Shifts in the media environment are one key factor explaining Americans' declining engagement with state and local politics.

Media Effects and Nationalization

Writing in 2007, Markus Prior explains that his "central claim . . . is that the media environment—the types of media to which people have access— explains many 'systematic variations in the amount of free information

received.' The media content available to people, its quantity, and the
ease with which it can be obtained varies over time" (6). Building on
that insight, this chapter considers what the changing media environment
means for information about the different levels of the federal system.
Earlier research has been largely silent on that question, focusing almost
exclusively on polarization and other questions of national-level politics
(DellaVigna and Kaplan 2007; Prior 2007; Ho and Quinn 2009; Stroud
2011; Arceneaux, Johnson, and Murphy 2012; Ladd 2012; Arceneaux and
Johnson 2013; Levendusky 2013b; Hopkins and Ladd 2014; Arceneaux
et al. 2015; Mutz 2015; Guess 2016; Mummolo 2016; Lelkes, Sood, and
Iyengar 2017). Still, despite its national focus, existing research has provided some hints and facts about the likely role of media environments
in shaping citizens' relative engagement with state and local politics (e.g.,
Simon and Stern 1955; Carpini, Keeter, and Kennamer 1994; Mondak
1995a; Baum 2003; Strömberg 2004; Prior 2006; Snyder and Strömberg
2010; Gentzkow, Shapiro, and Sinkinson 2011; Hayes and Lawless 2015).
This section draws out the expectations gleaned from prior research.

  In a political community large enough that most citizens don't know
most other citizens personally, mass media outlets are essential in transmit-
ting information. That is why scholars from Benedict Anderson (1991) to
Ernest Gellner (1983) emphasize the role of print media in the formation
of nations. It stands to reason that the structure of the media environment
is a potentially powerful determinant of voters' information about and interest in politics at each level of the federal system. When that environment facilitates the acquisition of political information about a given level
of government, voters are likely to be more informed and engaged with
respect to that government. People who have more information about a
given level of politics are more likely to be invested in it and understand
their role in it. If one doesn't know who is running for governor, it is hard
to care much about who wins (Verba, Schlozman, and Brady 1995; Delli
Carpini and Keeter 1996; Prior 2007; Hayes and Lawless 2015). Practically
speaking, informed people are also more likely to know how and when to
participate. For those reasons, this chapter focuses on the connection between media markets and political knowledge and engagement. Existing
evidence reinforces the link between information sources and engagement.
For example, Gentzkow, Shapiro, and Sinkinson (2011) show that the introduction of a local newspaper increased voter turnout in presidential as
well as congressional elections between 1869 and 1928, a period that runs
from just after the Civil War until the eve of the Great Depression (see

also Schulhofer-Wohl and Garrido 2013; Drago, Nannicini, and Sobbrio 2014; Shaker 2014). This positive effect on presidential turnout diminished as radios and then televisions proliferated, suggesting that voters acquired alternative information sources. But importantly, Gentzkow, Shapiro, and Sinkinson (2011) find no such decline in the effect on congressional turnout, quite possibly because congressional races received far less attention from radio and television (Hayes and Lawless 2015). Similarly, Gentzkow (2006) examines the impact of the rapid expansion of television in the 1950s on voter turnout. That research finds a generally negative effect of television on turnout, with an especially strong effect for congressional voting. That is likely because television partly replaced the lost information about national politics while providing far less coverage of local candidates.

At the same time, television might have proven to be a nationalizing influence for another reason, as Putnam (2000) details. In *Bowling Alone*, he contends that the introduction of television had a powerful privatizing effect on Americans' leisure (see also Olkean 2009). The sudden proliferation of TV led to more nights in the living room and fewer nights at the bowling alley or a church's recreation room. And that, in turn, clipped the density of local social networks, reducing a mechanism for the transmission of localized political information (Putnam 1966).

Still, it is critical not to think of a given media source as deterministically shaping political content. At root, consumer demand is a powerful influence on the provision of political news (Hamilton 2004; Mullainathan and Shleifer 2005; Gentzkow and Shapiro 2010). As a consequence, media outlets commonly adapt to that demand, albeit within the constraints of existing technologies. For instance, in response to the national distribution of the *New York Times*, local newspapers sought a new competitive advantage by increasing their local coverage (George and Waldfogel 2006).

Television provides another example of how the same mode of communication can have different impacts depending on its content. When it was first introduced in the late 1940s and 1950s, television programming was highly national. As a consequence, in counties where television had been introduced in the early 1950s, the relationship between national economic conditions and voting patterns was stronger (Song 2014). But then local programming emerged, and by the 1960s, members of Congress were making use of the Capitol's television studio to increase their visibility back home and feed the growing demand for locally oriented content (Prior 2006). Technology is not destiny, as the same technology can carry quite different content.

In a similar vein, Strömberg (2004) finds that radio's introduction in the 1930s increased voter turnout in gubernatorial races. Additionally, Prior (2007) demonstrates that the expansion of television increased political engagement among less-knowledgeable voters, voters who picked up political information as a by-product of the ubiquity of network news programs during prime time. Depending partly on its content and the available alternatives, the same technology can have a nationalizing or denationalizing impact. What is more, new modes of communication can sometimes displace existing modes and at other times coexist with or even complement them. Television's effects hinge on what is shown and on what else viewers might be doing with their time and attention.

The media environment varies powerfully over time, with new sources like radio, broadcast television, cable television, and the Internet disrupting existing markets. Yet the availability of political information might depend on media outlets' ownership structures and business models as well. Recent decades have seen significant consolidation in the ownership of both local television stations (Matsa 2014) and local newspapers (Ho and Quinn 2009; Mitchell and Holcomb 2016). As of 2014, 12 companies owned 589 local television stations; those companies had owned just 304 a decade earlier (Matsa 2014). That consolidation, in turn, may increase media outlets' incentives to substitute national for local news in the name of cost cutting. In 2014, newspapers' newsrooms employed around 33,000 people, a figure that is down by approximately 20,000 reporters since the mid-1990s (Mitchell and Holcomb 2016). It is possible that the dramatic decline of statehouse reporters is one outgrowth of this broader transformation (Enda, Matsa, and Boyles 2014). To understand whether and when media changes are a nationalizing force, it is thus critical to examine media content and to do so over substantial periods of time.

The media market varies across space as well, with voters exposed to different political information depending on the place where they happen to live. For one thing, it is considerably less expensive to cover state politics from the state capital, so it makes sense that voters who are in their state capital's media market are more knowledgeable about state politics (Delli Carpini, Keeter, and Kennamer 1994). On the flip side, it is far harder for a member of Congress to win coverage in a large media market with dozens of other members—and, indeed, prior research consistently finds less coverage of members of Congress in larger television markets (Schaffner and Sellers 2003; Althaus, Cizmar, and Gimpel 2009; Snyder and Strömberg 2010; Hayes and Lawless 2015). Such differences across communities are evidence that even in recent years, nationalization is incomplete. In the subsequent analyses, we make use of these geographic differences as a time-varying measure of the extent of nationalization. But first, we need to understand the relative attention to different levels of government in the various types of media, a task we turn to now.

Historical Media Attention across Levels of Government

How have newspapers covered politics and policy making across the federal system, and how has that distribution of coverage changed over time? Prior research has generated conflicting predictions but limited evidence. To provide an initial metric of newspapers' relative attention to different levels of government, this section presents analyses of two larger regional newspapers in the United States, the *Chicago Tribune* and the *Los Angeles Times*. We first chose a date at random from the spring months, which are less likely to be dominated by federal or state-level political campaigns. That date was March 10. We then used ProQuest Historical Newspapers to download all of the articles that contained any one of thirty-two word stems suggestive of political content.[1] We performed optical character recognition on each article to allow for automated analyses. Given the time-intensive nature of this work, we limit our analysis to just two big-city newspapers beginning in 1930, allowing us to observe any shifts that accompany the New Deal. There were 4,617 such articles between 1930 and 1989 in the *Chicago Tribune* and 9,017 such articles in the *Los Angeles Times*. These analyses end in 1989 for a practical reason: that was the final year of availability via ProQuest.

As an initial metric of the relative attention to the different levels of government, we then estimate the frequency of the terms "president," "governor," and "mayor" for each year and present the results for the *Chicago Tribune* in figure 9.1. The top panel compares the use of "president" with "governor" while the bottom panel compares "president" with "mayor." To be sure, these words are sometimes used in nonpolitical contexts, but as we will confirm below, our search procedure effectively identified articles about politics. As the figure makes clear, throughout this period, there are many more articles mentioning the president than those mentioning the mayor or the governor. Governors receive more attention earlier in the period and then receive occasional blips of attention. That said, there is essentially no year in which governors receive as much attention as mayors.

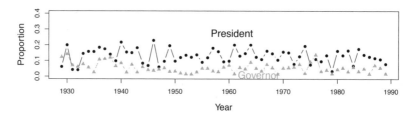

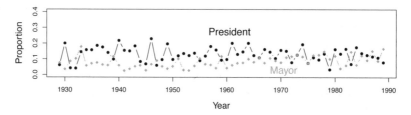

FIGURE 9.1. Attention to executives, *Chicago Tribune*
The top panel shows the share of political articles mentioning "president" (*black circles*)
and "governor" (*gray triangles*), while the bottom panel shows mentions of "president" and
"mayor" (*gray diamonds*).

Source: 4,617 articles appearing on March 10 of each year, obtained via ProQuest Historical.

Moreover, since the 1940s, the *Chicago Tribune* has given more attention
to the mayor of Chicago than to the governor of Illinois. This finding is
in keeping with prior research emphasizing that state government gets
more attention within the state capital's media market (Carpini, Keeter,
and Kennamer 1994)—although it doesn't necessarily get a lot of attention
(Gormley 1978). The primary conclusion is that as early as the 1930s, the
presidency appears to receive the lion's share of political coverage in the
Tribune—and that coverage remains similar across this period.

In figure 9.2's panels, we see the estimates for the *Los Angeles Times*.
The *Times* demonstrates the same basic pattern we saw with the *Chicago
Tribune*, as the presidency receives the most attention in almost all years.
It is also usually the case that the term "mayor" is used more frequently
than "governor," although not always. Still, the *Times* displays more over-
time variation than does the *Tribune*.

Such word counts are admittedly crude measures of attention. To get a
more developed picture of the clusters of coverage over time, we next consider the topics that appear in both papers and their over-time evolution.

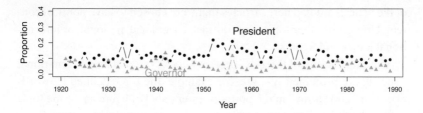

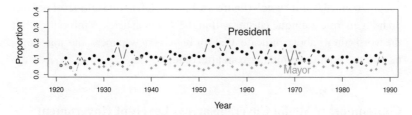

FIGURE 9.2. Attention to executives, *Los Angeles Times*
The top panel shows the share of political articles mentioning "president" (*black circles*) and "governor" (*gray triangles*), while the bottom panel shows mentions of "president" and "mayor" (*gray diamonds*).

Source: 9,017 articles appearing on March 10 of each year, obtained via ProQuest Historical.

To do so, we fit a multilevel model with a strong track record for clustering text—Latent Dirichlet Allocation (LDA; Blei, Ng, and Jordan 2003)—separately to the *Chicago Tribune* and *Los Angeles Times* articles described above. As we saw in chapter 7, LDA identifies clusters of words that co-occur in documents and has proven effective at identifying topics in a wide range of different collections of documents.[2] Users must choose a number of topics; to get a fine-grained view of the articles, we use forty.

The results are detailed in appendix figures 37–41 for the *Chicago Tribune* and figures 42–46 for the *Los Angeles Times*. Overall, the results strongly affirm the conclusions of the keyword analyses: national politics gets consistently more attention than local politics, which in turn gets more attention than state politics. National and international politics appear in the clusters at the center and top right of figure 38, for example. Local issues emerge in the center-right cluster in figure 39 as well as in various issue-specific clusters. For the *Chicago Tribune*, there is only a single cluster that seems indicative of state politics, using words like "state," "Illinoi," and "governor" (see figure 37, top-right cluster). It accounts for only 2 percent of the articles studied here, articles that were chosen to have political content. Numerous other topics, by contrast, cover local, national, or international issues and figures.

The same is true of the *Los Angeles Times*. National and international issues figure prominently—see, for example, the topic defined by words like "war" and "army" in the bottom-center panel of figure 42, or the topic defined by "soviet" and "china" in the top-center panel of figure 45. Local issues also appear repeatedly, including in the topic defined by words like "city," "council," and "vote" (figure 45, bottom left). Yet state-level politics do not generate a unique cluster within the *Times* articles, reinforcing what the word counts above indicate: that for big-city newspapers, the state capital and the politics within it are an afterthought.

Contemporary Media Coverage across Levels of Government

The analyses above stop in 1989. For more recent years, digitized databases of newspaper articles vastly expand the range of newspapers we can consider. Specifically, by searching the databases of *Newsbank*, we can estimate the relative share of coverage of local and state politics for fifty-one of the sixty-seven largest US newspapers by circulation. For some newspapers, the *Newsbank* archive extends into the early 1980s, allowing us to examine changes in coverage over decades. Importantly, these are typically the largest newspaper in a given metropolitan area: they are papers with an audience that is defined by its geography. If anyone has the means and motivation to cover subnational politics, it should be these papers.

As Ridout, Fowler, and Searles (2012) document, online databases like *Newsbank* are not perfect representations of the print newspapers that actually circulate. As those authors explain, coverage in such databases is partial, with "national and international coverage . . . more likely to be missing than local or statewide/provincial coverage" (451). In particular, newspapers commonly use wire services to provide national and international news, and those articles are underrepresented in *Newsbank*. But the resulting bias runs against the presumption of our study: if we can find evidence of nationally oriented coverage here, we should suspect that we are underestimating the extent of the actual emphasis on national news in print.

We first identified words typical of coverage of national, state, and local politics.[3] The use of keyword-based searches will invariably generate some errors, as these terms will include articles about company presidents as well as those about US presidents. They will almost certainly miss some stories as well. But spot checks confirmed that the overwhelming majority of the categorizations are appropriate.

We next calculated the number of articles of each type in each year. Appendix figures 47, 48, and 49 present the resulting ratios of local to national and state to national coverage for specific newspapers. Overall, there is substantially more local- than state-level coverage. The median local–national ratio across newspapers is 0.52, indicating just over five local articles for every ten nationally oriented articles. State-level politics receives only a fraction of that coverage, with its ratio being 0.18. There is some suggestion that newspapers located in or near state capitals cover state politics more (Carpini, Keeter, and Kennamer 1994), as illustrated by the *Denver Post*, Minneapolis's *Star Tribune*, the *St. Paul Pioneer Press*, and Rhode Island's *Providence Journal*.

To summarize the overall trends, and to measure the difference for newspapers in state capitals precisely, we then pooled the data across years and newspapers, generating a data set with 1,220 observations from fifty-one newspapers between 1981 and 2013. We use linear regression to estimate which newspaper-level factors make them more or less likely to provide state- and local-level coverage. On average, as table 9.1 makes clear, newspapers located in state capitals provide substantially more state-level coverage than others, with the ratio increasing by 0.09 on average. Emblematic of this trend is the *Sacramento Bee*, a paper renowned for its in-depth coverage of California state politics. On the other hand, newspapers in state capitals also provide markedly less coverage of local politics.

TABLE 9.1 **Regression results, attention to state and local news**

	State ratio	Local ratio
Intercept	1.325*	1.574*
	(0.193)	(0.586)
In state capital	0.093*	−0.183*
	(0.018)	(0.054)
Logged circulation	−0.091*	−0.059*
	(0.010)	(0.029)
N	1,220	1,220

Note: This table shows the results of linear regressions predicting the ratio of state to national (first column) or local to national (second column) keywords in fifty-one newspapers. The models include indicator variables for each year between 1982 and 2013, but the corresponding coefficients are suppressed here. $*p < 0.05$

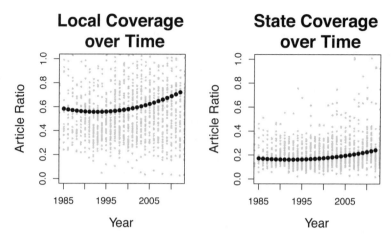

FIGURE 9.3. Ratio of state/local to national coverage in newspapers
For fifty-one of the sixty-seven largest newspapers by circulation, this figure presents the ratio
of local coverage to national coverage (*left*) and of state coverage to national coverage (*right*)
over time as obtained by *Newsbank*. The gray dots indicate specific observations, while the
black dots indicate the predicted ratio using a linear model. The ratios were estimated using
the *Newsbank* archive.

Newspapers with larger circulations are less likely to cover either state or
local politics. That could be because their audiences are more likely to
span multiple jurisdictions.

Examining individual papers, there is not a clear time trend. Many appear
to maintain roughly similar coverage ratios over time, including the *Houston
Chronicle* and the *Tampa Tribune*. And while some clearly reduce their local
coverage—consider the *St. Louis Post-Dispatch* or the *Oklahoman*—others
seem to increase it. Yet the pooled data set also enables us to estimate a time
trend across the newspapers, as illustrated in figure 9.3. In the left panel of
the figure, we see the observed ratios (in gray) and the average predicted
ratio estimated from a linear model.[4] For these fifty-one newspapers, local
coverage actually appears to be on the uptick, quite possibly as these papers
emphasize local content in the face of increased competition for national
coverage (George and Waldfogel 2006). So, too, does state coverage, although it begins at a much lower baseline.

Aside from local newspapers, the other major media source with a
spatially bounded audience—and thus a strong incentive to cover state
and local politics—is local television news. Here, the transcripts through
Newsbank are available only since 2006. Transcripts are also available for

just eleven states, only one of which is in the Northeast.[5] Still, they afford us an opportunity to see whether the trends identified above are specific to newspapers or represent a more general feature of the media environment. Accordingly, we apply similar techniques to the transcripts of seventy local television news programs between 2006 and 2013. The keywords are identical to those employed above for newspapers. Appendix figures 50–54 illustrate the results for specific stations.

Local television news does appear to give more attention to state and local politics than newspapers, with ratios of nearly 1 being common. In fact, the median ratio observed here is 0.83, indicating more attention to national news but not markedly so. Local attention usually outstrips state-level attention. But even state-level politics and government receive significant attention, at least from the observations here: the median ratio of state to national keywords is 0.55. To be fair, the stations included in this data set are disproportionately state capitals, from Little Rock, Arkansas, and St. Paul, Minnesota, to Austin, Texas. We again find that outlets in state capitals are more likely to cover state politics and government, although the substantive magnitude of the difference—0.03—is smaller than that uncovered for newspapers.

Turning to figure 9.4, we consider trends over time, although in this case, we only observe the eight-year period between 2006 and 2013. As the panels of the figure make clear, levels of local coverage are quite consistent over time, while state coverage appears to be growing slightly relative to national coverage. If there is a single type of outlet that appears most likely to cover state-level politics, it is local television news. Even in recent years, people watching local television news are likely to get at least some information about state and local politics, although admittedly, that does not always mean they are getting information about the states and localities where they themselves live. Certainly, residents of northern New Jersey might pick up significant information about New York City's mayor (Zukin and Snyder 1984), but that doesn't necessarily improve their capacity as local citizens.

To be sure, these analyses do nothing to rule out the possibility of more subtle shifts in how state or local politics have been covered by local TV news or newspapers. It is possible, for instance, that even when covering state and local politics, today's journalists often employ national-level frames. Perhaps governors' races are covered with an eye toward their national, partisan implications rather than their state-level impacts. Or else coverage of local and state politics might be increasingly boilerplate,

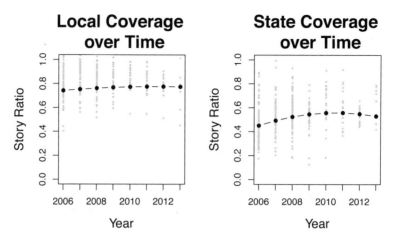

FIGURE 9.4. Ratio of state/local to national coverage on local TV
For seventy local TV affiliates observed between 2006 and 2013, this figure illustrates the ratios of local to national keywords (*left*) and state to national keywords (*right*) in local news transcripts obtained via *Newsbank*. The gray dots indicate observed ratios, while the black dots indicate predicted ratios by year for the full data set.

as coverage based on press releases replaces more in-depth, investigative journalism. Those are critical questions for future research. But based on the evidence presented here, we can conclude that the volume of coverage of the different levels of government in print newspapers and local TV news has been roughly similar for decades.

Americans' Changing Media Sources

Since at least 1930, the presidency has been a central focus of newspapers' political coverage, with mayors and governors receiving less coverage than the president does. That said, the evidence above suggests that there have not been dramatic shifts in the volume of newspaper or local TV news coverage devoted to state and local politics in recent decades. Nonetheless, if Americans are switching from media outlets that do cover state and local politics to those that do not, the consequences for their engagement with subnational politics could be pronounced. This section considers that possibility. It details that as Americans have shifted from broadcast television to cable television and from print newspapers to online news sources, they have also significantly reduced their exposure to information about state and local government. It seems self-evident that some media sources have spatially bounded audiences and thus are far more likely to cover local or state politics. Still, it is worth assessing that claim empirically, which we do here using responses to a question included in the January 2014 GfK survey. Specifically, the question asked respondents, "From which of the following do you get news about national/state/local politics?" Respondents were randomly assigned to read the question about national, state, or local politics, such that each respondent only answered with one frame of reference.

To be sure, assessing media consumption through self-reported survey data is imperfect (Prior 2009b). In general, respondents are likely to move quickly through surveys, sometimes missing the nuances of the questions. That takes on particular importance when measuring media exposure, as respondents might not be attentive to subtle distinctions among media outlets. For example, a respondent might easily confuse a national network broadcast like NBC's *Nightly News* with the broadcast of a local NBC affiliate.

Table 9.2 demonstrates that there are notable differences as to which media sources are perceived to provide information about which levels of government. By "network television," we mean nationally televised broadcasts that are accessible without a cable connection, such as ABC's *World News*. In the survey, 50 percent of respondents say that those national broadcasts are one of their sources for news about national politics. Only 42 percent say the same about local news broadcasts, such as Albuquerque,

TABLE 9.2 **Information sources across levels of government**

	National	State	Local
Network TV news	0.503	0.442	0.386
Cable TV news	0.424	0.306	0.291
Local TV news	0.418	0.513	0.528
Print newspaper	0.299	0.288	0.326
Online newspaper	0.235	0.190	0.223
Radio	0.238	0.249	0.243
Magazines	0.058	0.053	0.036
TV talk shows	0.189	0.172	0.125
Websites	0.241	0.214	0.228

Note: This table reports responses to the question "From which of the following do you get news about national/state/local politics?" From the January 2014 GfK survey, $n = 1,002$.

New Mexico's, Fox affiliate KQRE or Des Moines, Iowa's, KCCI, a CBS affiliate. Similarly, cable television news sources like CNN and the Fox News
cable channel are among the most cited sources of news about national
politics (42 percent) but are much less likely to be mentioned as sources
about state or local politics (29 percent). There is certainly evidence of
slippage, with 39 percent of respondents citing network TV news as a
source of information about local politics. That is likely the product of respondents not always differentiating between national networks and their
local affiliates. But overall, this sample thinks of network television, cable
television, and TV talk shows primarily as sources of national information. Local TV news and newspapers, by contrast, are among respondents'
primary sources when it comes to state and local politics. Any changes in
the media market that influence Americans' balance of media sources are
likely to have implications for their exposure to information about different levels of government as well.

That brings us to the question of how Americans' media sources have
changed in recent decades. Figure 9.5 presents the share of respondents

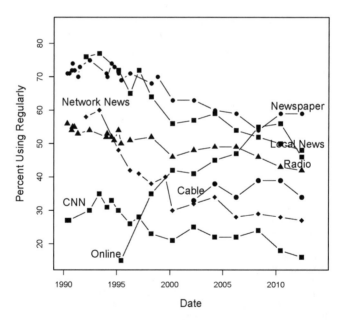

FIGURE 9.5. Consumption by media type

Source: Various Pew Research Center surveys.

to several nationally representative telephone surveys conducted by the Pew Research Center who indicate that they regularly use various media sources. As the figure makes clear, since 1990, there have been declines in some of the most prominent news sources, including newspapers and local television news. These media sources have spatially bounded audiences: owing to the limits of technology, they are distributed over discrete markets with clear geographic boundaries. Unsurprisingly, the largest growth has come in those reporting going online for their news—and while CNN usage is generally in decline over this period, cable television overall is not. Critically, these growing media sources do not have spatially bounded audiences. Websites like Yahoo! News and Huffington Post and cable channels like Fox News and CNN provide largely the same content to people in all parts of the United States (Hindman 2011). Even allowing for overreporting,[6] these trends demonstrate that Americans' relative consumption of news from spatially bounded media sources has declined notably since 1990. As novelist Jonathan Franzen observes in *Freedom*, "The urban gentry of Ramsey Hill were not so loyal to their city as not to read the *New York Times*" (2010, 3).

Generational replacement is one explanation for these changes in media consumption: younger, computer-friendly voters take the place of older voters more likely to subscribe to print newspapers. To see evidence of that, we turn back to the GfK data on media consumption across venues and estimate the average age of respondents who cite a particular media source in figure 9.6. As the figure makes clear, some of the core sources of local news—for instance, print newspapers but also local TV news—have self-reported audiences that are substantially older than those for more nationally oriented news sources, such as cable television. The median age of those who cite print newspapers as an information source is fifty-seven; for network news, it is fifty-one. For online newspapers, by contrast, it is forty-three, and for the Internet, it is thirty-eight. To the extent that people's primary media sources are habitual, generational replacement is likely to mean fewer magazine and print newspaper readers and more online news consumers over time.

But generational replacement is not the whole story. The shift in preferred media sources has taken place even for specific individuals, as table 9.3 demonstrates. It uses panel survey data—the 2008 National Annenberg Election Study and the follow-up 2012 Institute for the Study of Citizens and Politics Survey—to demonstrate that individuals' media consumption patterns are changing as well. Of the 2,217 respondents who

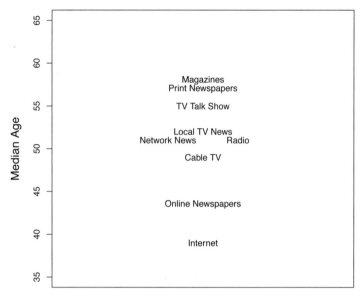

FIGURE 9.6. Media use by age
Using the January 2014 GfK survey, the figure illustrates the median age for respondents citing different media sources.

TABLE 9.3 **Change in information sources, 2008–2012**

	Mean January–March 2008	Mean October 2012	*p*-value
TV news	0.85	0.86	0.55
Newspapers	0.60	0.56	0.01
TV talk shows	0.49	0.56	0.00
Radio	0.46	0.45	0.51
Internet	0.39	0.38	0.81
Magazines	0.18	0.16	0.13
No political news	0.02	0.03	0.10

Source: 2,217 respondents to 2008 Annenberg Panel study reinterviewed in 2012 as part of the Institute for the Study of Citizens and Politics Survey. The panel was conducted through Knowledge Networks/GfK.

were interviewed in early 2008 and again in October 2012, 60 percent reported having heard something about the presidential campaign through newspapers in 2008. When asked that same question again in October 2012, 56 percent of respondents reported hearing about the presidential campaign through newspapers, a statistically significant decline. By contrast, there was a 7 percentage point uptick in respondents citing TV talk shows. Even within individuals' consumption patterns, we see evidence of a shift from newspapers to national television—and away from spatially bound media sources.

Media Use, Knowledge, and Engagement

The evidence so far indicates that Americans are shifting away from the media sources that provide at least a modicum of state and local coverage. But do such changes actually have consequences for Americans' knowledge about and engagement with state and local politics? To consider that question, we turn back to the 1,002 American adults surveyed through GfK's nationally sampled online panel in 2014. We start by asking a basic question: Are Americans more interested in national news relative to state and local news? We then consider the relationship between Americans' media sources and their knowledge about state and local politics.

The 2014 survey included an experiment in which respondents saw four headlines and were asked to indicate which they would be most likely to read. Three of the headlines were seen by everyone, and they captured different areas of interest, from sports ("Coach fired after disappointing season") to entertainment ("Singer denies rumors of divorce") and business ("Tech stocks up sharply"). The fourth headline was political, and it varied experimentally: some respondents saw "President apologizes for remark," while others saw "Governor" and still others saw "Mayor." The outcome of interest is the share of people choosing the political headline depending on who is doing the apologizing. As figure 9.7 illustrates, the respondents are more interested in the headline about the president, with 63 percent opting for it as opposed to 55 percent ($p = 0.03$) when it is a governor and 56 percent ($p = 0.07$) when it is a mayor. In the last chapter, we saw the weakness of Americans' place-based identities. This experiment demonstrates a related fact: Americans are more interested in news about the president than about a governor or mayor. The shift away from state and local news has both supply-side and demand-side explanations.

But what are the consequences of Americans' declining consumption of information about state and local politics? To answer that question, we employ several logistic regressions predicting whether the survey respondents knew their governor or mayor.[7] To measure that knowledge, respondents were randomly assigned to answer one of three open-ended

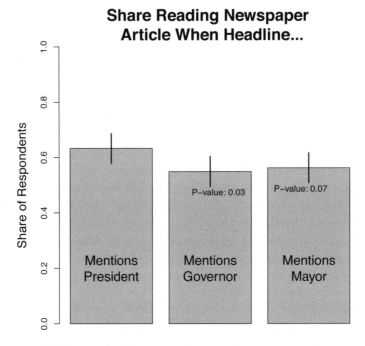

FIGURE 9.7. Headline experiment
In the January 2014 GfK survey, respondents were asked which of four headlines they would be most likely to read: "Coach fired after disappointing season," "Singer denies rumors of divorce," "Tech stocks up sharply," or "(President/Governor/Mayor) apologizes for remark," where respondents were randomly assigned to see one of the three offices in the final option. As the results make clear, respondents are more likely to be interested in the story when it is the president who apologizes.

questions. The first read, "Without looking it up, do you happen to know the name of your state's governor? Don't worry about spelling, and if you don't know, please write 'don't know.'" In response, 74 percent of respondents were able to name their governor. The second variant of the question asked them to both name and describe their governor.[8] Having to describe the governor was a slight deterrent, with 67 percent of respondents naming their governor when asked that version of the question.[9] For these analyses, we combine the two gubernatorial knowledge questions and include an independent variable measuring which version the respondent saw. The question about the respondents' mayor was worded similarly, and 36 percent named their mayor successfully. All three of these knowledge measures are binary, with 1 indicating respondents who know their governor or mayor.

Substantively, we are interested in the relationship between people's media options and choices and their knowledge of state and local politics. The costs of covering state politics are markedly lower for media outlets located in the state capital, so one key measure in these analyses is an indicator of whether the respondent lives in a TV market—technically, a designated market area or DMA—that is centered on the state's capital (Carpini, Keeter, and Kennamer, 1994). To the extent that people are getting information from local TV news, we might expect that those who live in the same media market as their state capital will be exposed to more information about state politics. If so, that would constitute evidence that quirks of geography and media availability—and not simply Americans' taste for state and local news—shape their knowledge. US TV markets vary dramatically in size, from a market like Glendive, Montana, with approximately eighty-four hundred viewers to one like New York City, with some 16.5 million, so we also include a logged measure of the media market's size.

There are ongoing debates among scholars about how best to measure people's media consumption (Prior 2009a, 2009b; Dilliplane, Goldman, and Mutz 2013; Prior 2013; Goldman, Mutz, and Dilliplane 2013). Here again, we recognize the limitation of self-reported data (Prior 2009a, 2013) but nonetheless exploit a series of self-reported media consumption measures. While people might well overstate their total exposure to political media, there is less reason to doubt their ability to identify which media sources they emphasize relative to others.

Our primary measures ask respondents, "From which of the following sources do you get information about state politics and government?" or "local politics and government?" For statistical power, we combine respondents who were asked about "state politics and government" with those asked about "local politics and government." We then generate binary indicators for each of nine media sources: national network television news, cable television news, local television news, print newspapers, online newspapers, radio news or talk shows, news magazines, television talk shows, and Internet sites, chat rooms, and blogs. In addition, our models also include a wide variety of individual-, county-, and market-level measures to reduce the chance that the associations we focus on are spurious.[10] Our main model is estimated using 503 observations.

The key results are illustrated in figure 9.8, with the full regression results available in appendix table 2. First, geography leaves a major imprint, with respondents living in a TV market centered on their state's capital a striking 11.9 percentage points more likely to know their governor's

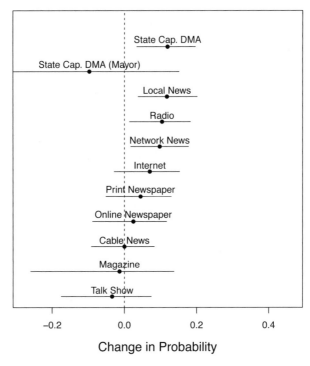

FIGURE 9.8. Correlates of knowing one's governor
Using the January 2014 GfK survey, the figure illustrates the correlates of knowing the name of one's governor.

name.[11] At the same time, from a separate model, we see that people who live in their state capital's TV market are no more likely to know their mayor,[12] a finding that gives us some confidence that the result for governors is not spurious but instead reflects the increased coverage of governors in their home media markets. The fact that people's place of residence shapes their knowledge of their governor even accounting for a host of individual- and community-level factors is indicative. It is not just that people who are interested in state politics seek them out in all settings. Instead, structural factors such as the relationship between the state capital and the media market play a major role in shaping Americans' knowledge of their governor. If that is true, then perhaps changes in the structure of media markets can influence knowledge as well.

Whether one lives near her state capital is just one way in which the media environment might shape knowledge of and engagement with state and local politics. We turn next to the differences in respondents' probability of naming their governor based on self-reported media sources for state and local politics. As figure 9.8 demonstrates, those who report watching local TV news, listening to radio, or watching network news are all demonstrably more likely to know their governor's name. Some of these effects are undoubtedly reflections of the differences in knowledge across the audiences of these different media.[13]

Still, it is noteworthy that local television news is positively associated with knowing one's governor, with an average increase of 8.9 percentage points among the 53.9 percent of respondents who report getting state or local political information from local television.[14] By contrast, the 34 percent of respondents who report watching cable news are no more or less likely to be able to name their state's governor. Here, too, we see the centrality of local TV news as a source of state-level political information. To the extent that local TV news viewership is declining, that decline might be a particular harbinger of waning knowledge of state politics.

Another way to approach the relationship between Americans' media consumption and their engagement with politics is by exploiting the design of the US Congress. Congressional leaders and a few other members are well known nationally (Grimmer 2013), while most US senators and representatives are principally known in their home states or districts. Accordingly, our 2014 GfK survey asked respondents an open-ended question designed to gauge whether they were more attentive to national figures in Congress (such as the party leaders) or their own congressional representatives. It read, "Please name up to three current members of Congress— either people in the US House of Representatives or in the US Senate— who first come to mind. There is no need to look up members' names if you don't happen to know three." We then coded responses based on the number of representatives and senators from the respondents' own state as well as the number from other states. Using linear regression models similar to those employed just above, we then estimate models in which the key dependent variable is the number of in-state or out-of-state representatives and senators named. As the key independent variable, we code responses to an open-ended question about "the source of information about state/local politics and government that you use most often" as either outlets that offer exclusively national coverage (such as Fox News) or outlets that offer some state and local coverage (such as the *Dallas Morning News*). Admittedly, the question itself asked about sources of information on state and local politics. But if respondents give answers

TABLE 9.4 **Regression results predicting local knowledge and engagement**

	Out of state	In state	Least favorite
Intercept	−1.383	−0.904	0.056
	(0.833)	(0.790)	(0.234)
Primary source: state media	0.238	0.414*	−0.016
	(0.143)	(0.136)	(0.040)
Primary source: national media	0.363*	0.290*	−0.067
	(0.134)	(0.127)	(0.039)
State capital DMA	−0.032	0.143	−0.048
	(0.126)	(0.119)	(0.039)
Logged market size	0.039	−0.043	−0.007
	(0.053)	(0.050)	(0.015)
Education	0.068*	0.060*	0.015*
	(0.024)	(0.023)	(0.007)
Income	0.856	2.256*	0.167
	(1.178)	(1.117)	(0.353)
Age	0.692	1.513*	−0.007
	(0.390)	(0.369)	(0.117)
Male	0.214*	0.133	−0.009
	(0.108)	(0.103)	(0.031)
Black	−0.108	−0.008	0.048
	(0.198)	(0.187)	(0.046)
Hispanic	−0.095	0.147	−0.002
	(0.185)	(0.175)	(0.051)
Party ID	0.012	0.007	−0.037
	(0.028)	(0.026)	(0.019)
Has children	−0.161	0.213	−0.015
	(0.128)	(0.121)	(0.039)
Married	0.029	−0.041	0.090*
	(0.123)	(0.116)	(0.036)
Homeowner	−0.094	0.027	0.013
	(0.132)	(0.125)	(0.037)
County total population	−0.076	0.069	−0.006
	(0.040)	(0.038)	(0.010)
R^2	0.116	0.168	0.075
N	332	332	357

Note: OLS regression results predicting different measures of knowledge about and engagement with local politics. The data are from the 2014 GfK survey, and the measures of national and state media come from an open-ended question about people's primary media sources. *$p < 0.05$

that nonetheless are nationally targeted outlets, that is a strong indication of the national orientation of their media diet.

The first two columns in table 9.4 show the results for the number of in-state or out-of-state representatives named. For in-state representatives, reporting a primary media source that has at least some state-level coverage—say, a local newspaper or television news program—leads to a marked 0.41 (SE = 0.14) increase in the number of in-state senators and US representatives named. Certainly, reporting a national media source is also positively correlated with naming in-state senators and representatives (β = 0.29, SE = 0.13), likely because most people's media diets include multiple sources. Still, when it comes to naming out-of-state senators and representatives, the magnitudes of the effects switch, with those whose primary media source is national more likely to name out-of-state figures.

The survey also asked people about their least favorite politician at any level of government. For Republicans, the answer is very commonly the sitting Democratic president. But for Democrats, there is variation in whether they name a politician within their state or on the national stage. As the third column of table 9.4 shows, Democrats who report that their primary media source is a national one are 0.07 less likely to name a least favorite politician within their home state (SE = 0.04). Substantively, this last effect is not enormous. But given the measurement error inherent in using people's self-reported primary media source to approximate their actual media consumption, the results overall are quite informative: people whose primary news source contains more state and local content are more likely to display state-specific political knowledge (see also Mondak 1995b; Shaker 2009).

The Effects of Television Markets over Time

Voter turnout is a habit sustained by various civic, social, and political institutions and should respond slowly to changes in media markets and the resulting shifts in political information (e.g., Rosenstone and Hansen 1993; Putnam 2000; Meredith 2009). Still, we should expect that as American voters shifted to and then away from local television news as an important source of information in the second half of the twentieth century, those changes would be reflected in their relative participation in gubernatorial elections.

But how might we test this changing relationship over broad swaths of time? In this section, we exploit previously observed relationships between media market structure and political knowledge and engagement (e.g., Carpini, Keeter, and Kennamer 1994; Althaus and Trautman 2008; Althaus, Cizmar, and Gimpel 2009) to estimate the changing effects of local television markets from 1928 to 2012. Specifically, we consider whether two patterns noted in prior cross-sectional studies have in fact

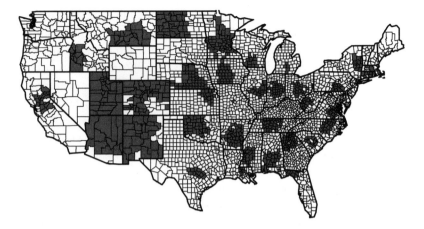

FIGURE 9.9. Counties in DMAs centered on state capital
This map illustrates those US counties in a DMA centered on their state capital.

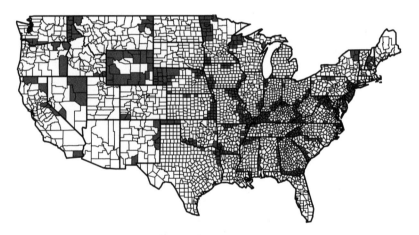

FIGURE 9.10. Counties in DMAs centered in other states
This map illustrates those US counties that are located in a DMA whose primary audience is in another state.

varied over time. The first is the effect of being in the same DMA as one's state capital: to the extent that voters are exposed to local television news, those in such counties are likely to receive more information about state-level politics and more likely to be more engaged in gubernatorial elections as a result (e.g., Carpini, Keeter, and Kennamer 1994). The second is the inverse: people in counties in an out-of-state media market are less likely to be exposed to news about their own state's politics. Here, we test the thesis of nationalization by considering whether these effects of media market geography on gubernatorial turnout have declined in recent years.

In figures 9.9 and 9.10, we map the 25 percent of US counties that are within a DMA centered on their state's capital and the 18 percent of US counties in a DMA that primarily covers another state, respectively. As the figures make clear, there is substantial geographic variation to exploit: thirty-eight states have at least some counties within the DMA centered on their state capital, and forty-one states have at least some counties whose media markets have larger populations in other states.

We then estimate the ratio between gubernatorial and presidential two-party turnout for each county in twelve-year periods between 1928 and 2012. We drop only gubernatorial elections held concurrently with presidential elections, as their turnout ratio will be very close to 1. As in chapter 3, we use the data set of county-level gubernatorial and presidential election returns introduced in Hirano and Snyder (2007) and augment it using various sources. By using turnout ratios, we can set aside challenging questions in estimating the voting-eligible population (McDonald and Popkin 2001) and instead focus on our core quantity of interest: turnout and engagement in gubernatorial elections relative to presidential elections. For consecutive sets of three four-year presidential cycles, we then estimate the effect of sharing a DMA with the state capital on the gubernatorial–presidential turnout ratio using models that include state fixed effects and year fixed effects. These data sets include southern as well as northern counties and range in size from 1,678 to 7,471 depending on the number of gubernatorial elections in a given twelve-year period.

Figure 9.11 presents each of the coefficients measuring the difference in state capital media markets. The trend tracks developments in the history of television with uncanny accuracy. In the decades prior to the proliferation of television in the 1940s and 1950s, there is essentially no difference between gubernatorial turnout in state capital media markets and elsewhere. The effect of being in a state capital DMA then becomes positive in the early 1960s, which is precisely when local television affiliates were coming online and beginning their own news broadcasts (Prior 2006, 2007; Song 2014). By the twelve-year period centered on 1972, the effect increased to 0.009 (SE = 0.007). In other words, in the period from 1968 to 1979, counties in their state capital DMA saw a 0.9 percentage point boost in gubernatorial turnout, all else equal. The DMA effect increased

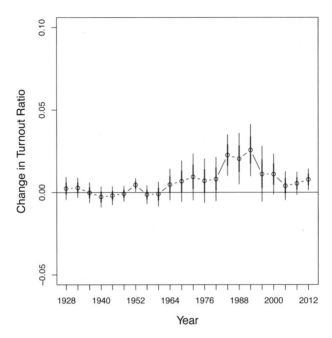

FIGURE 9.11. Gubernatorial turnout premium in state capital media markets
This figure illustrates the effect of being located in a DMA centered on the state capital on the ratio between gubernatorial and presidential turnout. These coefficients are estimated from linear models with fixed effects for states and years.

further to 0.023 (SE = 0.006) or 2.3 percentage points in 1984 before declining to 0.007 (SE = 0.003) for the comparable period around 2012. The downward trend makes sense as well given the introduction of cable television in the 1980s and the widespread use of the Internet beginning in the 1990s. Comparing 1984 to 2012, the effect declined markedly, with a corresponding two-sided p-value of 0.03. The difference is statistically significant—and precisely what we would expect if voters were relying less on local television broadcasts and were less informed about subnational politics as a result.

Figure 9.12 illustrates the results from similar models when we estimate the effects of being in a DMA in which the audience primarily lives in another state. Here, we see relationships that are generally the inverse of those observed above. Counties with out-of-state TV news always report lower gubernatorial turnout relative to presidential turnout, even before television was introduced. But that deficit grew precisely as local television expanded in the 1960s, and it has declined in recent years. As

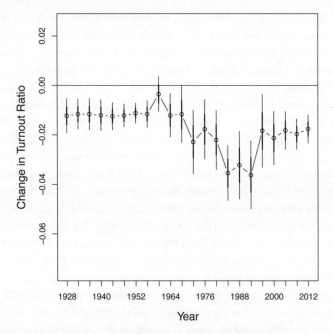

FIGURE 9.12. Gubernatorial turnout deficit in out-of-state media markets
This figure illustrates the effect of being in a DMA centered in another state on the ratio between gubernatorial and presidential turnout. These coefficients are estimated from linear models with fixed effects for states and years.

late as the elections surrounding 1984, it was −0.035 (SE = 0.006), while by those around 2012, it had declined to −0.018 (SE = 0.003). That difference has a two-sided p-value of 0.006, which is again statistically significant. The overall trend is highly indicative, especially when coupled with the results on state capital media markets reported above. The deficit induced by out-of-state media markets is now shrinking, a finding that we would expect if media content is increasingly nationalized irrespective of one's county of residence. With a variety of new national media options, one's local TV content matters less than it did in the 1980s.

Conclusion

In chapter 2, we detailed two separate facets of nationalization. The first was the nationalization of political divisions and voting patterns, while the second was declining interest in state and local politics. One advantage to that distinction is that the causes of nationalization's two faces might differ—and indeed, this chapter's evidence reinforces that contention.

On their own, technologically deterministic explanations do not seem well suited to explain nationalization's first face, the nationalization of voting behavior. In particular, the 1960s and 1970s stand out as a period in which gubernatorial elections were becoming less nationalized, even as television was captivating national audiences like never before (Prior 2007; Song 2014). The 1960s and 1970s are thus an informative outlier—a time of relatively nationalized media sources but meaningful state-to-state variation in voting patterns. What's more, as we discussed in chapter 6, countries like Britain and Canada have seen similar transformations in their media markets while also experiencing denationalization in their voting behavior at times during recent decades. Television alone didn't prevent the emergence of the Parti Quebecois in Quebec or the two referenda on sovereignty there; the Internet didn't stave off a referendum on sovereignty in Scotland in 2014. So, while the medium may shape the message, it does not determine the message. As the examples of Canada and Scotland suggest—and as we detailed in chapters 6 and 8—the structure of people's identities and interests is crucial in shaping their reactions to the changing media environment.

Our evidence here demonstrates that the relative inattention to state politics is nothing new: big-city papers like the *Los Angeles Times* and the *Chicago Tribune* gave state politics short shrift since the New Deal, and that trend holds in more recent years for larger local newspapers and some local television news outlets. Nonetheless, the transformation and fragmentation of American media markets has far-reaching consequences for the information citizens are exposed to about state and local politics. The primary change is simply in the types of media we consume, not the coverage of state or local politics within a given type. As we shift to cable news and online news sources, we are leaving behind the sources of what little state and local political information we do receive. The effects of that shift are evident in Americans' knowledge about state-level politics, in their political engagement, and in the geography of gubernatorial turnout. While citizens' places of residence still shape their engagement in state-level politics somewhat, they do so to a decidedly lesser extent than in decades past. Changes in the media market are thus an important part of the explanation for the second face of nationalization, the declining engagement with state and local politics. In his emphasis on media, political scientist Donald Stokes had the right cause—just not the right effect.

CHAPTER TEN

Conclusion

Tip O'Neill is best known for serving in a decidedly national role as the Speaker of the US House of Representatives from 1977 to 1987. But in the early 1930s, after losing a campaign for city council in Cambridge, Massachusetts, his father gave him a piece of advice: "Let me tell you something that I learned years ago. All politics is local" (BC University Libraries 2002). That phrase remains associated with O'Neill to this day, and it has taken on a wide variety of meanings, from emphasizing the importance of local connections to bemoaning the political peculiarities of different communities. As O'Neill (1988) explained, "I had received a tremendous vote in the other sections of the city, but I hadn't worked hard enough in my own backyard" (26).

The advice O'Neill received to cultivate local connections was well suited to the pre–New Deal era when it was first offered. Nor was it wide of the mark in the late 1970s, when O'Neill ascended to the Speakership. In recent years, however, American political behavior has nationalized in two different respects, both defined in chapter 2. First, politics is increasingly animated by the same fundamental divisions across the federal system. We saw evidence of that in chapter 3, as voting for down-ballot offices like governor has come to mirror voting for president. Chapter 5 reinforced that claim by showing that so few ostensibly local issues generate distinctive political interests.

Still, there is a second element to nationalized political behavior. As chapter 4 demonstrated, Americans' engagement with state and local politics has waned relative to their engagement with national politics. In recent decades, scholars and commentators have bemoaned America's relatively low levels of participation at the national level. But it turns out that participation in state and local politics is lower still. And unlike participation in national politics, participation at the state and local levels has continued to fall.

After detailing the two faces of nationalization, this book considered their likely causes. To explain the growing correspondence between presidential and subnational voting, chapters 6 and 7 pointed to political polarization and America's changing political parties. As the national parties have staked out increasingly clear and distinctive ideologies, the state parties and their candidates have had less room to craft their own brands. You can place the same order in almost any McDonald's throughout the country. Similarly, you can now vote for a party with a consistent national platform in all fifty states.

The second face of nationalization—the declining interest in state and local politics—requires a separate explanation. Chapter 8 demonstrated that contemporary Americans are strongly connected to their nation but not to their states or localities. Against that backdrop of subnational identities that are weak and apolitical, chapter 9 illustrated how America's media market has transformed. In earlier eras, Americans' primary news sources competed for spatially defined audiences, whether they were local television broadcasts or print newspapers. News outlets had clear economic incentives to cover the news of interest to people living in particular places. As a result, people who followed the news at all were likely to be exposed to at least some information about local and state politics. But as Americans' media options have proliferated, they have shifted to outlets with national audiences, such as cable television and the Internet. Absent strong attachments to their states or localities, Americans have little reason to stick with local newspapers or local television news. Engagement in local politics has suffered as a result.

In short, this book has demonstrated two pathways through which American political behavior nationalized. Here, we shift from the causes of nationalization to its consequences. As we have seen at moments throughout the book, nationalization touches on many political phenomena, including the declining incumbency advantage (chapter 2), the apparent Republican advantage in the House of Representatives (chapter 3), and the shift to a nationalized campaign finance system (chapter 4). Nationalized political behavior also has broader implications for questions of social science, from the optimal size of political communities (Dahl and Tufte 1973; Levy 2006) to sources of social solidarity in modern societies (Durkheim 1984). Rather than briefly mentioning the many potential implications of nationalized political behavior, though, this conclusion focuses narrowly on two of the most consequential: its implications for representation in subnational politics and for polarization and gridlock in federal politics.

Some of nationalization's consequences for accountability and political representation are straightforward. When political behavior is nationalized along the first dimension, voters' default is to support the same political party at all levels of government. Nationalized voters have less knowledge of state and local politics as well, making those defaults harder to overcome. As state and local politicians adapt to nationalized political behavior, they may well see less reason to cater to their own constituents, as those constituents are unlikely to vote on the basis of their performance in office. Indeed, after concluding that their actions in office are only weakly related to their ability to win votes, politicians might focus on the priorities of their campaign contributors, fellow partisans, or social networks instead.

There are other, subtler ways in which nationalized political behavior shapes subnational representation. One strength of federalist political institutions is that they allow states and localities to address the varied issues facing their particular electorates. If voters in one state are concerned about promoting development while in another state they want to secure sufficient water, a federalist division of authority should facilitate those differing issue agendas. Federalism would seem a natural fit for a nation that spans a continent and has fifty states confronting widely varying challenges. But that line of thinking assumes that states and localities can have quite different issue agendas. Nationalized politics might make such idiosyncratic issue agendas harder to sustain—and so might induce a mismatch between political institutions designed to address a plethora of issues and a political debate stubbornly limited to just a few. Nationalization is also likely to affect the types of issues that states address, as it advantages symbolic issues resonant nationwide over more tangible distributive issues.

Even at the federal level, nationalized political behavior has the potential to influence governance by fostering political polarization and gridlock. Both houses of the US Congress elect their members from geographically defined constituencies, whether they are states or districts. When building majority coalitions, one time-honored tactic has been to appeal to legislators' particular interests as local representatives. While legislators may not be favorable to a given piece of legislation's overall goal, they may still support the bill if it protects or advances key local interests. Yet as American political behavior nationalizes, legislators have less to gain from championing a local interest in the face of opposition from their fellow partisans. Nationalization seems to help explain why legislators' votes on bills have become so predictable—and why Congresses between 2011 and 2017 have been so gridlocked. Without alternative, local dimensions on which to evaluate legislation, legislators rely on their partisanship and ideology, making each roll call a test of partisan strength. Before turning to nationalization's two primary implications, though, we briefly detour to consider what it could mean for political science.

Implications for Studying Politics

Among its many implications, nationalized political behavior is likely to shape how we study American politics. In a localized political system, the fifty states are well described as "laboratories of democracy," to borrow Justice Louis Brandeis's phrase.[1] Their politics are relatively independent, making studies that compare political behavior across states quite sensible. If some states experience higher levels of some factor of interest—say, immigration or income inequality—comparing those states with others is eminently practical. But Brandeis was writing in 1932—and as we have seen, American political behavior was nationalizing within years of that opinion. Today, political behavior more often reflects national trends and events, meaning that political activity across states is often quite highly correlated (Hertel-Fernandez 2014, 2016; Garlick 2015; Rogers 2016). This fact inveighs against studies premised on the assumption that the American states provide us with fifty independent polities.

That said, nationalized political behavior also provides scholars with potential opportunities. Survey research is a mainstay of studies of American public opinion and political behavior; this book itself would not be possible without surveys. But with response rates to surveys declining (Curtin, Presser, and Singer 2005), and with the costs of nationally representative samples on the rise, researchers have been turning to convenience samples (Mullinix et al. 2015). To the extent that political behavior is nationalized, similar people are likely to respond to similar information in similar ways, irrespective of their place of residence. As a result, geographically targeted surveys and experiments that are balanced on key individual-level demographics should increasingly generalize to comparable individuals elsewhere.

This book's results might also motivate a particular set of surveys, experiments, and analyses: those aimed at evaluating policy interventions that might reduce the tension between our federalist institutions and our nationalized political behavior. Some such policy interventions might seek to improve the information that voters have about state and local politics and government, whether through education or regulatory changes in media markets. Others might aim to strengthen the connection between campaign donors and the candidates who actually represent them, perhaps by incentivizing donations to candidates whom prospective donors are eligible to vote for (Fontana, forthcoming). When assessing policies more generally, it is valuable to consider whether they serve to clarify or obscure lines of accountability in our federal system (Henig 2013).

As this conclusion transitions from nationalization's causes to its consequences, it shifts the spotlight to elected officials. It is not simply voters' behavior but also politicians' interpretations of that behavior that is likely to shape their actions while in office. In recent years, political science has devoted far more attention to mass behavior than to the question of how it is perceived or interpreted by political elites (but see Butler and Nickerson 2011; Broockman and Skovron 2013; Butler and Powell 2014). But as this conclusion demonstrates, documenting citizens' behavior is necessary without being sufficient. To fully assess nationalization's impacts, we need to know how politicians perceive and make sense of the trends documented throughout this book. That, too, is a key question for future research.

Representation in a Federalist System

Whether they are local, state, or national governments, a cornerstone of representative democracies generally is the link between what voters want and how politicians act while in office. Elections provide a central mechanism through which voters can hold both individual politicians and political parties accountable: when voters disapprove of an incumbent politician's performance, they can back the opposing candidate or party (Mayhew 1974). But this raises a critical question: on what issues and under what conditions will voters punish incumbents (Mayhew 1974; Healy and Malhotra 2009; Healy, Malhotra, and Mo 2010; Ashworth 2012; Achen and Bartels 2016)?

In the United States, voters at all levels of government typically face a choice between no more than two credible candidates. In such a setting, it becomes difficult for voters to send nuanced messages across multiple policy areas simultaneously (Key and Cummings 1966). With a single vote, they cannot simultaneously punish the incumbent for declining test scores and reward her for fixing potholes. Candidates represent bundles of various positions, experiences, and other attributes, making it difficult to disentangle precisely what a vote for or against a given candidate means (see also Hainmueller, Hopkins, and Yamamoto 2014).

In theory, federalist political institutions could either help or hinder political accountability. They do provide multiple venues for political representation, meaning that social groups that wield little influence at one level of government might gain a hearing at another. Today, federalist institutions mean that many Americans who do not share their president's partisanship do share their governor's. In that respect, federalism facilitates a closer match between public attitudes and policy making, as state officials can tailor their policies to residents' preferences (Nugent 2009).

Federalist systems do demand more of voters, as they need to participate in multiple elections and to know which level of government to hold accountable for which outcomes (Carsey and Wright 1998; Arceneaux 2005, 2006; Malhotra and Kuo 2008; Rogers 2016; Sances 2016; Hopkins and Pettingill, forthcoming). But a federalist division of authority also allows each level of government to specialize. Local governments can address education or zoning, for example, while state governments can tackle highways and the federal government can concern itself with foreign affairs (see also Henig 2013). That specialization, in turn, can help voters solve the problem of attributing particular outcomes to particular actors (Rodden 2006; Berry and Howell 2007; Burnett and Kogan 2016).

We might observe specialization within a given level of government as well as across levels. America's fifty states face a dizzying array of public policy challenges. In New Mexico, the concern might be about wildfires, while in Delaware the focus might be on legalizing sports gambling. Federalism has the potential to facilitate representation under such conditions, as it allows for the expression of varying political interests and concerns in each state. The top priorities in some places are likely to be ignored entirely in others.

America's political institutions have enjoyed remarkable stability during the roughly 230 years since the US Constitution was written and ratified. But during that same period, American society, and the political behavior that emerged from it, has nationalized. Nationalization, in turn, has the potential to undercut political accountability in our federalist system in two distinct ways. First, it can dampen the electoral connection between voters and elected officials in subnational politics (see also Rogers 2016). And second, it can reshape the political agenda in states and localities in ways that obscure the division of responsibility across the federal system.

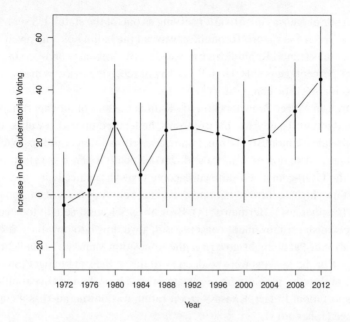

Year

FIGURE 10.1 Correlation between gubernatorial and presidential elections at state level

To see how nationalized voting patterns imperil state-level account-ability, consider politics from the viewpoint of a governor. In figure 10.1, we show the growing relationship between voting for president and vot-ing for governor. Specifically, we predict the two-party share of the vote for governor going to the Democrat using presidential voting for eight-year windows of elections. We focus here on the state level, as this basic pattern is roughly illustrative of what gubernatorial candidates and party operatives are likely to perceive. As recently as 1972, the relationship was essentially zero: knowing which way a state leaned in presidential politics told one nothing about the likely outcome in the gubernatorial race. In that setting, governors had strong incentives to craft their own reputa-tions. But the correlation coefficient has grown sharply since then, giving one party or the other a built-in advantage in many states. Given those advantages and disadvantages, today's gubernatorial candidates may well decide that their career prospects hinge more on their relationships with donors or activists outside their state than on voters within it.

The consequences of this shift are evident in many examples, includ-ing that of Sam Brownback, a conservative Republican. He was elected governor of Kansas in 2010 after serving as one of the state's US senators. The year 2010 saw a pro-Republican wave at the ballot box, and given that Kansas has leaned Republican for decades, Brownback won by a staggering 31 percentage points. He fell just shy of receiving twice as many votes as his Democratic competitor.

Once in office, Brownback made Kansas the site of an experiment in tax reduction. To develop his proposals, he teamed up with a well-known supply-side economist, Arthur Laffer, as well as interest groups backed by conservative donors Charles and David Koch (Goldfarb 2014). As a result, the GOP-controlled state cut income taxes dramatically in 2012, with the state's highest income tax rate dropping from 6.45 percent to 4.90 percent (Cooper 2012; Berman 2015). Brownback's Kansas sought to become "a petri dish for movement conservatism, a window into how the national Republican Party might govern if the opposition vanished" (Suellentrop 2015). But the tax cuts were so deep as to throw the state budget into disarray and to threaten funding for state priorities, including education and transportation. In fact, Kansas's credit rating was downgraded as a consequence (Jones 2014).

By 2014, with Brownback up for reelection, political opposition mounted. Democrat Paul Davis managed to win the endorsement of many disaffected Republican politicians, but he nonetheless fell short at the ballot box, losing by 3.7 percentage points. To be sure, Davis's performance was a dramatic improvement over that of the Democrat four years prior. But it was not enough to beat a Republican incumbent in a Republican state in a Republican year. The state remained in a budgetary crisis well into Brownback's second term, when one leading GOP official lamented, "In the end, we had a governor, held hostage by East Coast ideologues, who would not consider a correction to his tax policy" (Suellentrop 2015). By 2015, the resulting budget gap had ballooned to more than 10 percent of the state's total budget.

Sam Brownback's tenure as Kansas governor demonstrates some of nationalization's likely consequences. A governor, embedded in networks of national policy activists, brought their prescriptions to his state. The agenda reflected the ideological priorities of a partisan national network more than it reflected any indigenous interests in Kansas. Key to the Kansas story was Brownback's sizable cushion of support in a GOP-leaning state: it afforded his party unified control over the state, and it meant that he could win reelection despite seeing his support drop by more than 13 percentage points from the previous election. Even the Democrats' pickup of twelve seats in the Kansas House of Representatives in 2016—a shift widely seen as a reaction to Brownback—left them with fewer than half as many seats as the Republicans (Smith 2016).

Nationalized political behavior changes the incentives for politicians like Governor Brownback and so can dampen the electoral connection between voters and subnational officials. But to what extent is it incompatible with our federalist institutions? There are varied arguments about the conditions under which federalist institutions are advantageous (e.g., Riker 1964; Elazar 1966; Beer 1993; Derthick 2004; Rodden 2006; Levy 2006, 2007; Berry 2009; Feeley and Rubin 2009; Greve 2012; Bednar 2015)—and nationalized political behavior is more of a threat under some theoretical perspectives than others. To address that question, though, it is critical to distinguish between what we might term "institutional federalism" and "behavioral federalism." This book has had little to say on governance or policy making, so assessing the operation of contemporary federalist institutions is beyond its scope (see instead Nugent 2009; Greve 2012; Henig 2013). Nonetheless, it does provide substantial evidence on political behavior in subnational politics, behavior that some scholars see as a keystone of federalism. Put differently, this book's evidence provides a direct assessment of behavioral federalism. It speaks to institutional federalism only insofar as it depends on behavioral federalism.

As we saw at the book's outset, institutional federalism relies on a delicate balance between the forces of centralization and disintegration (Kollman 2013; Bednar 2015). To several commentators, public loyalty to the states serves as a critical counterweight to the centralization of authority in Washington, DC, meaning that this book's evidence on the weakness of state-level identities itself attests to the fragility of American federalism (Levy 2006, 2007; Feeley and Rubin 2009). In the words of Riker (1964), "It is very likely that the basic condition that allows for both centralization and resistance to centralization is the degree of popular identification with the national and state governments. If citizens, when asked their citizen-identification, reply, 'I am an American,' to the exclusion of 'I am a Hoosier' or 'I am a Texan,' the scene is set for centralization. But if they reply first and foremost 'I am a Buckeye,' then it is difficult to imagine much centralization occurring" (104). To scholars in this tradition, there is now a critical disjoint between Americans' political institutions and their loyalties. Americans are political monogamists, not the polygamists their institutions presuppose.

From other theoretical vantage points, however, this book's evidence on political behavior is less concerning, at least on its own. In some accounts, federalist institutions provide a critical check on government generally (Beer 1993; Nugent 2009; Greve 2012). In such views, federalism should be considered less an expression of dueling popular loyalties and more an institutional configuration adopted by a single nation to put competitive pressure on government. According to this way of thinking, federalism is akin to the separation of powers at the federal level: it is an institution to hold the various elements of the nation's government in check. Given these alternative justifications for federalism, this book's results do not by any means counsel an abandonment of federalist institutions. But they do encourage a reassessment of the grounds under which federalist institutions are justified.

One ostensible advantage of federalism is that it protects a variety of political venues in which different issues can be addressed. That, in turn, allows for the expression of varying political conflicts across America's states and localities. But as American political behavior has nationalized, and as politicians and political coalitions have adapted to the new nationalization, American federalism is no longer facilitating the expression of various issues and conflicts. Instead, the debates in states and even some localities have taken on a national hue, as state political conflicts become an extension of national conflicts, albeit with a different balance of forces. Kansas during Sam Brownback's tenure is one example among many.

Nationalization is likely to standardize the political agenda across the federal system. That, in turn, mutes the capacity of federalist institutions to express the diverse disagreements of a diverse country. At the same time, nationalization is also likely to affect the types of issues that are prominent in politics, as chapter 5 indicated. Local political issues are often tangible and concrete—they are distributional questions of school boundaries and home values (Fischel 2001; Oliver, Ha, and Callen 2012). National issues, by contrast, need to be engaging to a wide range of people, meaning that they are often symbolic issues imbued with meaning for the status of different social groups (see especially Carmines and Stimson 1980; Sears 1993). In this respect, too, contemporary nationalization has the potential to induce a consequential mismatch between the issues Americans face in our daily lives and the issues that structure our choices at the ballot box.

Political Polarization

Nationalized political behavior has clear consequences for state and local governance. But its impacts don't stop there: they are also evident in federal policy making. And there, too, the career of Tip O'Neill is instructive.

As the Speaker of the House during the first six years of the Reagan administration, O'Neill was a critical player in several major pieces of legislation, including the Tax Reform Act of 1986 and the Immigration Reform and Control Act of the same year. Any legislation during that period had to run a policy-making gauntlet, as it required the backing of the Democratic-controlled House of Representatives, the GOP-controlled Senate, and President Ronald Reagan. And that decade's more localized politics is a key part of the explanation for how those bills managed to become laws.

Take the 1986 tax reform, whose broad goals were to close tax loopholes and reduce tax rates. As the bill was being formulated, one key source of dissent came from New York representatives of both political parties. New York imposed high state taxes on its residents, meaning that the proposal to end the federal income tax deduction for state and local taxes was of particular concern. New Yorkers stood to see even higher tax bills if the deduction were eliminated. But by shifting gears and preserving the deduction, O'Neill lieutenant Dan Rostenkowski managed to secure key New Yorkers' support (Birnbaum and Murray 1987). A variety of other side deals also provided perks to specific localities—and smoothed the way for the bill's passage. As Birnbaum and Murray (1987) note, the Reagan administration "wisely turned its head when it came to the dirty business of negotiating transition rules. Even the most committed congressional reformers realized that these relatively small provisions were a necessary price to pay. If ten or fifteen billion dollars in temporary transition rules would enable Congress to close several hundred billions of dollars' worth of permanent tax loopholes, then they were willing to go along" (243). This story is by no means unique to the passage of tax reform. When building majority coalitions, it often helps if legislators have district-level preferences that can override their general partisan or ideological orientation (Lee 2000, 2005; Evans 2004; Waxman 2009).

In the years leading up to 2017, the story has been very different (Binder 2003; McCarty, Poole, and Rosenthal 2006; Lapinski 2008). The only legislation that can build cross-party coalitions today is the essential business of funding the government—and even those bills are increasingly subject to high-stakes brinksmanship, shutdowns of the federal government, and threats of federal default. Scholars and observers alike point to elite-level political polarization as a key culprit (McCarty, Poole, and Rosenthal 2006; Mann and Ornstein 2016). Yet, while there is widespread agreement that political elites are highly polarized, the term "polarization" itself can mean different things (DiMaggio, Evans, and Bryson 1996; Levendusky 2009; Noel 2013; Lee 2015). Most commonly, political scientists measure polarization by looking at the divergence in roll-call voting between the two parties along a single dimension (e.g., McCarty, Poole, and Rosenthal 2006; Shor and McCarty 2011; Lee 2015). As the two parties become more homogeneously liberal and conservative, the ability of congressional leaders to fashion cross-party coalitions has declined. But the experience of Tip O'Neill suggests that if we conceive of polarization simply as increasing divergence along one dimension, we neglect a critical question: what happened to the alternative, local dimensions with which party leaders like Tip O'Neill were once able to fashion majorities? Notice that for each legislator, the local dimension is idiosyncratic. It may be increased Medicaid funding in one congressional district and tariffs on foreign-made steel in another.

At all levels of government, America's political institutions inscribe a central role for local, place-based interests. The use of geographically defined districts to elect legislators at the state and federal level, for instance, affords place-based interests a privileged position in policy making. As Rehfeld (2005) notes, "The truth of Tip O'Neill's aphorism, that all politics is local, depends not on the nature of politics per se, but on the institutional incentives that lead politicians to serve local interests over nonlocal interests, incentives that arise only because electoral constituents are defined territorially" (8). When members of Congress allow local interests to override their national ideological or partisan incentives, they are simply following the grooves defined by our political system.

Members of Congress have long felt the dueling pulls of local and national commitments (see especially Howell, Jackman, and Rogowski 2013). But the evidence detailed throughout this book helps explain why legislators have deemphasized local interests in recent years: their constituents are less attentive to those interests at the same time that their campaign contributors are less likely to be local. Nationalized political behavior is likely to make legislators more unequivocally focused on national partisan and ideological questions and so can undermine a foundation of legislative bargaining. Legislators are no longer as willing to buck their party in favor of a local interest. Every vote becomes a partisan test of strength rather than an opportunity to fashion a bill-specific coalition (see especially Lee 2009). Polarization, in this view, is driven not simply by increasing divergence along the primary dimension of conflict but by the disappearance of other dimensions. Nationalized political behavior is a key missing link that enriches our understanding of polarization and helps make sense of contemporary gridlock in federal politics.

In late 2009, as the sweeping health care reform bill was being taken up in the US Senate, Nebraska senator Ben Nelson saw an opportunity. Nelson's Democrats held exactly the sixty votes in the Senate that they needed to pass health care reform—and with scant GOP support for the measure, his vote would be pivotal. As a Democrat from a reliably Republican state, Nelson sought a concrete achievement to bring home to his constituents. He succeeded, securing a deal worth $100 million in Medicaid funding for Nebraska alone. In fact, the deal was so lucrative it was nicknamed the "Cornhusker Kickback" (Fabian 2010). But politics in 2009 was nationalized in a way that politics in the 1980s was not. What should have been a triumph under Tip O'Neill's playbook was a failure in a more nationalized age. Not only were the Nebraska-specific payments attacked and scrapped from the final health reform bill, but Nelson saw the writing on the wall and retired rather than seeking reelection in 2012. The days of building cross-party legislative coalitions in Congress seem as outdated as Nelson's strategy for protecting his seat. Nationalization is an element in recent political polarization that is as critical as it is overlooked.

Notes

Chapter One

1. In fact, both Gellner (1983) and Anderson (1991) emphasize the role of print media in making national communities conceivable in the first place.

Chapter Two

1. Writing about the period from 1888 to 1896, Jensen (1971) notes that "the prevalence of party loyalty was evident in the focus on national issues in races where national problems had no bearing. Candidates for state and local office were more likely to take stands on the tariff than on local taxation" (8).

2. None of this is intended to romanticize urban political machines: in truth, those organizations typically lacked both the incentives and the resources to mobilize broad swaths of the electorate (Erie 1988). Even so, it remains the case that prior to the 1960s, the political parties could count on extensive networks of local organizations and activists in many places (Mayhew 1986).

3. It is true that party voting and incumbency are not necessarily opposites, as Ansolabehere and Snyder (2002) point out. In fact, Ansolabehere et al. (2006) report that when Minnesota switched to using partisan primaries and ballots in 1973, both party-line voting and the incumbency advantage rose.

Chapter Three

1. A 2 denotes weak Democrats, while a 3 denotes Democratic leaners, a 4 denotes pure Independents, a 5 denotes Republican leaners, and a 6 denotes weak Republicans. For more, see Keith et al. 1992.

2. Multilevel models differ from classical regression models in that they

incorporate random errors at different levels of the data, such as at the individual and state levels simultaneously.

3. Specifically, education was measured using a six-category measure, income was measured using a five-category measure, race was measured using binary indicators for African Americans and respondents who identify as "other," gender was measured using an indicator variable for males, and religious identification was measured using indicator variables for Catholic, Protestant, and Jewish identifiers.

4. Even including respondents from the South, the ICC for 2012 rises only to 0.016.

5. On this point, see Fiorina, Abrams, and Pope (2005), who write that "rather, unmeasured changes in the positions of the candidates make it appear that voters have changed. The point has extremely important (and damaging) implications for literally hundreds of electoral analyses carried out over the past forty years. Because candidate positions generally are not measured . . . even when studies use identical measures of voter attitudes, statistical estimates will confound voter change with candidate change" (127–28).

6. On differences between midterm and presidential electorates, see Campbell (1960), Erikson (1988), Campbell (1991), and Rogers (2013).

7. Virginia currently holds its gubernatorial elections in the year immediately following the presidential election but held midterm gubernatorial elections between 1954 and 1970.

8. Specifically, the exit polls were conducted in select precincts in person by Voter Research and Surveys, Voter News Service, and then Edison Media Research and Mitofsky International.

9. Both the variables of interest are binary, so we use a polychoric correlation.

10. The list includes partisan identification, income, education, race, Hispanic ethnicity, age, and urban and suburban residence.

11. Specifically, the dependent variable is the share of the two-party vote going to the Democratic candidate. The regression models include the presidential candidates' home states at the time of the election (coded 1 for Democrats and −1 for Republicans), the vice presidential candidate's home states (coded 1 for Democrats and −1 for Republicans), and fixed effects for states and years.

12. The excluded states are the six New England states as well as Alaska, Kansas, and Mississippi. In all, we employ 2,853 counties in these analyses. The 2016 data are from Pettigrew (2017).

Chapter Four

1. Both questions asked if respondents "happened to know" the name of the vice president of the United States, and neither provided response options. The

1945 poll was conducted between February 3 and February 8 using 1,500 telephone interviews. The 1996 poll was conducted between June 27 and June 30 and included 1,004 telephone interviews.

2. McCutcheon et al. v. Federal Election Commission (U.S. District Court for the District of Columbia, June 22, 2012), Verified Complaint for Declaratory and Injunctive Relief.

3. Lee Drutman performed the calculation. Contributions below $200 are not individually reported, making a comparable analysis impossible. However, as Gimpel, Lee, and Pearson-Merkowitz (2008) note, contributions in amounts less than $200 accounted for no more than 12 percent of campaigns' total funds between 2000 and 2004 (377).

4. The remaining states elect their governors in odd years, whether in the year following the presidential election (New Jersey and Virginia) or in the year preceding it (Kentucky, Louisiana, and Mississippi).

5. The data are available online at http://www.electproject.org/ (accessed December 13, 2014).

Chapter Five

1. One exception comes from states like New York that allow third parties to "fuse" and endorse major-party candidates (Sifry 2013).

2. In the words of King (1996), "The geographic variation is usually quite large to begin with, but after we control for what we have learned about voters, there isn't much left for contextual effects" (160).

3. For examples, see Wright (1977); Giles and Buckner (1993); Glaser (1994); Bledsoe, Welch, and Sigelman (1995); Glaser and Gilens (1997); Hero (1998); Taylor (1998); Burns and Gimpel (2000); Oliver and Mendelberg (2000); Oliver and Wong (2003); Tolbert and Grummel (2003); Marschall and Stolle (2004); Branton and Jones (2005); Campbell, Wong, and Citrin (2006); Gay (2006); Putnam (2007); Bafumi and Herron (2009); Dancygier (2010); Ha (2010); Hopkins (2010, 2011b); Newman (2012); Enos (2014, 2015); Dinesen and Sonderskov (2015); Acharya et al. (2016); Hersh and Nall (2016).

4. Technically, this means assuming "ignorability" conditional on the included variables; see Imbens (2004).

5. Also, the effect of living in a changing community might differ from the effect of moving to a new community, even though both fall under the heading of contextual effects.

6. The specific question read, "Should federal spending on defense be increased, decreased, or kept about the same?"

7. For binary outcomes, we use logistic regression. Otherwise, we use ordinary least squares. For examples of the statistical models, see appendix table 1.

8. By "parsimonious," we mean the model with fewer variables.

9. Age and income are included as continuous measures, and the change in income between 2000 and 2004 is included in models of 2004 responses from the ANES panel.

10. For a similar statistical modeling approach, see Putnam (2007). With the possible exception of income, all of these variables are causally prior to the contextual measures of interest, making their inclusion reasonable.

11. In the appendix, we also present results in which we vary the distances and thresholds for measuring each local context (see also Dinesen and Sonderskov 2015). The goal of these analyses is to show that the broad pattern of results is not the product of specific measurement decisions.

12. Specifically, the question read: "Listed below are various areas of government spending. Please indicate whether you would like to see more or less government spending in each area. Remember that if you say 'much more,' it might require a tax increase to pay for it . . . the police and law enforcement."

13. Here, too, the result is not especially sensitive to our definition of high crime. As appendix figure 14 shows, for a substantively meaningful range from the 60th percentile to the 85th percentile threshold for high crime rates, the results are statistically significant.

14. Of the respondents, 464 did not provide a valid ZIP code.

15. Specifically, the question asked: "How would you rate economic conditions in this country today . . . as excellent, good, only fair, or poor?"

16. Those values are similar for other years.

17. This question was asked of subsets of respondents in 1993, 1994, and 2000.

18. It was asked of subsets in 1993, 1994, 1996, 1998, and 2000.

19. In fact, appendix figures 16 and 17 illustrate that there is no meaningful threshold at which people living in more heavily polluted areas are demonstrably more likely to perceive air pollution as a threat.

20. The specific language asked, "As I name some issues that are in the news these days, please tell me how important the issue is to you personally. . . . Global warming."

21. Again, to see this result's robustness to different thresholds, see appendix figure 18. For any distance threshold examined here, people who live within that distance from an ocean coastline are in fact more likely to say that climate change is important. Statistically, the difference is only significant for those living in a ZIP code within two miles of the coastline.

22. As appendix figure 19 makes clear, those who live near nuclear power plants are no less supportive of building more nuclear plants—and for thresholds of between 57 and 84 miles, they are significantly more supportive.

23. The researcher was unable to directly supervise any aspect of the survey implementation, so all details are as reported by the call center. To complete the survey, 4,324 randomly selected phone numbers were called. Of them, 860 people

refused to participate, 1,333 calls reached an answering machine, 1,159 calls were not answered, and 572 calls reached a disconnected number. The AAPOR RR1 Response Rate is 10.4 percent.

24. Specifically, the survey question read: "As you might know, the states of Idaho and Montana recently approved hunting to reduce the number of wolves in this region. Some people argue that the wolf population needs to be reduced to prevent attacks on livestock and big game animals. Other people argue that wolves are too endangered and too important to the environment to allow wolf hunting. Thinking about the wolf population in this region, do you feel that wolf hunting 1) should stop immediately; 2) should continue until the wolf population is reduced slightly; 3) should continue until the wolf population is reduced substantially; or 4) should continue until the wolf population is eliminated."

25. In appendix figure 21, we see that across a variety of distance thresholds, respondents living near federal lands are never less likely to prefer the federal government, but we also see no significant effects.

26. This procedure requires identifying a unique ZIP code for each census tract, which we do by finding the ZIP code that contains the largest share of residences for each census tract. The crosswalk file we use is at http://www.huduser.org /portal/datasets/usps_crosswalk.html.

Chapter Six

1. In the words of Hernan (2015), "Social sciences, on the other hand, tend to ask questions that do not lend themselves to experimentation or even to emulation of an experiment using observational data. Hence, there is greater dependence on theoretical models to fill in the gaps and to provide a scaffolding to organize the various empirical findings" (103–4).

2. In the former case, regional differences in voting are the result of clustering where different types of people live. In the latter case, those differences stem instead from the fact that political candidates and parties only target people in certain places.

3. Like Chhibber and Kollman (2004), Schattschneider (1960) was also attentive to the changing distribution of authority in the federal system, noting that "one of the most remarkable developments in recent American politics is the extent to which the federal, state, and local governments have become involved in doing the same kinds of things in large areas of public policy" (10). Those words are surely more true today than they were in 1960, as the intervening decades have seen increased federal involvement in education, criminal justice, health care, and other areas that were traditionally the purview of the states (Lunch 1987; Greve 2012).

4. The data were drawn from the Tax Policy Center, http://www.taxpolicycenter .org/statistics/source-revenue-share-gdp (accessed September 14, 2016).

5. On the highly localized voting patterns of the New Deal, see Darmofal (2008).

6. The data were obtained via VoteView, http://www.voteview.com/political _polarization_2015.html (accessed September 19, 2016).

Chapter Seven

1. Loughry 2006, 11.

2. There is also no evidence of convergence over time: the standard deviation of the average ideal point across state Republican parties actually grows slightly over this period.

3. Dan Coffey, Daniel Galvin, Gerald Gamm, John Henderson, and Justin Phillips helpfully shared many platforms as well.

4. To improve the quality of the topics LDA returns, we manually divided the platforms into segments addressing the same issue, resulting in a total of 37,092 platform segments. We also performed standard preprocessing techniques, such as stemming the words and removing punctuation (Hopkins and King 2010; Grimmer and Stewart 2013). LDA uses a multilevel model to identify clusters of words that tend to occur within documents. We recover similar results when using the structural topic model developed by Roberts et al. (2014).

5. For additional details about estimation, see Hopkins and Schickler (2016).

6. For a different statistical approach to analyzing state party platforms between 1952 and 2014, see Hatch (2016).

7. Specifically, the first question read as follows: "If you had to describe the Democratic/Republican Party in your state in one sentence, what would you say?"

8. The corresponding standard errors are 0.39 and 0.33.

9. They also correlate with the scores for gubernatorial candidates reported by Bonica (2014) at 0.71 for Democrats and 0.55 for Republicans. Using those scores derived from campaign donations produces the same substantive conclusions.

10. As independent variables, we include indicator variables for Democrats, Republicans, respondents with incomes under $50,000, respondents who did not complete high school, respondents who did complete high school, respondents who completed college, males, blacks, Hispanics, respondents ages 18–29, respondents ages 30–44, and respondents ages 45–64. The models are clustered at the state level.

Chapter Eight

1. https://books.google.com/ngrams.

2. When we use the similar "I am an American," we get a Pearson's correlation of 0.66. Note, however, that adding the "an" leads to a much larger number of examples and so swamps the variation in the state-level metrics.

3. SSI recruits panelists willing to take online surveys through various procedures including emails lists and online advertisements, making these opt-in samples likely to overrepresent people who are politically engaged. The sample sizes are 812 respondents for the September 2013 survey and 1,106 respondents for the 2015 survey.

4. The importance of family roles echoes the 1995 results for a nationally representative sample reported by Abrams and Fiorina (2012).

5. The other statements were "I'm not very interested in what others think about my state/country," "When someone criticizes the state/country where I live, I don't take it as a personal insult," "When someone praises my state/country, it feels like a personal compliment," and "I act like a person from my state/country to a great extent."

6. Specifically, the questions were all formatted in parallel to this one: "We'd like to know how important various things are to your sense of who you are. When you think about yourself, how important is your place of residence to your sense of who you are?" Respondents were also asked about their occupation, ethnic or racial background, religion, and about being American.

7. In a pilot survey with an online convenience sample conducted via SSI in September 2013, we assessed the strength of local identities using a six-item battery that has been widely used and validated (Mael and Tetrick 1992). It includes true-or-false questions, such as "I'm not very interested in what others think about my community" and "My community's successes are my successes." A Pearson's correlation is a measure of linear association between two variables. Here, the Pearson's correlation between the overall scale and the "insult" item is 0.59, making the item a reasonable (if imperfect) stand-in for the scale as a whole.

8. These results on the dominance of national identity echo findings from both the 1996 and 2004 General Social Survey. The latter of those surveys found that 51 percent of Americans reported feeling very close to America, while 23 percent reported feeling very close to both their state and their city or town.

9. Technically, these are ordinary least squares (OLS) models in which we identify how an outcome variable changes as a linear function of several independent variables.

10. This finding is especially noteworthy given arguments that white southerners are more likely to adhere to an "honor culture" in which protecting one's reputation is paramount (Nisbett and Cohen 1996).

11. Since we are not considering state or regional attachments, we omit the indicator for living in the South.

12. While we do not have a manipulation check, respondents took the task seriously. Only 8 percent failed to provide a response, and a significant majority of the responses provided were meaningful, positive aspects of communities, such as their safety, diversity, landscapes, or amenities.

13. A randomly selected 478 respondents were asked to first write about what they were most proud of about their community, while 536 were simply asked about

the chance they would support their incumbent member of Congress. The mean score on the 0–4 scale in the pride condition was 2.21, while in the control condition it was 2.12, producing a gap highly similar to the experiment above. The corresponding *p*-value is 0.19.

14. Specifically, it asked, "Thinking about [the United States of America/your state], what are you most proud of?"

Chapter Nine

1. These word stems included any word that begins with the following letters: "Congress," "Democrat," "governor," "gov.," "gubernatorial," "legislature," "mayor," "president," "rep.," "representative," "Republican," "Senat," "assembly," "ald," "city manager," "commission," "council," "delegate," "incumben," "municipal," "ordinance," "ward," "local government," "township," "department," "budget," "apportionment," "partisan," "local politics," "public officials," "non-partisan," "nonpartisan," "campaign," and "election." The presidency received more attention in the 1930s, 1950s, and 1960s than in other decades. And in both outlets, while the presidency tends to attract the most attention, there is some level of attention to subnational political figures as well.

2. In its basic version, LDA is an unsupervised, multilevel approach to text analysis that models each document as a draw from a corpus-level topic distribution and then models words within each document as drawn from those topics.

3. For national politics, we chose the terms "president," "Congress," "Senate," "Bush," "Clinton," "Reagan," "Cheney," "Gore," "Quayle," "White House," "congressman," "Democrat," and "Republican." At the state level, we chose "governor," "lieutenant governor," "assembly," "legislature," "statehouse," and "delegate." At the local level, we chose "mayor," "city manager," "council," "alderman," "municipal," "county government," "City Hall," "commissioner," "councilmember," "township," and "ordinance."

4. Specifically, we do so using a linear model that includes the year, the year squared, and fixed effects for each newspaper except one.

5. These states include Arkansas, Colorado, Florida, Hawaii, Massachusetts, Minnesota, Nevada, Oklahoma, Tennessee, Texas, and Washington.

6. While there is reason to think that survey respondents overstate their actual media consumption (Prior 2009b), there is less reason to think that their overreporting will vary across media types.

7. Logistic regressions are linear models designed to analyze binary outcomes.

8. Specifically, it read, "Do you happen to know the name of your state's governor? If so, please write that person's name and then describe him or her to someone from elsewhere in one sentence. Don't worry about spelling, and if you don't happen to know who your governor is, there is no need to look it up—please just write 'don't know.'"

9. Notice that both of these estimates are in the range we would expect given other surveys, as detailed in figure 4.1 in chapter 4.

10. Specifically, at the individual level, our models include measures of education, income, age, gender, race/ethnicity, partisan identification, the extremity of partisan identification, having children, being married, and owning a home. We also include county-level measures, such as each respondent's county's percentage of black residents, its percentage of Hispanic residents, its percentage of residents with a bachelor's degree, its median income, its population density, and its total population. All of these variables have been connected to political engagement in at least some research (Oliver 2001; Hopkins and Williamson 2012).

11. The associated 95 percent confidence interval runs from 3.4 to 19.7 percentage points.

12. The estimated effect is −9.7 percentage points, with a wide 95 percent confidence interval from −31.3 to 15.1.

13. Again, given the question wording, it is also possible that some share of the respondents didn't understand the distinction between network news and local television news, as network TV news named stations such as ABC, NBC, and CBS with local affiliates.

14. The 95 percent confidence interval is between 2.5 percentage points and 15.6 percentage points.

Chapter Ten

1. New State Ice Co. v. Liebmann, 285 U.S. 262 (1932) (Brandeis, J., dissenting).

References

Abdelal, Rawi, Yoshiko M. Herrera, Alastair Iain Johnston, and Rose McDermott. 2006. "Identity as a Variable." *Perspectives on Politics* 4 (4): 695–711.

Abrajano, Marisa A., and R. Michael Alvarez. 2010. *New Faces, New Voices: The Hispanic Electorate in America*. Princeton, NJ: Princeton University Press.

Abramowitz, Alan I., and Kyle L. Saunders. 2008. "Is Polarization a Myth?" *Journal of Politics* 70 (2): 542–55.

Abramowitz, Alan, and Steven Webster. 2016. "All Politics Is National: The Rise of Negative Partisanship and the Nationalization of US House and Senate Elections in the 21st Century." *Electoral Studies* 41:12–22.

Abrams, Samuel J., and Morris P. Fiorina. 2012. "'The Big Sort' That Wasn't: A Skeptical Reexamination." *PS: Political Science & Politics* 45 (2): 203–10.

Acharya, Avidit, Matthew Blackwell, and Maya Sen. 2016. "The Political Legacy of American Slavery." *Journal of Politics* 78 (3): 621–41.

Achen, Christopher H., and Larry M. Bartels. 2016. *Democracy for Realists: Why Elections Do Not Produce Responsive Government*. Princeton, NJ: Princeton University Press.

Achen, Christopher H., and W. Phillips Shively. 1995. *Cross-Level Inference*. Chicago: University of Chicago Press.

Adams, Greg D. 1997. "Abortion: Evidence of an Issue Evolution." *American Journal of Political Science* 41 (3): 718–37.

Ahler, Douglas J., and Broockman, David E. 2017. "The Delegate Paradox: Why Polarized Politicians Can Represent Citizens Best." Stanford University Graduate School of Business Research Paper No. 17-30. Available at SSRN: https://ssrn.com/abstract=2958017.

Aisch, Gregor, and Robert Gebeloff. 2014. "Mapping Migration in the United States." *New York Times*, August 15.

Albertson, Bethany, and Shana Kushner Gadarian. 2015. *Anxious Politics: Democratic Citizenship in a Threatening World*. New York: Cambridge University Press.

Alderman, Derek H., and Robert Maxwell Beavers. 1999. "Heart of Dixie Revisited: An Update on the Geography of Naming in the American South." *Southeastern Geographer* 39 (2): 190–205.

Aldrich, John H. 1993. "Rational Choice and Turnout." *American Journal of Political Science* 5 (7): 246–78.

———. 1995. *Why Parties? The Origin and Transformation of Party Politics in America*. Chicago: University of Chicago Press.

Althaus, Scott L., Anne M. Cizmar, and James G. Gimpel. 2009. "Media Supply, Audience Demand, and the Geography of News Consumption in the United States." *Political Communication* 26 (3): 249–77.

Althaus, Scott L., and Todd C. Trautman. 2008. "The Impact of Television Market Size on Voter Turnout in American Elections." *American Politics Research* 36 (6): 824–56.

Anderson, Benedict. 1991. *Imagined Communities: Reflections on the Origin and Spread of Nationalism*. New York: Verso.

Ansolabehere, Stephen, Shigeo Hirano, James M. Snyder, and Michiko Ueda. 2006. "Party and Incumbency Cues in Voting: Are They Substitutes?" *Quarterly Journal of Political Science* 1 (2): 119–37.

Ansolabehere, Stephen, Marc Meredith, and Erik Snowberg. 2011. "Sociotropic Voting and the Media." In *Improving Public Opinion Surveys: Interdisciplinary Innovation and the American National Election Studies*, edited by John Aldrich and Kathleen McGraw, 175–90. Princeton, NJ: Princeton University Press.

Ansolabehere, Stephen, and James M. Snyder. 2002. "The Incumbency Advantage in US Elections: An Analysis of State and Federal Offices, 1942–2000." *Election Law Journal* 1 (3): 315–38.

Anzia, Sarah F. 2013. *Timing and Turnout: How Off-Cycle Elections Favor Organized Groups*. Chicago: University of Chicago Press.

Arceneaux, Kevin. 2005. "Using Cluster Randomized Field Experiments to Study Voting Behavior." *Annals of the American Academy of Political and Social Science* 601 (1): 169–79.

———. 2006. "The Federal Face of Voting: Are Elected Officials Held Accountable for the Functions Relevant to Their Office?" *Political Psychology* 27 (5): 731–54.

Arceneaux, Kevin, and Martin Johnson. 2013. *Changing Minds or Changing Channels? Partisan News in an Age of Choice*. Chicago: University of Chicago Press.

Arceneaux, Kevin, Martin Johnson, René Lindstädt, and Ryan J. Vander Wielen. 2016. "The Influence of News Media on Political Elites: Investigating Strategic Responsiveness in Congress." *American Journal of Political Science* 60 (1): 5–29.

Arceneaux, Kevin, Martin Johnson, and Chad Murphy. 2012. "Polarized Political Communication, Oppositional Media Hostility, and Selective Exposure." *Journal of Politics* 74 (1): 174–86.

Arceneaux, Kevin, and David W. Nickerson. 2009. "Who Is Mobilized to Vote? A

Re-Analysis of 11 Field Experiments." *American Journal of Political Science* 53 (1): 1–16.

Ashworth, Scott. 2012. "Electoral Accountability: Recent Theoretical and Empirical Work." *Annual Review of Political Science* 15:183–201.

Bafumi, Joseph, and Michael Herron. 2009. "Prejudice, Black Threat, and the Racist Voter in the 2008 Presidential Election." *Journal of Political Marketing* 8 (4): 334–48.

Bafumi, Joseph, and Robert Y. Shapiro. 2009. "A New Partisan Voter." *Journal of Politics* 71 (1): 1–24.

Banfield, Edward C. 1961. *Political Influence*. Piscataway, NJ: Transaction.

Barber, Michael, and Nolan McCarty. 2013. "Causes and Consequences of Polarization." In *Task Force on Negotiating Agreement in Politics*, edited by Jane Mansbridge and Cathie Jo Martin, 19–53. Washington, DC: American Political Science Association.

Barro, Robert J., Xavier Sala-i Martin, Olivier Jean Blanchard, and Robert E. Hall. 1991. "Convergence across States and Regions." *Brookings Papers on Economic Activity* 22 (1): 107–82.

Bartels, Larry. 1998. "Panel Attrition and Panel Conditioning in American National Election Studies." Paper prepared for the 1998 meetings of the Society for Political Methodology, San Diego.

———. 2002. "Beyond the Running Tally: Partisan Bias in Political Perceptions." *Political Behavior* 24 (2): 117–50.

———. 2006. "What's the Matter with Kansas?" *Quarterly Journal of Political Science* 1 (2): 201–26.

———. 2008. *Unequal Democracy: The Political Economy of the New Gilded Age*. New York: Russell Sage Foundation.

Baum, Matthew. 2003. *Soft News Goes to War: Public Opinion and American Foreign Policy in the New Media Age*. Princeton, NJ: Princeton University Press.

Baumgartner, Frank R., and Bryan D. Jones. 1993. *Agendas and Instability in American Politics*. Chicago: University of Chicago Press.

———. 2013. "Policy Agendas Project." Accessed January 15, 2013. http://www.policyagendas.org/.

Baybeck, Brady, and Robert Huckfeldt. 2002. "Spatially Dispersed Ties among Interdependent Citizens: Connecting Individuals and Aggregates." *Political Analysis* 10 (3): 261–75.

BC University Libraries. 2002. "Tip O'Neill and BC." http://www.bc.edu/libraries/about/exhibits/burnsvirtual/oneill/4.html.

Beard, Charles A. 1913. *An Economic Interpretation of the Constitution of the United States*. New York: Macmillan.

Bednar, Jenna. 2015. "The Resilience of the American Federal System." In *Oxford Handbook of the United States Constitution*, edited by Mark Tushnet, Sanford Levinson, and Mark Graber, 283–302. Oxford, UK: Oxford University Press.

Bednar, Jenna, and Elisabeth R. Gerber. 2015. "Geography, Campaign Contributions and Representation." Working paper, University of Michigan.

Beer, Samuel Hutchison. 1993. *To Make a Nation: The Rediscovery of American Federalism*. Cambridge, MA: Harvard University Press.

Bensel, Richard F. 1984. *Sectionalism and American Political Development*. Madison: University of Wisconsin Press.

Berelson, Bernard, Paul Felix Lazarsfeld, and William N. McPhee. 1954. *Voting: A Study of Opinion Change in a Presidential Election*. Chicago: University of Chicago Press.

Berinsky, Adam J., and Donald R. Kinder. 2006. "Making Sense of Issues through Media Frames: Understanding the Kosovo Crisis." *Journal of Politics* 68 (3): 640–56.

Berman, Russell. 2015. "Kansas's Failed Experiment." *Atlantic*, April 9. https://www.theatlantic.com/politics/archive/2015/04/kansass-failed-experiment/389874/.

Bernstein, Jonathan. 2000. "The New New Presidential Elite." In *In Pursuit of the White House 2000: How We Choose Our Presidential Nominees*, edited by William G. Mayer, 145–78. New York: Chatham House.

Berry, Christopher R. 2009. *Imperfect Union: Representation and Taxation in Multilevel Governments*. New York: Cambridge University Press.

Berry, Christopher R., and William G. Howell. 2007. "Accountability and Local Elections: Rethinking Retrospective Voting." *Journal of Politics* 69 (3): 844–58.

Bertrand, Marianne, and Adair Morse. 2013. "Trickle-Down Consumption." Working paper, University of Chicago.

Binder, Sarah A. 2003. *Stalemate: Causes and Consequences of Legislative Gridlock*. Washington, DC: Brookings Institution.

Birkhead, Nathaniel. 2011. "Party Polarization in State and Nation." Paper presented at the State Politics and Policy Conference, Dartmouth University, Dartmouth, New Hampshire, June 2.

Birnbaum, Jeffrey H., and Alan S. Murray. 1987. *Showdown at Gucci Gulch: Lawmakers, Lobbyists, and the Unlikely Triumph of Tax Reform*. New York: Vintage Books.

Bishop, Bill. 2009. *The Big Sort: Why the Clustering of Like-Minded America Is Tearing Us Apart*. New York: Houghton Mifflin Harcourt.

Black, Earl, and Merle Black. 2009. *The Rise of Southern Republicans*. Cambridge, MA: Harvard University Press.

Blalock, Hubert M. 1967. *Toward a Theory of Minority-Group Relations*. New York: John Wiley and Sons.

Bledsoe, Timothy, Susan Welch, and Lee Sigelman. 1995. "Residential Context and Racial Solidarity among African Americans." *American Journal of Political Science* 39 (2): 434–58.

Blei, David M., Andrew Y. Ng, and Michael I. Jordan. 2003. "Latent Dirichlet Allocation." *Journal of Machine Learning Research* 3:993–1022.

Bond, Robert M., Christopher J. Fariss, Jason J. Jones, Adam D. I. Kramer, Cameron Marlow, Jaime E. Settle, and James H. Fowler. 2012. "A 61-Million-Person Experiment in Social Influence and Political Mobilization." *Nature* 489 (7415): 295–98.

Bonica, Adam. 2014. "Mapping the Ideological Marketplace." *American Journal of Political Science* 58 (2): 367–86.

Books, John, and Charles Prysby. 1999. "Contextual Effects on Retrospective Economic Evaluations: The Impact of the State and Local Economy." *Political Behavior* 21 (1): 1–16.

Brader, Ted. 2006. *Campaigning for Hearts and Minds: How Emotional Appeals in Political Ads Work*. Chicago: University of Chicago Press.

Brader, Ted, Nicholas Valentino, and Elizabeth Suhay. 2008. "Is It Immigration or the Immigrants? The Emotional Influence of Groups on Public Opinion and Political Action." *American Journal of Political Science* 52 (4): 959–78.

Brady, David W., Robert D'Onofrio, and Morris P. Fiorina. 2000. "The Nationalization of Electoral Forces Revisited." In *Continuity and Change in House Elections*, edited by David W. Brady, John F. Cogan, and Morris P. Fiorina, 130–48. Palo Alto, CA: Stanford University Press.

Branton, Regina P., and Bradford S. Jones. 2005. "Re-examining Racial Attitudes: The Conditional Relationship between Diversity and Socioeconomic Environment." *American Journal of Political Science* 49 (2): 359–72.

Broockman, David E., and Christopher Skovron. 2013. "What Politicians Believe about Their Constituents: Asymmetric Misperceptions and Prospects for Constituency Control." Working paper, University of California, Berkeley.

Brosius, Hans-Bernd, and Anke Bathelt. 1994. "The Utility of Exemplars in Persuasive Communications." *Communication Research* 21 (1): 48–78.

Bui, Quoctrung, and Margot Sanger-Katz. 2016. "Why the Government Owns So Much Land in the West." *New York Times*, January 6, A14.

Burden, Barry C., and David C. Kimball. 1998. "A New Approach to the Study of Ticket Splitting." *American Political Science Review* 92 (3): 533–44.

———. 2002. *Why Americans Split Their Tickets: Campaigns, Competition, and Divided Government*. Ann Arbor: University of Michigan Press.

Burden, Barry C., and Amber Wichowsky. 2010. "Local and National Forces in Congressional Elections." In *The Oxford Handbook of American Elections and Political Behavior*, edited by Jan E. Leighley, 453–70. New York: Oxford University Press.

Burnett, Craig M., and Vladimir Kogan. 2017. "The Politics of Potholes: Service Quality and Retrospective Voting in Local Elections." *Journal of Politics* 79 (1): 302–14.

Burns, Nancy. 1994. *The Formation of American Local Governments: Private Values in Public Institutions*. New York: Oxford University Press.

Burns, Peter, and James G. Gimpel. 2000. "Economic Insecurity, Prejudicial

Stereotypes, and Public Opinion on Immigration Policy." *Political Science Quarterly* 115 (2): 201–25.

Butler, Daniel M., and David W. Nickerson. 2011. "Can Learning Constituency Opinion Affect How Legislators Vote? Results from a Field Experiment." *Quarterly Journal of Political Science* 6 (1): 55–83.

Butler, Daniel M., and Eleanor Neff Powell. 2014. "Understanding the Party Brand: Experimental Evidence on the Role of Valence." *Journal of Politics* 76 (2): 492–505.

Callis, Robert R., and Melissa Kresin. 2015. "Residential Vacancies and Home-ownership in the Third Quarter 2015." *U.S. Census Bureau News*, October 27.

Campbell, Andrea L. 2007. "Parties, Electoral Participation, and Shifting Voting Blocs." In *The Transformation of American Politics: Activist Government and the Rise of Conservatism*, edited by Paul Pierson and Theda Skocpol, 68–102. Princeton, NJ: Princeton University Press.

Campbell, Andrea L., Cara Wong, and Jack Citrin. 2006. "'Racial Threat,' Partisan Climate, and Direct Democracy: Contextual Effects in Three California Initiatives." *Political Behavior* 28:129–50.

Campbell, Angus. 1960. "Surge and Decline: A Study of Electoral Change." *Public Opinion Quarterly* 24 (3): 397–418.

Campbell, Angus, Phillip E. Converse, Warren E. Miller, and Donald E. Stokes. 1960. *The American Voter*. New York: Wiley.

Campbell, David E. 2006. *Why We Vote: How Schools and Communities Shape Our Civic Life*. Princeton, NJ: Princeton University Press.

Campbell, James E. 1991. "The Presidential Surge and Its Midterm Decline in Congressional Elections, 1868–1988." *Journal of Politics* 53 (2): 477–87.

Caramani, Daniele. 2004. *The Nationalization of Politics: The Formation of National Electorates and Party Systems in Western Europe*. New York: Cambridge University Press.

Carmines, Edward G., and James A. Stimson. 1980. "The Two Faces of Issue Voting." *American Political Science Review* 74 (1): 78–91.

———. 1989. *Issue Evolution: Race and the Transformation of American Politics*. Princeton, NJ: Princeton University Press.

Carnes, Nicholas. 2013. *White-Collar Government: The Hidden Role of Class in Economic Policy Making*. Chicago: University of Chicago Press.

Caro, Robert A. 2012. *The Years of Lyndon Johnson: The Passage of Power*. New York: Alfred A. Knopf.

Carpini, Michael X. Delli, Scott Keeter, and J. David Kennamer. 1994. "Effects of the News Media Environment on Citizen Knowledge of State Politics and Government." *Journalism & Mass Communication Quarterly* 71 (2): 443–56.

Carsey, Thomas M. 1995. "The Contextual Effects of Race on White Voter Behavior: The 1989 New York City Mayoral Election." *Journal of Politics* 57 (1): 221–28.

Carsey, Thomas M., and Geoffrey C. Layman. 2006. "Changing Sides or Changing Minds? Party Identification and Policy Preferences in the American Electorate." *American Journal of Political Science* 50 (2): 464–77.

Carsey, Thomas M., and Gerald C. Wright. 1998. "State and National Factors in Gubernatorial and Senatorial Elections." *American Journal of Political Science* 4 (3): 994–1002.

Carson, E. Ann. 2015. "Prisoners in 2014." September 17. Bureau of Justice Statistics, US Department of Justice, Washington, DC.

Caselli, Francesco, and Wilbur John Coleman II. 2001. "The US Structural Transformation and Regional Convergence: A Reinterpretation." *Journal of Political Economy* 109 (3): 584–616.

Caughey, Devin. 2015. "The Dynamics of State Policy Liberalism, 1936–2014." *American Journal of Political Science* 60 (4): 899–913.

Cawley, R. McGreggor. 1993. *Federal Land, Western Anger: The Sagebrush Rebellion and Environmental Politics.* Lawrence: University Press of Kansas.

Chang, Jonathan, Sean Gerrish, Chong Wang, Jordan L. Boyd-Graber, and David M. Blei. 2009. "Reading Tea Leaves: How Humans Interpret Topic Models." In *Neural Information Processing Systems*, edited by Y. Bengio, D. Schuurmans, J. D. Lafferty, C. K. I. Williams, and A. Culotta, 288–96. Vancouver: Curran Associates.

Chen, Jowei, and Jonathan Rodden. 2013. "Unintentional Gerrymandering: Political Geography and Electoral Bias in Legislatures." *Quarterly Journal of Political Science* 8 (3): 239–69.

Chetty, Raj, and Nathaniel Hendren. 2015. "The Impacts of Neighborhoods on Intergenerational Mobility: Childhood Exposure Effects and County-Level Estimates." Technical report working paper. Accessed May 5, 2015. http://www .equality-of-opportunity.org/images/nbhdspaper.pdf.

Chetty, Raj, Nathaniel Hendren, and Lawrence F. Katz. 2015. "The Effects of Exposure to Better Neighborhoods on Children: New Evidence from the Moving to Opportunity Experiment." Technical report, National Bureau of Economic Research.

Chhibber, Pradeep, and Ken Kollman. 2004. *The Formation of National Party Systems: Federalism and Party Competition in Canada, Great Britain, India, and the United States.* Princeton, NJ: Princeton University Press.

Cho, Wendy K. Tam, and James G. Gimpel. 2010. "Rough Terrain: Spatial Variation in Campaign Contributing and Volunteerism." *American Journal of Political Science* 54 (1): 74–89.

———. 2012. "Geographic Information Systems and the Spatial Dimensions of American Politics." *Annual Review of Political Science* 15:443–60.

Cho, Wendy K. Tam, James G. Gimpel, and Iris S. Hui. 2012. "Voter Migration and the Geographic Sorting of the American Electorate." *Annals of the Association of American Geographers* 103 (4): 856–70.

Cho, Wendy K. Tam, and Thomas J. Rudolph. 2008. "Emanating Political Participation: Untangling the Spatial Structure behind Participation." *British Journal
of Political Science* 38 (2): 273–89.

Chwe, Michael. 2001. *Rational Ritual: Culture, Coordination, and Common Knowledge.* Princeton, NJ: Princeton University Press.

Citrin, Jack, and Donald Philip Green. 1990. "The Self-Interest Motive in American Public Opinion." *Research in Micropolitics* 3 (1): 1–28.

Coffey, Daniel J. 2007. "State Party Activists and State Party Polarization." In *The
State of the Parties,* 5th ed., edited by John C. Green and Daniel J. Coffey, 75–
92. New York: Rowman and Littlefield.

———. 2014. "Issue Ownership vs. Conflict Extension: Understanding State Party
Polarization." Paper presented at the State Politics and Policy Conference,
May 15, Bloomington, Indiana.

Cohen, Lizabeth. 2004. "A Consumers' Republic: The Politics of Mass Consumption in Postwar America." *Journal of Consumer Research* 31 (1): 236–39.

Cohen, Marty, David Karol, Hans Noel, and John Zaller. 2009. *The Party Decides:
Presidential Nominations Before and After Reform.* Chicago: University of Chicago Press.

———. 2016. "Party versus Faction in the Reformed Presidential Nominating System." *Political Science and Politics* (October): 701–8.

Cohn, Nate. 2016. "There Are More White Voters Than People Think. That's Good
News for Trump." *New York Times,* June 9. http://www.nytimes.com/2016/06/10
/upshot/there-are-more-white-voters-than-people-think-thats-good-news-for
-trump.html.

Combs, David J. Y., Caitlin A. J. Powell, David Ryan Schurtz, and Richard H.
Smith. 2009. "Politics, Schadenfreude, and Ingroup Identification: The Sometimes Happy Thing about a Poor Economy and Death." *Journal of Experimental Social Psychology* 45 (4): 635–46.

Congressional Budget Office. 2014. "The Federal Budget: An Infographic." Technical report, April 18. https://www.cbo.gov/publication/45278.

Conover, Pamela Johnston, and Stanley Feldman. 1984. "How People Organize
the Political World: A Schematic Model." *American Journal of Political Science*
28 (1): 95–126.

Converse, Philip E. 1964. "The Nature of Belief Systems in Mass Publics." In
Ideology and Discontent, edited by David Apter, 206–61. New York: Free
Press.

———. 1972. "Change in the American Electorate." In *The Human Meaning of
Social Change,* edited by Angus Campbell and Philip E. Converse, 263–338.
New York: Russell Sage Foundation.

Cooper, Brad. 2012. "Brownback Signs Big Tax Cut in Kansas." *Kansas City Star,*
May 23. http://www.kansascity.com/latest-news/article303137/Brownback-signs
-big-tax-cut-in-Kansas.html.

Cooper, Christopher A., and H. Gibbs Knotts. 2010. "Declining Dixie: Regional Identification in the Modern American South." *Social Forces* 88 (3): 1083–101.

Costa, Dora L., and Matthew E. Kahn. 2010. *Heroes and Cowards: The Social Face of War*. Princeton, NJ: Princeton University Press.

Cotter, Cornelius P., James L. Gibson, John F. Bibby, and Robert J. Huckshorn. 1984. *Party Organizations in American Politics*. Pittsburgh, PA: University of Pittsburgh Press.

Cowie, Jefferson. 2001. *Capital Moves: RCA's Seventy-Year Quest for Cheap Labor*. New York: The New Press.

Craig, Tim. 2013. "Mara, Silverman Spar over Romney, Barry in D.C. Council Race." *Washington Post*, April 4. http://www.washingtonpost.com/local/dc-pol itics/mara-silverman-spar-over-romney-barry-in-dc-council-race/2013/04/04 /679375ba-9d49-11e2-a941-a19bce7af755_story.html.

Cramer, Katherine T. 2016. *The Politics of Resentment: Rural Consciousness in Wisconsin and the Rise of Scott Walker*. Chicago: University of Chicago Press.

Cramer Walsh, Katherine. 2012. "Putting Inequality in Its Place: Rural Consciousness and the Power of Perspective." *American Political Science Review* 106 (3): 517–32.

Crano, William D. 1995. "Attitude Strength and Vested Interest." In *Attitude Strength: Antecedents and Consequences*, edited by Richard E. Petty and Jon A. Krosnick, 131–57. Mahwah, NJ: Lawrence Erlbaum.

Crenson, Matthew A. 1971. *The Un-politics of Air Pollution: A Study of Nondecisionmaking in the Cities*. Baltimore: Johns Hopkins Press.

Currie, Janet, and Reed Walker. 2011. "Traffic Congestion and Infant Health: Evidence from EZPass." *American Economic Journal* 3 (1): 65–90.

Curtin, Richard, Stanley Presser, and Eleanor Singer. 2005. "Changes in Telephone Survey Nonresponse over the Past Quarter Century." *Public Opinion Quarterly* 69 (1): 87–98.

Dahl, Robert. 1961. *Who Governs? Democracy and Power in an American City*. New Haven, CT: Yale University Press.

Dahl, Robert Alan, and Edward R. Tufte. 1973. *Size and Democracy*. Palo Alto, CA: Stanford University Press.

Dancygier, Rafaela. 2010. *Immigration and Conflict in Europe*. Princeton, NJ: Princeton University Press.

Darmofal, David. 2008. "The Political Geography of the New Deal Realignment." *American Politics Research* 36 (6): 934–61.

Dawson, Michael C. 1994. *Behind the Mule: Race and Class in African-American Politics*. Princeton, NJ: Princeton University Press.

Deaux, Kay. 2000. "Models, Meanings and Motivations." In *Social Identity Processes: Trends in Theory and Research*, edited by D. Capozza and R. Brown, 2–14. London: SAGE.

DeBlasio, Bill. 2014. "Text of Bill DeBlasio's Inauguration Speech." *New York*

Times, January 1. http://www.nytimes.com/2014/01/02/nyregion/complete-text
-of-bill-de-blasios-inauguration-speech.html?_r=0.

DellaVigna, Stefano, and Ethan Kaplan. 2007. "The Fox Effect: Media Bias and
Voting." *Quarterly Journal of Economics* 122 (3): 1187–234.

DellaVigna, Stefano, John A. List, Ulrike Malmendier, and Gautam Rao. 2014.
"Voting to Tell Others." Technical report, National Bureau of Economic
Research.

Delli Carpini, Michael X., and Scott Keeter. 1996. *What Americans Know about
Politics and Why It Matters*. New Haven, CT: Yale University Press.

Delli Carpini, Michael X., Scott Keeter, and J. David Kennamer. 1994. "Effects
of the News Media Environment on Citizen Knowledge of State Politics and
Government." *Journalism & Mass Communication Quarterly* 71 (2): 443–56.

Denvir, Daniel. 2015. "Voter Turnout in U.S. Mayoral Elections Is Pathetic, But
It Wasn't Always This Way." *City Lab*, May 22. http://www.citylab.com/politics
/2015/05/mayoral-election-voting-turnout/393737/.

Derthick, Martha. 2004. *Keeping the Compound Republic: Essays on American
Federalism*. Washington, DC: Brookings Institution Press.

Desmet, Klaus, and Marcel Fafchamps. 2005. "Changes in the Spatial Concentration of Employment across US Counties: A Sectoral Analysis 1972–2000."
Journal of Economic Geography 5 (3): 261–84.

de Souza Briggs, Xavier, Susan J. Popkin, and John Goering. 2010. *Moving to Opportunity: The Story of an American Experiment to Fight Ghetto Poverty*. New
York: Oxford University Press.

De Wit, John B. F., Enny Das, and Raymond Vet. 2008. "What Works Best: Ob-
jective Statistics or a Personal Testimonial? An Assessment of the Persuasive
Effects of Different Types of Message Evidence on Risk Perception." *Health
Psychology* 27 (1): 110.

Dilliplane, Susanna, Seth K. Goldman, and Diana C. Mutz. 2013. "Televised Exposure to Politics: New Measures for a Fragmented Media Environment." *American Journal of Political Science* 57 (1): 236–48.

DiMaggio, Paul, John Evans, and Bethany Bryson. 1996. "Have Americans' Social
Attitudes Become More Polarized?" *American Journal of Sociology* 102 (3):
690–755.

Dinesen, Peter Thisted, and Kim Mannemar Sonderskov. 2015. "Ethnic Diversity
and Social Trust: Evidence from the Micro-Context." *American Sociological
Review* 80 (3): 550–73.

Downs, Anthony. 1957. *An Economic Theory of Democracy*. New York: Harper.

Drago, Francesco, Tommaso Nannicini, and Francesco Sobbrio. 2014. "Meet the
Press: How Voters and Politicians Respond to Newspaper Entry and Exit."
American Economic Journal: Applied Economics 6 (3): 159–88.

Druckman, James N. 2003. "The Power of Television Images: The First Kennedy-
Nixon Debate Revisited." *Journal of Politics* 65 (2): 559–71.

Drutman, Lee. 2013. "The Political 1% of the 1%." Sunlight Foundation blog, June 24. http://sunlightfoundation.com/blog/2013/06/24/1pct_of_the_1pct/.

Duranton, Gilles, and Diego Puga. 2005. "From Sectoral to Functional Urban Specialisation." *Journal of Urban Economics* 57 (2): 343–70.

Durkheim, Emile. 1984. *The Division of Labor in Society*. New York: Free Press.

Edsall, Thomas B. 2015. "What If All Politics Is National?" *New York Times*, September 29. https://www.nytimes.com/2015/09/30/opinion/what-if-all-politics-is-national.html?_r=0.

Egan, Patrick J., and Megan Mullin. 2012. "Turning Personal Experience into Political Attitudes: The Effect of Local Weather on Americans Perceptions about Global Warming." *Journal of Politics* 1 (1): 1–14.

Einhorn, Robin L. 2001. *Property Rules: Political Economy in Chicago, 1833–1872*. Chicago: University of Chicago Press.

Einstein, Katherine Levine, and Vladimir Kogan. 2015. "Pushing the City Limits: Policy Responsiveness in Municipal Government." *Urban Affairs Review* 52 (1): 3–32.

Elazar, Daniel J. 1966. *American Federalism: A View from the States*. New York: Crowell. Reprint, New York: Harper & Row, 1972.

Enda, Jodi, Katerina Eva Matsa, and Jan Lauren Boyles. 2014. "American's Shifting Statehouse Press." Washington, DC: Pew Research Center.

Enos, Ryan D. 2014. "Causal Effect of Intergroup Contact on Exclusionary Attitudes." *Proceedings of the National Academy of Sciences* 111 (10): 3699–704.

———. 2015. "What the Demolition of Public Housing Teaches Us about the Impact of Racial Threat on Political Behavior." *American Journal of Political Science* 60 (1): 123–42.

Enos, Ryan D., and Anthony Fowler. 2014. "Pivotality and Turnout: Evidence from a Field Experiment in the Aftermath of a Tied Election." *Political Science Research and Methods* 2 (2): 309–19.

Epstein, Leon D. 1986. *Political Parties in the American Mold*. Madison: University of Wisconsin Press.

Erie, Stephen P. 1988. *Rainbow's End: Irish-Americans and the Dilemmas of Urban Machine Politics, 1840–1985*. Berkeley: University of California Press.

Erikson, Robert S. 1988. "The Puzzle of Midterm Loss." *Journal of Politics* 50 (4): 1011–29.

———. 2017. "The Congressional Incumbency Advantage over Sixty Years: Measurement, Trends, and Implications." In *Governing in a Polarized Age: Elections, Parties, and Political Representation in America*, edited by Alan S. Gerber and Eric Schickler, 65–89. New York: Cambridge University Press.

Erikson, Robert S., Gerald C. Wright, and John P. McIver. 1993. *Statehouse Democracy*. New York: Cambridge University Press.

Ethier, Kathleen A., and Kay Deaux. 1994. "Negotiating Social Identity When Contexts Change: Maintaining Identification and Responding to Threat." *Journal of Personality and Social Psychology* 67 (2): 243.

Evans, Diana. 2004. *Greasing the Wheels: Using Pork Barrel Projects to Build Majority Coalitions in Congress*. New York: Cambridge University Press.

Fabian, Jordan. 2010. "Obama Healthcare Plan Nixes Ben Nelson's 'Cornhusker Kickback' Deal." *The Hill*, February 22. http://thehill.com/blogs/blog-briefing-room/news/82621-obama-healthcare-plan-nixes-ben-nelsons-cornhusker-kickback-deal.

Faulkner, William. 1936. *Absalom! Absalom!* New York: Random House.

Feeley, Malcolm, and Edward Rubin. 2009. *Federalism: Political Identity and Tragic Compromise*. Ann Arbor: University of Michigan Press.

Feinstein, Brian D., and Eric Schickler. 2008. "Platforms and Partners: The Civil Rights Realignment Reconsidered." *Studies in American Political Development* 22 (1): 1–31.

Feller, Avi, Andrew Gelman, and Boris Shor. 2012. "Red State/Blue State Divisions in the 2012 Presidential Election." *Forum* 10 (4): 127–31.

Fenno, Richard F. 1978. *Home Style: House Members in Their Districts*. Harlow, UK: Pearson Longman.

Ferejohn, John. 1986. "Incumbent Performance and Electoral Control." *Public Choice* 50 (1): 5–25.

Fiorina, Morris P. 1981. *Retrospective Voting in American National Elections*. New Haven, CT: Yale University Press.

Fiorina, Morris P., Samuel J. Abrams, and Jeremy C. Pope. 2005. *Culture War?* New York: Pearson Longman.

Fischel, William A. 2001. *The Homevoter Hypothesis: How Home Values Influence Local Government Taxation, School Finance, and Land-Use Policies*. Cambridge, MA: Harvard University Press.

Fischer, Claude S. 2002. "Ever-More Rooted Americans." *City & Community* 1 (2): 177–98.

Fischer, Mary J. 2003. "The Relative Importance of Income and Race in Determining Residential Outcomes in US Urban Areas, 1970–2000." *Urban Affairs Review* 38 (5): 669.

Foner, Eric. 1988. *Reconstruction: Americas Unfinished Revolution, 1863–1877*. Vol. 9. New York: Harper & Row.

Fontana, David. Forthcoming. "The Geography of Campaign Finance Law." *Southern California Law Review*.

Fowler, Anthony. 2016. "A Bayesian Explanation for Incumbency Advantage." Working paper, Harris School of Public Policy Studies, University of Chicago.

Fox17. 2014. "3 Tennessee Supreme Court Judges Up for Election." http://www.fox17.com/news/features/top-stories/stories/3-tennessee-supreme-court-judges-up-election-sky-arnold-22442.shtml.

Frank, Robert H. 1985. *Choosing the Right Pond: Human Behavior and the Quest for Status*. New York: Oxford University Press.

Franklin, Mark N. 2004. *Voter Turnout and the Dynamics of Electoral Competition in Established Democracies since 1945*. New York: Cambridge University Press.

Franzen, Jonathan. 2010. *Freedom*. New York: Farrar, Straus and Giroux.

Frey, William H. 2009. "The Great American Migration Slowdown: Regional and Metropolitan Dimensions." Report, Brookings Institution, Washington, DC.

Fuller, Jamie. 2014. "Candidates Aren't Talking about Obamacare Much, So Why Won't the Ads Go Away?" *The Fix* (blog), *Washington Post*, July 25. http://www.washingtonpost.com/blogs/the-fix/wp/2014/07/25/candidates-arent-talking-about-obamacare-much-so-why-wont-the-ads-go-away/.

Gadarian, Shana K. 2010. "The Politics of Threat: How Terrorism News Shapes Foreign Policy Attitudes." *Journal of Politics* 72 (2): 469–83.

Gadarian, Shana Kushner, and Bethany Albertson. 2014. "Anxiety, Immigration, and the Search for Information." *Political Psychology* 35 (2): 133–64.

Gagnon, V. P. 1994. "Ethnic Nationalism and International Conflict: The Case of Serbia." *International Security* 19 (3): 130–66.

Gainsborough, Juliet F. 2001. *Fenced Off: The Suburbanization of American Politics*. Washington, DC: Georgetown University Press.

Gamm, Gerald. 1999. *Urban Exodus: Why the Jews Left Boston and the Catholics Stayed*. Cambridge, MA: Harvard University Press.

Garlick, Alex. 2015. "National Policies, Agendas and Polarization in American State Legislatures: 2011–2014." Paper presented at the Annual Meeting of the American Political Science Association, San Francisco, September 3–6.

Gay, Claudine. 2006. "Seeing Difference: The Effect of Economic Disparity on Black Attitudes toward Latinos." *American Journal of Political Science* 50:982–97.

———. 2012. "Moving to Opportunity: The Political Effects of a Housing Mobility Experiment." *Urban Affairs Review* 48 (2): 147–79.

Gellner, Ernest. 1983. *Nations and Nationalism*. Ithaca, NY: Cornell University Press.

Gelman, Andrew, and Jennifer Hill. 2006. *Data Analysis Using Regression and Multilevel/Hierarchical Models*. New York: Cambridge University Press.

Gelman, Andrew, and Zaiying Huang. 2008. "Estimating Incumbency Advantage and Its Variation as an Example of a Before-After Study." *Journal of the American Statistical Association* 103 (482): 437–46.

Gelman, Andrew, David Park, Boris Shor, Joseph Bafumi, and Jeronimo Cortina. 2008. *Red State, Blue State, Rich State, Poor State: Why Americans Vote the Way They Do*. Princeton, NJ: Princeton University Press.

Gentzkow, Matthew. 2006. "Television and Voter Turnout." *Quarterly Journal of Economics* 121 (3): 931–72.

Gentzkow, Matthew, and Jesse M. Shapiro. 2010. "What Drives Media Slant? Evidence from US Daily Newspapers." *Econometrica* 78 (1): 35–71.

Gentzkow, Matthew, Jesse M. Shapiro, and Michael Sinkinson. 2011. "The Effect of Newspaper Entry and Exit on Electoral Politics." *American Economic Review* 101:2980–3018.

Gentzkow, Matthew, Jesse M. Shapiro, and Matt Taddy. 2016. "Measuring Polarization in High-Dimensional Data: Method and Application to Congressional Speech." Working paper, Stanford University.

George, Lisa M., and Joel Waldfogel. 2006. "The New York Times and the Market for Local Newspapers." *American Economic Review* 96 (1): 435–47.

Gerber, Alan S., and Donald P. Green. 2000. "The Effects of Canvassing, Telephone Calls, and Direct Mail on Voter Turnout: A Field Experiment." *American Political Science Review* 94 (3): 653–63.

Gerber, Alan S., Donald P. Green, and Christopher W. Larimer. 2008. "Social Pressure and Voter Turnout: Evidence from a Large-Scale Voter Turnout Experiment." *American Political Science Review* 102 (1): 33–48.

Gerber, Alan S., and Gregory A. Huber. 2010. "Partisanship, Political Control, and Economic Assessments." *American Journal of Political Science* 54 (1): 153–73.

Gerber, Elisabeth R., and Daniel J. Hopkins. 2011. "When Mayors Matter: Estimating the Impact of Mayoral Partisanship on City Policy." *American Journal of Political Science* 55 (2): 326–39.

Giles, Michael W., and Melanie A. Buckner. 1993. "David Duke and Black Threat: An Old Hypothesis Revisited." *Journal of Politics* 55 (3): 702–13.

Gillion, Daniel Q., Jonathan M. Ladd, and Marc Meredith. Forthcoming. "Party Polarization, Ideological Sorting and the Emergence of the Partisan Gender Gap." *British Journal of Political Science.*

Gimpel, James G. 1996. *National Elections and the Autonomy of American State Party Systems*. Pittsburgh, PA: University of Pittsburgh Press.

Gimpel, James G., Frances E. Lee, and Joshua Kaminski. 2006. "The Political Geography of Campaign Contributions in American Politics." *Journal of Politics* 68 (3): 626–39.

Gimpel, James G., Frances E. Lee, and Shanna Pearson-Merkowitz. 2008. "The Check Is in the Mail: Interdistrict Funding Flows in Congressional Elections." *American Journal of Political Science* 52 (2): 373–94.

Gimpel, James G., and Jason E. Schuknecht. 2003. *Patchwork Nation*. Ann Arbor: University of Michigan Press.

Glaeser, Edward L., and Bryce A. Ward. 2005. "Myths and Realities of American Political Geography." Technical report, National Bureau of Economic Research, Cambridge, Massachusetts.

Glaser, James M. 1994. "Back to the Black Belt: Racial Environment and White Racial Attitudes in the South." *Journal of Politics* 56 (1): 21–41.

———. 1998. *Race, Campaign Politics, and the Realignment in the South*. New Haven, CT: Yale University Press.

Glaser, James M., and Martin Gilens. 1997. "Interregional Migration and Political Resocialization: A Study of Racial Attitudes under Pressure." *Public Opinion Quarterly* 61 (1): 72–86.

Goldfarb, Zachary A. 2014. "In Kansas, Brownback Tried a Red-State 'Experiment.' Now He May Be Paying a Political Price." *Washington Post*, July 30. https://www.washingtonpost.com/politics/in-kansas-gov-brownbacks-reelection-race-is-case-study-in-republican-party-shift/2014/07/30/3192d86c-1420-11e4-8936-26932bcfd6ed_story.html?utm_term=.d8d5bc739da9.

Goldmacher, Shane. 2016. "Rubio: 'We're Not Going to Fix America with Senators and Congressmen.'" *Politico*, January 5. http://www.politico.com/story/2016/01/marco-rubio-senate-congress-217357.

Goldman, Seth K. 2012. "Effects of the 2008 Obama Presidential Campaign on White Racial Prejudice." *Public Opinion Quarterly* 76 (4): 663–87.

Goldman, Seth K., and Daniel J. Hopkins. 2016. "Past Threat, Present Prejudice: The Impact of Adolescent Racial Context on White Racial Attitudes." SSRN Working Paper 2799347.

Goldman, Seth K., and Diana C. Mutz. 2014. *The Obama Effect: How the 2008 Campaign Changed White Racial Attitudes.* New York: Russell Sage Foundation.

Goldman, Seth K., Diana C. Mutz, and Susanna Dilliplane. 2013. "All Virtue Is Relative: A Response to Prior." *Political Communication* 30 (4): 635–53.

Goldstein, Noah J., Robert B. Cialdini, and Vladas Griskevicius. 2008. "A Room with a Viewpoint: Using Social Norms to Motivate Environmental Conservation in Hotels." *Journal of Consumer Research* 35 (3): 472–82.

Gormley, William T. 1978. "Television Coverage of State Government." *Public Opinion Quarterly* 42 (3): 354–59.

Gould, Ingrid Ellen. 2000. *Sharing America's Neighborhoods: The Prospects for Stable Racial Integration.* Cambridge, MA: Harvard University Press.

Green, Donald P., and Alan S. Gerber. 2008. *Get Out the Vote: How to Increase Voter Turnout.* Washington, DC: Brookings Institution Press.

Green, Donald P., Bradley Palmquist, and Eric Schickler. 2002. *Partisan Hearts and Minds.* New Haven, CT: Yale University Press.

Green, Donald P., Dara Z. Strolovitch, and Janelle S. Wong. 1998. "Defended Neighborhoods, Integration, and Racially Motivated Crime." *American Journal of Sociology* 104 (2): 372–403.

Greve, Michael S. 2012. *The Upside-Down Constitution.* Cambridge, MA: Harvard University Press.

Grimmer, Justin. 2013. "Appropriators Not Position Takers: The Distorting Effects of Electoral Incentives on Congressional Representation." *American Journal of Political Science* 57 (3): 624–42.

Grimmer, Justin, Solomon Messing, and Sean J. Westwood. 2012. "How Words and Money Cultivate a Personal Vote: The Effect of Legislator Credit Claiming on Constituent Credit Allocation." *American Political Science Review* 1 (1): 1–17.

Grimmer, Justin, and Brandon Stewart. 2013. "Text as Data: The Promise and Pitfalls of Automatic Content Analysis Methods for Political Texts." *Political Analysis* 21 (3): 267–97.

Grimmer, Justin, Sean J. Westwood, and Solomon Messing. 2014. *The Impression of Influence: Legislator Communication, Representation, and Democratic Accountability.* Princeton, NJ: Princeton University Press.

Grossmann, Matt, and David A. Hopkins. 2015. "Ideological Republicans and Group Interest Democrats: The Asymmetry of American Party Politics." *Perspectives on Politics* 13 (1): 119–39.

Guess, Andrew M. 2016. "Media Choice and Moderation: Evidence from Online Tracking Data." Working paper, New York University.

Ha, Shang E. 2010. "The Consequences of Multiracial Contexts on Public Attitudes toward Immigration." *Political Research Quarterly* 6 3(1): 29–42.

Hainmueller, Jens, Daniel J. Hopkins, and Teppei Yamamoto. 2014. "Causal Inference in Conjoint Analysis: Understanding Multidimensional Choices via Stated Preference Experiments." *Political Analysis* 22 (1): 1–30.

Hajnal, Zoltan L. 2007. *Changing White Attitudes toward Black Political Leadership.* New York: Cambridge University Press.

Hajnal, Zoltan L., and Taeku Lee. 2011. *Why Americans Don't Join the Party: Race, Immigration, and the Failure (of Political Parties) to Engage the Electorate.* Princeton, NJ: Princeton University Press.

Hajnal, Zoltan L., and Jessica Trounstine. 2010. "Who or What Governs? The Effects of Economics, Politics, Institutions, and Needs on Local Spending." *American Politics Research* 38 (6): 1130.

Hall, Andrew B. 2015. "What Happens When Extremists Win Primaries?" *American Political Science Review* 109 (1): 18–42.

Hamilton, Alexander, James Madison, and John Jay. 1788. *The Federalist Papers.* New York: Penguin.

Hamilton, James. 2004. *All the News That's Fit to Sell: How the Market Transforms Information into News.* Princeton, NJ: Princeton University Press.

Hatch, Rebecca S. 2015. "Party Organizational Strength and Technological Capacity: The Adaptation of the State-Level Party Organizations in the United States to Voter Outreach and Data Analytics in the Internet age." *Party Politics* 22 (2): 191–202.

———. 2016. "State Political Parties in American Politics: Innovation and Integration in the Party System." PhD dissertation, Duke University.

Hayes, Danny, and Jennifer L. Lawless. 2015. "As Local News Goes, So Goes Citizen Engagement: Media, Knowledge, and Participation in US House Elections." *Journal of Politics* 77 (2): 447–62.

Healy, Andrew, and Neil Malhotra. 2009. "Myopic Voters and Natural Disaster Policy." *American Political Science Review* 103 (3): 387–406.

Healy, Andrew J., Neil Malhotra, and Cecilia Hyunjung Mo. 2010. "Irrelevant Events Affect Voters' Evaluations of Government Performance." *Proceedings of the National Academy of Sciences* 107 (29): 12804–9.

Heim, Joe. 2016. "These Buildings Will Never, Ever Return to the Federal Government?" *Washington Post*, January 16. https://www.washingtonpost.com/local /these-buildings-will-never-ever-return-to-the-federal-government/2016/01/16 /101cb8f2-bbe4-11e5-829c-26ffb874a18d_story.html?utm_term=.1b9f9abd3a54.

Hendrickson, David C. 2003. *Peace Pact: The Lost World of the American Founding.* Lawrence: University of Kansas Press.

Henig, Jeffrey R. 2013. *The End of Exceptionalism in American Education: The*

Changing Politics of School Reform. Cambridge, MA: Harvard Education Press.

Hernan, Miguel A. 2015. "Invited Commentary: Agent-Based Models for Causal Inference—Reweighting Data and Theory in Epidemiology." *American Journal of Epidemiology* 181 (2): 103–5.

Hernandez, Raymond. 2012. "Bloomberg Backs Obama, Citing Fallout from the Storm." *New York Times*, November 1. http://www.nytimes.com/2012/11/02/ny region/bloomberg-endorses-obama-saying-hurricane-sandy-affected-decision .html.

Hero, Rodney E. 1998. *Faces of Inequality: Social Diversity in American Politics*. New York: Oxford University Press.

Hersh, Eitan. 2013. "Long-Term Effect of September 11 on the Political Behavior of Victims, Families and Neighbors." *Proceedings of the National Academy of Sciences* 110 (52): 20959–63.

———. 2015. *Hacking the Electorate*. New York: Cambridge University Press.

Hersh, Eitan D., and Clayton Nall. 2016. "The Primacy of Race in the Geography of Income-Based Voting: New Evidence from Public Voting Records." *American Journal of Political Science* 60 (2): 289–303.

Hertel-Fernandez, Alexander. 2014. "Who Passes Business's 'Model Bills'? Policy Capacity and Corporate Influence in U.S. State Politics." *Perspectives on Politics* 12 (3): 582–602.

———. 2016. "Explaining Durable Business Coalitions in U.S. Politics: Conservatives and Corporate Interests across America's Statehouses." *Studies in American Political Development* 30 (1): 1–18.

Hibbing, John R., and Elizabeth Theiss-Morse. 2002. *Stealth Democracy: Americans' Beliefs about How Government Should Work*. New York: Cambridge University Press.

Hindman, Matthew. 2009. *The Myth of Digital Democracy*. Princeton, NJ: Princeton University Press.

———. 2011. "Less of the Same: The Lack of Local News on the Internet." Report to the Federal Communications Commission. https://apps.fcc.gov/edocs_public /attachmatch/DOC-307476A1.pdf.

Hirano, Shigeo, and James M. Snyder. 2007. "The Decline of Third-Party Voting in the United States." *Journal of Politics* 69 (1): 1–16.

———. 2013. "The Direct Primary and Candidate-Centered Voting in U.S. Elections." Working paper, Columbia University, New York.

Hjorth, Frederik, Peter Thisted Dinesen, and Kim Mannemar Sonderskov. 2016. "The Content and Correlates of Subjective Local Contexts." Paper presented at the Annual Meeting of the American Political Science Association, Philadelphia, September 1–4.

Ho, Daniel E., and Kevin M. Quinn. 2009. "Viewpoint Diversity and Media Consolidation: An Empirical Study." *Stanford Law Review* 61 (4): 781–868.

Hoffman, Roy. 2016. "How to Be Liberal in Lower Alabama." *New York Times*, January 11, A23.

Hopkins, Daniel J. 2009. "No More Wilder Effect, Never a Whitman Effect: When and Why Polls Mislead about Black and Female Candidates." *Journal of Politics* 71(3): 769–81.

———. 2010. "Politicized Places: Explaining Where and When Immigrants Provoke Local Opposition." *American Political Science Review* 104 (1): 40–60.

———. 2011a. "The Limited Local Impacts of Ethnic and Racial Diversity." *American Politics Research* 39 (2): 344–79.

———. 2011b. "National Debates, Local Responses: The Origins of Local Concern about Immigration in Britain and the United States." *British Journal of Political Science* 41 (3): 499–524.

———. 2012. "Flooded Communities: Explaining Local Reactions to the Post-Katrina Migrants." *Political Research Quarterly* 65 (2): 443–59.

Hopkins, David A. 2017. *Red Fighting Blue: How Geography and Electoral Rules Polarize American Politics*. New York: Cambridge University Press.

Hopkins, Daniel J., and Gary King. 2010. "A Method of Automated Nonparametric Content Analysis for Social Science." *American Journal of Political Science* 54 (1): 229–47.

Hopkins, Daniel J., and Jonathan M. Ladd. 2014. "The Consequences of Broader Media Choice: Evidence from the Expansion of Fox News." *Quarterly Journal of Political Science* 9:115–35.

Hopkins, Daniel J., and Jonathan Mummolo. 2017. "Assessing the Breadth of Framing Effects." *Quarterly Journal of Political Science* 12 (1): 37–57.

Hopkins, Daniel J., and Lindsay M. Pettingill. Forthcoming. "Retrospective Voting in Big-City U.S. Mayoral Elections." *Political Science Research and Methods*.

Hopkins, Daniel J., and Eric Schickler. 2016. "The Nationalization of State Party Platforms, 1918–2014." Paper presented at the Annual Meeting of the American Political Science Association, Philadelphia, September 1–4.

Hopkins, Daniel J., and Thad Williamson. 2012. "Inactive by Design? Neighborhood Design and Political Participation." *Political Behavior* 34 (1): 79–101.

Horiuchi, Yusaku. 2005. *Institutions, Incentives and Electoral Participation in Japan: Cross-level and Cross-national Perspectives*. New York: Routledge.

Howell, William G. 2003. *Power without Persuasion: The Politics of Direct Presidential Action*. Princeton, NJ: Princeton University Press.

Howell, William G., Saul P. Jackman, and Jon C. Rogowski. 2013. *The Wartime President: Executive Influence and the Nationalizing Politics of Threat*. Chicago: University of Chicago Press.

Huber, Gregory A., and Kevin Arceneaux. 2007. "Identifying the Persuasive Effects of Presidential Advertising." *American Journal of Political Science* 51 (4): 957–77.

Huckfeldt, Robert, Paul E. Johnson, and John Sprague. 2004. *Political Disagreement: The Survival of Diverse Opinions within Communication Networks*. New York: Cambridge University Press.

Huckfeldt, Robert, and John Sprague. 1990. "Social Order and Political Chaos: The Structural Setting of Political Information." In *Information and Democratic Processes*, edited by John A. Ferejohn and James H. Kuklinski, 23–58. Chicago: University of Illinois.

———. 1995. *Citizens, Politics and Social Communication: Information and Influence in an Election Campaign*. New York: Cambridge University Press.

Huddy, Leonie. 2013. "From Group Identity to Political Cohesion and Commitment." In *Oxford Handbook of Political Psychology*, edited by Leonie Huddy, David O. Sears, and Robert Jervis, 738–63. New York: Oxford University Press.

Huddy, Leonie, Stanley Feldman, Theresa Capelos, and Colin Provost. 2002. "The Consequences of Terrorism: Disentangling the Effects of Personal and National Threat." *Political Psychology* 23 (3): 485–509.

Huddy, Leonie, Lilliana Mason, and Lene Aarøe. 2015. "Expressive Partisanship: Campaign Involvement, Political Emotion, and Partisan Identity." *American Political Science Review* 109 (1): 1–17.

Hurwitz, Jon, and Mark Peffley. 2005. "Playing the Race Card in the Post-Willie Horton Era." *Public Opinion Quarterly* 69 (1): 99–112.

Imbens, Guido W. 2004. "Nonparametric Estimation of Average Treatment Effects under Exogeneity: A Review." *Review of Economics and Statistics* 86 (1): 4–29.

Iyengar, Shanto. 1991. *Is Anyone Responsible? How Television Frames Political Issues*. Chicago: University of Chicago Press.

Iyengar, Shanto, and Donald R. Kinder. 1987. *News That Matters*. Chicago: University of Chicago Press.

Iyengar, Shanto, Gaurav Sood, and Yphtach Lelkes. 2012. "Affect, Not Ideology: A Social Identity Perspective on Polarization." *Public Opinion Quarterly* 76 (3): 405–31.

Jacobson, Gary. 2011. "Partisan Differences in Job Approval Ratings of George W. Bush and U.S. Senators in the States: An Exploration." In *Facing Up to the Challenge of Democracy*, edited by Paul M. Sniderman and Benjamin Highton, 153–84. Princeton, NJ: Princeton University Press.

———. 2015. "It's Nothing Personal: The Decline of the Incumbency Advantage in US House Elections." *Journal of Politics* 77 (3): 861–73.

———. 2016. "The Electoral Connection, Then and Now." In *Governing in a Polarized Age: Elections, Parties, and Political Representation in America*, edited by Alan S. Gerber and Eric Schickler, 15–34. New York: Cambridge University Press.

Javian, Katherine S. 2012. "Party Voting in the American States: How National Factors and Institutional Variation Affect State Elections." Dissertation, Temple University.

Jensen, Richard J. 1971. *The Winning of the Midwest: Social and Political Conflict, 1888–1896*. Chicago: University of Chicago Press.

Jessee, Stephen A. 2012. *Ideology and Spatial Voting in American Elections*. New York: Cambridge University Press.

Jochim, Ashley E., and Bryan D. Jones. 2013. "Issue Politics in a Polarized Congress." *Political Research Quarterly* 66 (2): 352–69.

Johnson, Kirk. 2006. "Democrats See Surge in Power at State Level." *New York Times*, November 8. http://www.nytimes.com/2006/11/08/us/politics/09statehouse cnd.html.

Johnson, Kirk, Richard Perez-Pena, and Erik Eckholm. 2016. "Cautious Response to Armed Oregon Protest." *New York Times*, January 4. https://www.nytimes .com/2016/01/05/us/in-oregon-law-enforcement-faces-dilemma-in-confronting -armed-group.html?_r=0.

Johnston, Richard, and Andre Blais. 2012. "Alignment, Realignment, and Dealignment in Canada: The View from Above." Paper prepared at the Festschrift Conference for Andre Blais, Montreal, Quebec, January 20–21.

Johnston, Richard, Michael G. Hagen, and Kathleen Hall Jamieson. 2004. *The 2000 Presidential Election and the Foundations of Party Politics*. New York: Cambridge University Press.

Jones, Tim. 2014. "Brownback's Tax Cuts Prompt S&P to Reduce Kansas's Rating." *Bloomberg*, August 6. https://www.bloomberg.com/news/articles/2014-08-06 /brownback-s-tax-cuts-prompt-s-p-to-reduce-kansas-s-credit-rating.

Kahneman, Daniel, and Amos Tversky. 1979. "Prospect Theory: An Analysis of Decision under Risk." *Econometrica* 47 (2): 263–92.

Kalin, Michael, and Nicholas Sambanis. Forthcoming. "How Should We Think about Social Identity?" *Annual Review of Political Science*.

Karol, David. 2009. *Party Position Change in American Politics: Coalition Management*. New York: Cambridge University Press.

Kaufmann, Karen M. 2004. *The Urban Voter: Group Conflict and Mayoral Voting Behavior in American Cities*. Ann Arbor: University of Michigan Press.

Kawachi, Ichiro, Bruce P. Kennedy, Kimberly Lochner, and Deborah Prothrow-Stith. 1997. "Social Capital, Income Inequality, and Mortality." *American Journal of Public Health* 87 (9): 1491–98.

Keith, Bruce E., David B. Magleby, Candice J. Nelson, Elizabeth Orr, Mark C. Westlye, and Raymond E. Wolfinger. 1992. *The Myth of the Independent Voter*. Berkeley: University of California Press.

Kellstedt, Lyman A., John C. Green, James L. Guth, and Corwin E Smidt. 1996. "Grasping the Essentials: The Social Embodiment of Religion and Political Behavior." In *Religion and the Culture Wars: Dispatches from the Front*, edited by John C. Green, 174–92. Lanham, MD: Rowman and Littlefield.

Kernell, Samuel. 1997. *Going Public: New Strategies of Presidential Leadership*. Washington, DC: CQ Press.

Key, V. O. 1949. *Southern Politics in State and Nation*. New York: A. A. Knopf.
———. 1964. *Politics, Parties, and Pressure Groups*. New York: Crowell.

Key, V. O., and Milton C. Cummings. 1966. *The Responsible Electorate*. Cambridge, MA: Belknap.

Kim, Sukkoo. 1998. "Economic Integration and Convergence: US Regions, 1840–1987." *Journal of Economic History* 58 (3): 659–83.

Kinder, Donald R., and Lynn M. Sanders. 1996. *Divided by Color: Racial Politics and Democratic Ideals*. Chicago: University of Chicago Press.

King, Gary. 1996. "Why Context Shouldn't Count." *Political Geography* 15 (2): 159–64.

———. 1997. *A Solution to the Ecological Inference Problem: Reconstructing Individual Behavior from Aggregate Data*. Princeton, NJ: Princeton University Press.

Klar, Samara. 2013. "The Influence of Competing Identity Primes on Political Preferences." *Journal of Politics* 75 (4): 1108–24.

———. 2014. "Identity and Engagement among Political Independents in America." *Political Psychology* 35 (4): 577–91.

Klar, Samara, and Yanna Krupnikov. 2016. *Independent Politics*. New York: Cambridge University Press.

Klinghard, Daniel. 2010. *The Nationalization of American Political Parties, 1880–1896*. New York: Cambridge University Press.

Kollman, Ken. 2013. *Perils of Centralization: Lessons from Church, State, and Corporation*. New York: Cambridge University Press.

Kornbluth, Mark L. 2000. *Why Americans Stopped Voting: The Decline of Participatory Democracy and the Emergence of Modern American Politics*. New York: New York University Press.

Kousser, Thad, and Justin H. Phillips. 2012. *The Power of American Governors: Winning on Budgets and Losing on Policy*. New York: Cambridge University Press.

Kriner, Douglas L., and Andrew Reeves. 2012. "The Influence of Federal Spending on Presidential Elections." *American Political Science Review* 106 (2): 348–66.

———. 2015a. *The Particularistic President: Executive Branch Politics and Political Inequality*. New York: Cambridge University Press.

———. 2015b. "Presidential Particularism and Divide-the-Dollar Politics." *American Political Science Review* 109 (1): 155–71.

Kriner, Douglas L., and Francis X. Shen. 2007. "Iraq Casualties and the 2006 Senate Elections." *Legislative Studies Quarterly* 32 (4): 507–30.

Kruse, Kevin M. 2005. *White Flight: Atlanta and the Making of Modern Conservatism*. Princeton, NJ: Princeton University Press.

LaCroix, Alison L. 2010. *The Ideological Origins of American Federalism*. Cambridge, MA: Harvard University Press.

Lacy, Dean. 2009. "Why Do Red States Vote Republican While Blue States Pay the Bills?" Paper presented at the Annual Meeting of the American Political Science Association, Toronto, September 3–6.

Ladd, Jonathan M. 2012. *Why Americans Hate the Media and How It Matters*. Princeton, NJ: Princeton University Press.

Lakoff, George, and Mark Johnson. 1980. *Metaphors We Live By*. Chicago: University of Chicago Press.

Lane, Robert E. 1961. *Political Ideology: Why the American Common Man Believes What He Does*. New York: Free Press of Glencoe.

Lapinski, John S. 2008. "Policy Substance and Performance in American Lawmaking, 1877–1994." *American Journal of Political Science* 52 (2): 235–51.

La Raja, Ray. 2003. "State Parties and Soft Money: How Much Party Building?" In *The State of the Parties*, edited by John C. Green and Rick Farmer, 132–50. Lanham, MD: Rowman and Littlefield.

La Raja, Raymond J., and Brian F. Schaffner. 2015. *Campaign Finance and Political Polarization: When Purists Prevail*. Ann Arbor: University of Michigan Press.

Lassiter, Matthew D. 2006. *The Silent Majority: Suburban Politics in the Sunbelt South*. Princeton, NJ: Princeton University Press.

Lavine, Howard G., Christopher D. Johnston, and Marco R. Steenbergen. 2012. *The Ambivalent Partisan: How Critical Loyalty Promotes Democracy*. New York: Oxford University Press.

Lee, Frances E. 2005. "Interests, Constituencies, and Policy Making." In *The Legislative Branch*, edited by Paul Quirk and Sarah A. Binder. New York: Oxford University Press.

———. 2009. *Beyond Ideology: Politics, Principles, and Partisanship in the US Senate*. Chicago: University of Chicago Press.

———. 2015. "How Party Polarization Affects Governance." *Annual Review of Political Science* 18:1–22.

———. 2016. *Insecure Majorities: Congress and the Perpetual Campaign*. Chicago: University of Chicago Press.

Lee, Frances E., and Bruce I. Oppenheimer. 1999. *Sizing Up the Senate: The Unequal Consequences of Equal Representation*. Chicago: University of Chicago Press.

Lee, Ronald D. 2000. "The Lee-Carter Method for Forecasting Mortality, with Various Extensions and Applications." *North American Actuarial Journal* 4 (1): 80–93.

Leighley, Jan, and Jonathan Nagler. 2014. *Who Votes Now? Demographics, Issues, Equality, and Turnout in the United States*. Princeton, NJ: Princeton University Press.

Lelkes, Yphtach, Gaurav Sood, and Shanto Iyengar. 2017. "The Hostile Audience: The Effect of Access to Broadband Internet on Partisan Affect." *American Journal of Political Science* 61 (1): 5–20.

Lenz, Gabriel S. 2013. *Follow the Leader? How Voters Respond to Politicians' Policies and Performance*. Chicago: University of Chicago Press.

Leuchtenburg, William E. 1989. *In the Shadow of FDR: From Harry Truman to Ronald Reagan*. Ithaca, NY: Cornell University Press.

Levendusky, Matthew. 2009. *The Partisan Sort: How Liberals Became Democrats and Conservatives Became Republicans*. Chicago: University of Chicago Press.

———. 2013a. *How Partisan Media Polarize America*. Chicago: University of Chicago Press.

———. 2013b. "Why Do Partisan Media Polarize Viewers?" *American Journal of Political Science* 57 (3): 611–23.

Levy, Jacob T. 2006. "Beyond Publius: Montesquieu, Liberal Republicanism and the Small-Republic Thesis." *History of Political Thought* 27 (1): 50–90.

———. 2007. "Federalism, Liberalism, and the Separation of Loyalties." *American Political Science Review* 101 (3): 459–77.

Lewis-Beck, Michael S., and Tom W. Rice. 1983. "Localism in Presidential Elections: The Home State Advantage." *American Journal of Political Science* 27 (3): 548–56.

Lodge, Milton, and Charles S. Taber. 2013. *The Rationalizing Voter*. New York: Cambridge University Press.

Loughry, Allen H. 2006. *Don't Buy Another Vote, I Won't Pay for a Landslide*. Parsons, WV: McCalin.

Lunch, William M. 1987. *The Nationalization of American Politics*. Berkeley: University of California Press.

Mael, Fred A., and Lois E. Tetrick. 1992. "Identifying Organizational Identification." *Educational and Psychological Measurement* 52 (4): 813–24.

Malhotra, Neil, and Alexander G. Kuo. 2008. "Attributing Blame: The Public's Response to Hurricane Katrina." *Journal of Politics* 70 (1): 120–35.

Mann, Thomas E., and Norman J. Ornstein. 2016. *It's Even Worse Than It Looks: How the American Constitutional System Collided with the New Politics of Extremism*. New York: Basic Books.

Marcus, George E. 2006. "Emotions in Politics." *Annual Review of Political Science* 3:221–50.

Marschall, Melissa J., and Dietlind Stolle. 2004. "Race and the City: Neighborhood Context and the Development of Generalized Trust." *Political Behavior* 26 (2): 125–53.

Masket, Seth. 2009. *No Middle Ground: How Informal Party Organizations Control Nominations and Polarize Legislatures*. Ann Arbor: University of Michigan Press.

Massey, Douglas, and Nancy Denton. 1993. *American Apartheid: The Making of the Underclass*. Cambridge, MA: Harvard University Press.

Matsa, Katerina Eva. 2014. "Market Is Still Hot for Buying Up Local TV Stations." Pew Research Center, December 23. http://www.pewresearch.org/fact-tank/2014/12/23/market-is-still-hot-for-buying-up-local-tv-stations.

Mayhew, David R. 1974. *Congress: The Electoral Connection*. New Haven, CT: Yale University Press.

———. 1986. *Placing Parties in American Politics: Organization, Electoral Settings, and Government Activity in the Twentieth Century*. Princeton, NJ: Princeton University Press.

McAdam, Doug. 1982. *Political Process and the Development of Black Insurgency, 1930–1970*. Chicago: University of Chicago Press.

McCarty, Nolan, Keith T. Poole, and Howard Rosenthal. 2006. *Polarized America: The Dance of Ideology and Unequal Riches*. Cambridge, MA: MIT Press.

McCormick, Richard Patrick. 1973. *The Second American Party System: Party Formation in the Jacksonian Era*. New York: W. W. Norton.

McDonald, Michael P., and Samuel L. Popkin. 2001. "The Myth of the Vanishing Voter." *American Political Science Review* 95 (4): 963–74.

McGirr, Lisa. 2001. *Suburban Warriors: The Origins of the New American Right*. Princeton, NJ: Princeton University Press.

Mendelberg, Tali. 2001. *The Race Card: Campaign Strategy, Implicit Messages, and the Norm of Equality*. Princeton, NJ: Princeton University Press.

Meredith, Marc. 2009. "Persistence in Political Participation." *Quarterly Journal of Political Science* 4 (3): 187–209.

———. 2013. "Heterogeneous Friends-and-Neighbors Voting." Working paper, University of Pennsylvania.

Merritt, Richard L. 1965. "The Emergence of American Nationalism: A Quantitative Approach." *American Quarterly* 17 (2): 319–35.

Mickey, Robert. 2015. *Paths out of Dixie*. Princeton, NJ: Princeton University Press.

Milfont, Taciano L., Laurel Evans, Chris G. Sibley, Jan Ries, and Andrew Cunningham. 2014. "Proximity to Coast Is Linked to Climate Change Belief." *PloS ONE* 9 (7): e103180.

Mill, John Stuart. 1869. *On Liberty*. London: Longmans, Green, Reader, and Dyer.

Miller, Joanne M., and Jon A. Krosnick. 2000. "News Media Impact on the Ingredients of Presidential Evaluations: Politically Knowledgeable Citizens Are Guided by a Trusted Source." *American Journal of Political Science* 44 (2): 301–15.

———. 2004. "Threat as a Motivator of Political Activism: A Field Experiment." *Political Psychology* 25 (4): 507–23.

Miller, Warren Edward, and J. Merrill Shanks. 1996. *The New American Voter*. Cambridge, MA: Harvard University Press.

Mitchell, Amy, and Jesse Holcomb. 2016. "State of the News Media 2016." Pew Research Center, June 23. http://www.journalism.org/2016/06/15/state-of-the-news-media-2016/.

Moen, Matthew C. 1992. *The Transformation of the Christian Right*. Tuscaloosa: University Alabama Press.

Mondak, Jeffery J. 1995a. "Media Exposure and Political Discussion in US Elections." *Journal of Politics* 57 (1): 62–85.

———. 1995b. "Newspapers and Political Awareness." *American Journal of Political Science* 39 (2): 513–27.

Moore, Ryan T., and Andrew Reeves. 2017. "Learning from Place in the Era of Geolocation." In *Analytics, Policy and Governance*, edited by Benjamin Ginsberg, Kathy Wagner Hill, and Jennifer Bachner, 118–36. New Haven, CT: Yale University Press.

Morris, Edmund. 1999. *Dutch: A Memoir of Ronald Reagan*. New York: Random House.

Mullainathan, Sendhil, and Andrei Shleifer. 2005. "The Market for News." *American Economic Review* 95 (4): 1031–53.

Mullinix, Kevin J., Thomas J. Leeper, James N. Druckman, and Jeremy Freese. 2015. "The Generalizability of Survey Experiments." *Journal of Experimental Political Science* 2 (2): 109–38.

Mummolo, Jonathan. 2016. "News from the Other Side: How Topic Relevance Limits the Prevalence of Partisan Selective Exposure." *Journal of Politics* 78 (3): 763–73.

Mutz, Diana C. 1992. "Mass Media and the Depoliticization of Personal Experience." *American Journal of Political Science* 32 (3): 483–508.

———. 1994. "Contextualizing Personal Experience: The Role of Mass Media." *Journal of Politics* 56 (3): 689–714.

———. 2011. *Population-Based Survey Experiments*. Princeton, NJ: Princeton University Press.

———. 2015. *In-Your-Face Politics: The Consequences of Uncivil Media*. Princeton, NJ: Princeton University Press.

Nagourney, Adam. 2014. "Midterms Give Parties Chance for Sweeping Control of States." *New York Times*, August 11.

Nall, Clayton. 2015. "The Political Consequences of Spatial Policies: How Interstate Highways Facilitated Geographic Polarization." *Journal of Politics* 77 (2): 394–406.

Nall, Clayton, and Jonathan Mummolo. 2016. "Why Partisans Don't Sort: The Constraints on Political Segregation." *Journal of Politics* 79 (1): 45–59.

National Park Service. 2016. "Military Bases in the Continental United States." Accessed May 31, 2017. https://www.nps.gov/nagpra/DOCUMENTS/BasesMap Index.htm.

Nettles, Curtis Putnam. 1962. *Emergence of a National Economy, 1775–1815*. Harper & Row.

Newman, Benjamin J. 2012. "Acculturating Contexts and Anglo Opposition to Immigration in the United States." *American Journal of Political Science* 57 (2): 374–90.

———. 2016. "Breaking the Glass Ceiling: Local Gender-Based Earnings Inequality and Women's Belief in the American Dream." *American Journal of Political Science* 60 (4): 1006–25.

Newman, Benjamin J., Christopher D. Johnston, and Patrick L. Lown. 2015. "False Consciousness or Class Awareness? Local Income Inequality, Personal Economic Position, and Belief in American Meritocracy." *American Journal of Political Science* 59 (2): 326–40.

Nickerson, David W. 2008. "Is Voting Contagious? Evidence from Two Field Experiments." *American Political Science Review* 102 (1): 49.

Niemi, Richard G., and M. Kent Jennings. 1991. "Issues and Inheritance in the Formation of Party Identification." *American Journal of Political Science* 35 (4): 970–88.

Niemi, Richard G., Stephen Wright, and Lynda W. Powell. 1987. "Multiple Party Identifiers and the Measurement of Party Identification." *Journal of Politics* 49 (4): 1093–103.

Nisbett, Richard E., and Dov Cohen. 1996. *Culture of Honor: The Psychology of Violence in the South*. Boulder, CO: Westview Press.

Nivola, Pietro S. 2002. *Tense Commandments: Federal Prescriptions and City Problems*. Washington, DC: Brookings Institution Press.

Noble, Jason. 2016. "Ted Cruz Calls on Oregon Activists to 'Stand Down.'" *USA Today*, January 4. https://www.usatoday.com/story/news/politics/onpolitics/2016/01/04/ted-cruz-oregon-standoff/78279632/.

Noel, Hans. 2013. *Political Ideologies and Political Parties in America*. New York: Cambridge University Press.

Noelle-Neumann, Elisabeth. 1993. *The Spiral of Silence: Public Opinion—Our Social Skin*. Chicago: University of Chicago Press.

Nugent, John D. 2009. *Safeguarding Federalism: How States Protect Their Interests in National Policymaking*. Norman: University of Oklahoma Press.

Nyhan, Brendan, Eric McGhee, John Sides, Seth Masket, and Steven Greene. 2012. "One Vote Out of Step? The Effects of Salient Roll Call Votes in the 2010 Election." *American Politics Research* 40 (5): 844–79.

Oliver, J. Eric. 2001. *Democracy in Suburbia*. Princeton, NJ: Princeton University Press.

Oliver, J. Eric, Shang E. Ha, and Zachary Callen. 2012. *Local Elections and the Politics of Small-Scale Democracy*. Princeton, NJ: Princeton University Press.

Oliver, J. Eric, and Tali Mendelberg. 2000. "Reconsidering the Environmental Determinants of White Racial Attitudes." *American Journal of Political Science* 44 (3): 574–89.

Oliver, J. Eric, and Janelle Wong. 2003. "Intergroup Prejudice in Multiethnic Settings." *American Journal of Political Science* 47 (4): 567–82.

Olkean, Benjamin A. 2009. "Do Television and Radio Destroy Social Capital? Evidence from Indonesian Villages." *American Economic Journal: Applied Economics* 1 (4): 1–33.

Olson, Mancur. 1965. *The Logic of Collective Action*. Cambridge, MA: Harvard University Press.

O'Neill, Tip. 1988. *Man of the House: The Life and Political Memoirs of Speaker Tip O'Neill*. New York: St. Martin's.

Paddock, Joel. 2005. *State & National Parties & American Democracy*. New York: Peter Lang.

Padula, Guy. 2002. *Madison v. Marshall: Popular Sovereignty, Natural Law, and the United States Constitution*. Lanham, MD: Lexington Books.

Page, Benjamin I., and Lawrence R. Jacobs. 2009. *Class War? What Americans Really Think about Economic Inequality*. Chicago: University of Chicago Press.

Patterson, Thomas E. 1993. *Out of Order*. New York: Vintage.

Patty, John W. 2006. "Loss Aversion, Presidential Responsibility, and Midterm Congressional Elections." *Electoral Studies* 25 (2): 227–47.

Perlstein, Rick. 2009. *Before the Storm: Barry Goldwater and the Unmaking of the American Consensus*. New York: Nation Books.

Peterson, Paul. 1981. *City Limits*. Chicago: University of Chicago Press.

Pettigrew, Stephen. 2017. "November 2016 General Election Results (County Level)." Harvard Dataverse, Harvard University Cambridge, MA. http://dx.doi.org/10.7910/DVN/MLLQDH.

Pettys, Todd E. 2003. "Competing for the People's Affection: Federalism's Forgotten Marketplace." *Vanderbilt Law Review* 56 (2): 329–91.

Phillips, Kevin P. 1969. *The Emerging Republican Majority*. New Rochelle, NY: Arlington House.

Piketty, Thomas, and Emmanuel Saez. 2003. "Income Inequality in the United States, 1913–1998." *Quarterly Journal of Economics* 118 (1): 1–39.

Poole, Keith, and Howard Rosenthal. 1997. *Congress: A Political-Economic History of Roll Call Voting*. New York: Oxford University Press.

———. 2016. "The Divisions in the House Republican Party." Voteview blog, January 8. https://voteviewblog.com/2016/01/08/the-divisions-in-thehouse-republican-party/.

Popkin, Samuel. 1994. *The Reasoning Voter: Communication and Persuasion in Presidential Campaigns*. Chicago: University of Chicago Press.

Porter, Michael. 2003. "The Economic Performance of Regions." *Regional Studies* 37 (6–7): 549–78.

Posner, Daniel N. 2004. "The Political Salience of Cultural Difference: Why Chewas and Tumbukas Are Allies in Zambia and Adversaries in Malawi." *American Political Science Review* 98 (4): 529–45.

Prior, Markus. 2006. "The Incumbent in the Living Room: The Rise of Television and the Incumbency Advantage in US House Elections." *Journal of Politics* 68 (3): 657–73.

———. 2007. *Post-broadcast Democracy: How Media Choice Increases Inequality in Political Involvement and Polarizes Elections*. New York: Cambridge University Press.

———. 2009a. "The Immensely Inflated News Audience: Assessing Bias in Self-Reported News Exposure." *Public Opinion Quarterly* 73 (1): 130–43.

———. 2009b. "Improving Media Effects Research through Better Measurement of News Exposure." *Journal of Politics* 71 (3): 893–908.

———. 2013. "The Challenge of Measuring Media Exposure: Reply to Dilliplane, Goldman, and Mutz." *Political Communication* 30 (4): 620–34.

Putnam, Robert D. 1966. "Political Attitudes and the Local Community." *American Political Science Review* 60 (3): 640–54.

————. 2000. *Bowling Alone: The Collapse and Revival of American Community*. New York: Simon and Schuster.

————. 2007. "E Pluribus Unum: Diversity and Community in the 21st Century: The 2006 Johan Skytte Prize Lecture." *Scandinavian Political Studies* 30 (2): 137–74.

Putnam, Robert D., and David E. Campbell. 2012. *American Grace: How Religion Divides and Unites Us*. New York: Simon and Schuster.

Rae, Douglas W. 2003. *City: Urbanism and Its End*. New Haven, CT: Yale University Press.

Reed, John Shelton. 1976. "The Heart of Dixie: An Essay in Folk Geography." *Social Forces* 54 (4): 925–39.

Reeves, Andrew, and James G. Gimpel. 2012. "Ecologies of Unease: Geographic Context and National Economic Evaluations." *Political Behavior* 34 (3): 507–34.

Rehfeld, Andrew. 2005. *The Concept of Constituency: Political Representation, Democratic Legitimacy, and Institutional Design*. New York: Cambridge University Press.

Ridout, Travis N., Erika Franklin Fowler, and Kathleen Searles. 2012. "Exploring the Validity of Electronic Newspaper Databases." *International Journal of Social Research Methodology* 15 (6): 451–66.

Rieder, Jonathan. 1987. *Canarsie*. Cambridge, MA: Harvard University Press.

Riker, William H. 1964. *Federalism: Origin, Operation, Significance*. Boston: Little, Brown.

————. 1986. *The Art of Political Manipulation*. New Haven, CT: Yale University Press.

Riker, William H., and Peter C. Ordeshook. 1968. "A Theory of the Calculus of Voting." *American Political Science Review* 62 (1): 25–42.

Ritzer, George. 2011. *The McDonaldization of Society*. Thousand Oaks, CA: Pine Forge Press.

Roberts, Margaret E., Brandon M. Stewart, Dustin Tingley, Christopher Lucas, Jetson Leder-Luis, Shana Kushner Gadarian, Bethany Albertson, and David G. Rand. 2014. "Structural Topic Models for Open-Ended Survey Responses." *American Journal of Political Science* 58 (4): 1064–82.

Roccas, Sonia, and Marilynn B. Brewer. 2002. "Social Identity Complexity." *Personality and Social Psychology Review* 6 (2): 88–106.

Rodden, Jonathan. 2006. *Hamilton's Paradox: The Promise and Peril of Fiscal Federalism*. New York: Cambridge University Press.

————. 2010. "The Geographic Distribution of Political Preferences." *Annual Review of Political Science* 13:321–40.

————. 2013. "The Long Shadow of the Industrial Revolution: Geography and the Representation of the Left." Book manuscript. Accessed September 15, 2015. http://www.stanford.edu/jrodden/wp/shadow.pdf.

Rogers, Steven. 2013. "Coattails, Raincoats, and Congressional Election Outcomes." Working paper, Vanderbilt University.

———. 2016. "National Forces in State Legislative Elections." *Annals of the American Academy of Political and Social Science* 667:207–25.

———. 2017. "Accountability in State Legislatures." Working paper, St. Louis University. Accessed May 31, 2017. http://www.stevenmrogers.com/www/book project.html.

Rosenblum, Nancy. 2008. *On the Side of the Angels*. Princeton, NJ: Princeton University Press.

Rosenstone, Steven J., and John M. Hansen. 1993. *Mobilization, Participation, and Democracy in America*. New York: Macmillan.

Rossiter, Clinton. 1956. *The First American Revolution: The American Colonies on the Eve of Independence*. Vol. 17. New York: Harcourt Brace.

Rozin, Paul, and Edward B. Royzman. 2001. "Negativity Bias, Negativity Dominance, and Contagion." *Personality and Social Psychology Review* 5 (4): 296–320.

Sampson, Robert J. 2012. *Great American City: Chicago and the Enduring Neighborhood Effect*. Chicago: University of Chicago Press.

Sampson, Robert J., Jeffrey D. Morenoff, and Thomas Gannon-Rowley. 2002. "Assessing 'Neighborhood Effects': Social Processes and New Directions in Research." *Annual Review of Sociology* 28:443–78.

Sampson, Robert J., Stephen W. Raudenbush, and Felton Earls. 1997. "Neighborhoods and Violent Crime: A Multilevel Study of Collective Efficacy." *Science* 277 (5328): 918–24.

Sances, Michael W. 2016. "Attribution Errors in Federalist Systems: When Voters Punish the President for Local Tax Increases." Working paper, University of Memphis.

Sands, Melissa. 2016. "Who Wants to Tax a Millionaire? Exposure to Inequality Reduces Support for Redistribution." Paper presented at the Annual Meeting of the American Political Science Association, Philadelphia, September 1–4.

Schaffner, Brian F., and Patrick J. Sellers. 2003. "The Structural Determinants of Local Congressional News Coverage." *Political Communication* 20 (1): 41–57.

Schattschneider, E. E. 1942. *Party Government*. Westport, CT: Greenwood Press.

———. 1960. "The Semi-Sovereign People: A Realist's View of Democracy in America." Boston: Wadsworth, Cengage Learning.

Schickler, Eric. 2016. *Racial Realignment: The Transformation of American Liberalism, 1932–1965*. Princeton, NJ: Princeton University Press.

Schildkraut, Deborah J. 2007. "Defining American Identity in the Twenty-First Century: How Much There Is There?" *Journal of Politics* 69 (3): 597–615.

———. 2011. *Americanism in the Twenty-First Century: Public Opinion in the Age of Immigration*. New York: Cambridge University Press.

———. 2014. "Boundaries of American Identity: Evolving Understandings of Us." *Annual Review of Political Science* 17:441–60.

Schleicher, David. 2008. "Why Is There No Partisan Competition in City Council Elections?" *Journal of Law and Politics* 15:419–73.

Schleifer, Theodore. 2014. "With Eyes on Seats in Maryland and West Virginia, Politicians Cross Borders." *New York Times*, August 1.

Schlozman, Daniel. 2015. *When Movements Anchor Parties: Social Movements, Political Parties, and Electoral Change*. Princeton, NJ: Princeton University Press.

Schuessler, Alexander A. 2000. *A Logic of Expressive Choice*. Princeton, NJ: Princeton University Press.

Schulhofer-Wohl, Sam, and Miguel Garrido. 2013. "Do Newspapers Matter? Short-Run and Long-Run Evidence from the Closure of the *Cincinnati Post*." *Journal of Media Economics* 26 (2): 60–81.

Sears, David O. 1993. "Symbolic Politics: A Socio-Psychological Theory." In *Explorations in Political Psychology*, edited by Shanto Iyengar and William J. McGuire, 113–49. Durham, NC: Duke University Press.

Sears, David O., and Carolyn L. Funk. 1991. "The Role of Self-Interest in Social and Political Attitudes." *Advances in Experimental Social Psychology* 24 (1): 1–91.

Sears, David O., and Sheri Levy. 2003. "Childhood and Adult Political Development." In *Oxford Handbook of Political Psychology*, edited by David O. Sears, Leonie Huddy, and Robert Jervis, 60–109. New York: Oxford University Press.

Self, Robert O. 2003. *American Babylon: Race and the Struggle for Postwar Oakland*. Princeton, NJ: Princeton University Press.

Sellers, Jeffrey M., Daniel Kubler, R. Alan Walks, Philippe Rochat, and Melanie Walter-Rogg. 2013. "Metropolitan Sources of Political Behavior." In *The Political Ecology of the Metropolis*, edited by Jeffrey M. Sellers, Daniel Kubler, R. Alan Walks, Philippe Rochat, and Melanie Walter-Rogg, 419–488. Colchester, UK: ECPR Press.

Shaker, Lee. 2009. "Citizens' Local Political Knowledge and the Role of Media Access." *Journalism & Mass Communication Quarterly* 86 (4): 809–26.

———. 2014. "Dead Newspapers and Citizens' Civic Engagement." *Political Communication* 31 (1): 131–48.

Shefter, Martin. 1994. *Political Parties and the State: The American Historical Experience*. New York: Cambridge University Press.

Sherif, Muzafer, Oliver J. Harvey, B. Jack White, William R. Hood, Carolyn W. Sherif, et al. 1961. *Intergroup Conflict and Cooperation: The Robbers Cave Experiment*. Vol. 10. Norman, OK: University Book Exchange.

Shor, Boris, and Nolan McCarty. 2011. "The Ideological Mapping of American Legislatures." *American Political Science Review* 105 (3): 530–51.

Sifry, Micah L. 2013. *Spoiling for a Fight: Third-Party Politics in America*. New York: Routledge.

Simon, Herbert A., and Frederick Stern. 1955. "The Effect of Television upon Voting Behavior in Iowa in the 1952 Presidential Election." *American Political Science Review* 49 (2): 470–77.

Sinclair, Betsy. 2012. *The Social Citizen*. Chicago: University of Chicago Press.

Skocpol, Theda. 1999. "Advocates without Members: The Recent Transformation of American Civic Life." In *Civic Engagement in American Democracy*, edited by Theda Skocpol and Morris Fiorina. Washington, DC: Brookings Institution Press.

———. 2003. *Diminished Democracy: From Membership to Management in American Civic Life*. Norman: University of Oklahoma Press.

Small, Deborah A., George Loewenstein, and Paul Slovic. 2007. "Sympathy and Callousness: The Impact of Deliberative Thought on Donations to Identifiable and Statistical Victims." *Organizational Behavior and Human Decision Processes* 102 (2): 143–53.

Smith, H. L. 1997. "Matching with Multiple Controls to Estimate Treatment Effects in Observational Studies." *Sociological Methodology* 27 (1): 325–53.

Smith, Mitch. 2016. "In Kansas, Where Republicans and Fiscal Woes Reign, Democrats Made Inroads." *New York Times Magazine*, December 22, A22.

Sniderman, Paul M., and Edward H. Stiglitz. 2012. *The Reputational Premium: A Theory of Party Identification and Policy Reasoning*. Princeton, NJ: Princeton University Press.

Snyder, James M., and David Strömberg. 2010. "Press Coverage and Political Accountability." *Journal of Political Economy* 118 (2): 355–408.

Song, B. K. 2014. "The Effect of Television on Electoral Politics." Working paper, Harvard University.

Squire, Peverill. 2014. "Electoral Career Movements and the Flow of Political Power in the American Federal System." *State Politics & Policy Quarterly* 14 (1): 72–89.

Steel, Ronald. 1980. *Walter Lippmann and the American Century*. New Brunswick, NJ: Transaction.

Stokes, Donald E. 1967. "Parties and the Nationalization of Electoral Forces." In *The American Party Systems: Stages of Political Development*, edited by W. N. Chambers and W. D. Burnham, 182–202. New York: Oxford University Press.

Strömberg, David. 2004. "Radio's Impact on Public Spending." *Quarterly Journal of Economics* 119 (1): 189–221.

Stroud, Natalie Jomini. 2011. *Niche News: The Politics of News Choice*. New York: Oxford University Press.

Suellentrop, Chris. 2015. "The Kansas Experiment." *New York Times Magazine*, August 5, 36.

Sugrue, Thomas J. 1996. *The Origins of the Urban Crisis: Race and Inequality in Postwar Detroit*. Princeton, NJ: Princeton University Press.

Taber, Charles S., and Milton Lodge. 2006. "Motivated Skepticism in the Evaluation of Political Beliefs." *American Journal of Political Science* 50 (3): 755–69.

Tajfel, Henri. 1981. *Human Groups and Social Categories: Studies in Social Psychology*. New York: Cambridge University Press.

Tam Cho, Wendy K., James G. Gimpel, and Iris S. Hui. 2013. "Voter Migration and the Geographic Sorting of the American Electorate." *Annals of the Association of American Geographers* 103 (4): 856–70.

Tausanovitch, Chris, and Christopher Warshaw. 2014. "Representation in Municipal Government." *American Political Science Review* 108 (3): 605–41.

———. 2015. "Does the Ideological Proximity Between Congressional Candidates and Voters Affect Voting Decisions in Recent U.S. House Elections?" Working paper, Massachusetts Institute of Technology.

Taylor, Marylee C. 1998. "How White Attitudes Vary with the Racial Composition of Local Populations: Numbers Count." *American Sociological Review* 63:512–35.

Tesler, Michael. 2016. *Post-Racial or Most-Racial? Race and Politics in the Obama Era.* Chicago: University of Chicago Press.

Theiss-Morse, Elizabeth. 2009. *Who Counts as an American? The Boundaries of National Identity.* New York: Cambridge University Press.

Theodoridis, Alexander. 2015. "The Political World through Red and Blue Colored Glasses: Measuring and Manipulating Partisan Bias." Working paper, University of California, Merced.

Tolbert, Caroline J., and John A. Grummel. 2003. "Revisiting the Racial Threat Hypothesis: White Voter Support for California's Proposition 209." *State Politics and Policy Quarterly* 3 (2): 183–92.

Trende, Sean, and David Byler. 2017. "How Trump Won: The Northeast." RealClear Politics, January 18. http://www.realclearpolitics.com/articles/2017/01/18 /how_trump_won_the_northeast_132827.html.

Trounstine, Jessica. 2008. *Political Monopolies in American Cities: The Rise and Fall of Bosses and Reformers.* Chicago: University of Chicago Press.

Turner, Mike. 2016. Website of Congressman Mike Turner. Accessed January 16, 2016. https://turner.house.gov/.

US Census Bureau. 1992. "1992 Census of Governments, Volume 1, Number 2: Popularly Elected Officials." US Department of Commerce.

———. 2016. "Fact Finder." Accessed December 1, 2016. www.census.gov.

US Department of Justice. 2014. "Uniform Crime Report, 2014." Accessed January 15, 2016. www.fbi.gov.

Vavreck, Lynn. 2009. *The Message Matters: The Economy and Presidential Campaigns.* Princeton, NJ: Princeton University Press.

———. 2014. "Candidates Ace Geography in Their Ads." *New York Time,* May 21.

Verba, Sidney, Kay Lehman Schlozman, and Henry E. Brady. 1995. *Voice and Equality: Civic Voluntarism in American Politics.* Cambridge, MA: Harvard University Press.

Ware, Alan. 2006. *The Democratic Party Heads North, 1877–1962.* New York: Cambridge University Press.

Waxman, Henry. 2009. *The Waxman Report: How Congress Really Works.* New York: Twelve.

Weaver, Vesla M. 2007. "Frontlash: Race and the Development of Punitive Crime Policy." *Studies in American Political Development* 21 (2): 230–65.

White, Richard D., Jr. 2006. *Kingfish: The Reign of Huey P. Long*. New York: Random House.

Wilcox, Clyde, and Carin Robinson. 2010. *Onward Christian Soldiers? The Religious Right in American Politics*. Boulder, CO: Westview Press.

Wildavsky, Aaron. 1965. "The Goldwater Phenomenon: Purists, Politicians, and the Two-Party System." *Review of Politics* 27 (3): 386–413.

Williams, Jennifer. 2016. "The Oregon Militia Standoff, Explained." *Vox*, January 3. https://www.vox.com/2016/1/3/10703712/oregon-militia-standoff.

Williams, Thomas Harry. 1981. *Huey Long*. New York: Vintage.

Wilson, James Q. 1962. *The Amateur Democrat: Club Politics in Three Cities*. Chicago: University of Chicago Press.

Wilson, William J. 1996. *When Work Disappears: The World of the New Urban Poor*. New York: Alfred A. Knopf.

Wilson, William Julius, and Richard P. Taub. 2007. *There Goes the Neighborhood: Racial, Ethnic, and Class Tensions in Four Chicago Neighborhoods and their Meaning for America*. New York: Vintage.

Winter, Nicholas G. 2008. *Dangerous Frames: How Ideas about Race and Gender Shape Public Opinion*. Chicago: University of Chicago Press.

Wolfinger, Raymond E., and Steven J. Rosenstone. 1980. *Who Votes?* Vol. 22. New Haven, CT: Yale University Press.

Wong, Cara. 2007. "Little and Big Pictures in Our Heads: Race, Local Context, and Innumeracy about Racial Groups in the U.S." *Public Opinion Quarterly* 71:392–412.

———. 2010. *Boundaries of Obligation in American Politics: Geographic, National, and Racial Communities*. New York: Cambridge University Press.

Wong, Cara, Jake Bowers, Tarah Williams, and Katherine Drake Simmons. 2012. "Bringing the Person Back In: Boundaries, Perceptions, and the Measurement of Racial Context." *Journal of Politics* 1 (1): 1–18.

Wright, Gerald C. 1977. "Contextual Models of Electoral Behavior: The Southern Wallace Vote." *American Political Science Review* 71 (2): 497–508.

Wright, Matthew, and Jack Citrin. 2010. "Saved by the Stars and Stripes? Images of Protest, Salience of Threat, and Immigration Attitudes." *American Politics Research* 39 (2): 323–43.

Wright, Matthew, Jack Citrin, and Jonathan Wand. 2012. "Alternative Measures of American National Identity: Implications for the Civic-Ethnic Distinction." *Political Psychology* 33 (4): 469–82.

Young, Ernest A. 2015. "The Volk of New Jersey? State Identity, Distinctiveness, and Political Culture in the American Federal System." Duke Law School Public Law and Legal Theory Series No. 2015–11.

Zaller, John. 1992. *The Nature and Origins of Mass Opinion*. New York: Cambridge University Press.

———. 2004. "Floating Voters in U.S. Presidential Elections, 1948–2000." In *Studies in Public Opinion: Attitudes, Nonattitudes, Measurement Error, and Change*, ed-ited by Willem E. Saris and Paul M. Sniderman, 166–212. Princeton, NJ: Princeton University Press.

Zorbaugh, Henry. 1929. *The Gold Coast and the Slum: A Sociological Study of Chicago's Near North Side*. Chicago: University of Chicago Press.

Zukin, Cliff, and Robin Snyder. 1984. "Passive Learning: When the Media Envi-ronment Is the Message." *Public Opinion Quarterly* 48 (3): 629–38.

Index

Abrams, Samuel J., 242n5, 247n4
Absalom, Absalom (Faulkner), 194
African Americans: attachment to place of residence and, 92, 187, 188; political importance of identities and, 173, 179
air pollution: correlation between local pollution and support for environmental spending, 109, 110f, 244n19; data sources, 108, 109f, 244n16; national salience of the issue, 108; questions asked of respondents, 108–9, 244nn17–18; statistical model and contextual covariates, 101, 244nn7–10
Alabama, 47, 165
Alberta, Canada, 124
American elections: connection between gubernatorial and presidential voting, 48–50, 49f, 242nn8–9; distinctiveness of the South in, 54; evidence of the nationalization of, 37, 53–55; gubernatorial voting (*see* gubernatorial elections); home-state advantage for presidential candidates, 52–53, 53f, 242n11; media's impact on nationalization, 55 (*see also* media markets); nationalized vote choices' impact on voter engagement, 57–58; political geography factor in election results, 56–57; question of the importance of geography to representation, 36–37; subnational clustering in partisanship (*see* partisan identification); trend towards nationalization, 55, 56–57
American Legislative Exchange Council (ALEC), 150

American National Election Study (ANES), 40, 100, 117–18, 160
American South. *See* South
Anderson, Benedict, 129, 200
Ansolabehere, Stephen, 30, 241n3
antiterrorism spending. *See* 9/11 targets and terrorism
Arkansas, 45, 47, 165
Atlas of U.S. Presidential Elections (Leip), 43
Australia, 64

Baltimore, MD, 104
Barber, Michael, 137
Bartels, Larry M., 25, 26, 37
Bensel, Richard, 139, 140
Bernstein, Jonathan, 139
Berry, Christopher R., 2
Birnbaum, Jeffrey H., 237
Bloc Quebecois, 24–25
Bloomberg, Michael, 81, 110
Bongino, Dan, 36, 55
Bonica, Adam, 77, 246n9
Bowling Alone (Putnam), 201
Brady, David W., 26, 64
Brady, Henry E., 64
Brandeis, Louis, 230
Brown, Scott, 167, 168
Brownback, Sam, 73, 75, 233–35
Bundy, Ammon, 88
Bundy, Cliven, 88, 121
Bundy, Ryan, 88
Burden, Barry C., 27
Bush, George W., 49, 63, 124
Byler, David, 54
Byrne, Jane, 59

Chicago Studies in American Politics

A SERIES EDITED BY BENJAMIN I. PAGE, SUSAN HERBST,
LAWRENCE R. JACOBS, AND ADAM J. BERINSKY

Series titles, continued from front matter: